A Guide To Record Collecting

by

Jerry Osborne

and

Bruce Hamilton

Victoria Erickson
Associate Editor

Published by

O'SULLIVAN
WOODSIDE
& COMPANY
Phoenix, Arizona

*This book is dedicated
to Alice Rogers and Darryl Stolper
with thanks
from Jerry, Bruce and Vicki.*

Jellyroll Productions cannot begin to acknowledge all of the people whose work in the preparation of our series of price guides has enabled us to put this compendium together, but there are a few we must especially thank in addition to the two above:

Don Newton, John Clark, Tom Koehler, Homer Kellogg, Victor Pearlin, Nay Nassar and Mike Obrenovich.

Manufactured in the United States of America.

First Edition
First Printing

ISBN: 0-89019-068-2

Follett T 1270

Distributed to Booksellers by:

Follett Publishing Company
1010 West Washington Blvd.
Chicago, Illinois 60607

CONTENTS

THE PEOPLE BEHIND THE BOOK

Jerry Osborne, former disc jockey, salesman, emcee and promoter, makes his home among the pine trees in the cool country of Prescott, Arizona. His time is mainly divided between the pressures of co-publishing a weekly fan tabloid, *MusicWorld*, and keeping up his end of the Jellyroll team.

Bruce Hamilton, also a disc jockey for many years, devotes his full time to the field of nostalgia, including overseeing Jellyroll's activities from his Scottsdale residence. His other publishing interests are related to the fields of comics and original art.

Victoria Erickson, a full-timer with Jellyroll for three years, has been part of the team since it was founded. Her background includes education in English, advertising and mass communications, plus a brief association with radio. She collects advertising and paper records from her home in Mesa.

Jerry

Bruce

Vicki

THE WORLD'S 50 MOST VALUABLE RECORDS

Scattered throughout this book are 57 records (eight are tied for 50th place) that qualify, in our judgment, for this distinctive class. They are easy to locate in color and are identified by number as shown by the example on the back cover. All ties, as in the case of the eight records tied for 18th through 25th place, are marked as tied for 18th.

This feature was a fun list to put together, and despite the title, we must qualify the statement. These *are* the most valuable records in the world in the fields covered by our guides and from the information available to us. For the statement to be literally true, though, we would need to have access to private auction lists in highly specialized areas, which, aside from being an impossibility, would leave us with a baffling list of improbables ... records that no one among the general public would ever have a possibility of finding.

We have ruled out private recordings, demonstration discs, and the field of jazz, which we are yet not fully qualified to judge (our first price guide on jazz is scheduled for publication in 1981). It's interesting to note, however, that we know of a King Oliver record that brought $1,500 several years ago!

The all-time champion is without doubt! The only known unbroken copy in existence of *Stormy Weather* by the Five Sharps (see the section on *Blacks and Blues*) brought over $3,800 in auction in 1977 for a VG copy. Our projected valuation of $4,500 for a mint copy is partially based on this sale, but also on outstanding offers that have been made for a copy, and the considered estimates of our sources.

Our latest, up-to-the-minute information has indicated some fluctuations in our listed prices and the order of the Top 50, but we've stuck with the order strictly as listed from all of our current guides. How will the list read next year? Let's wait and see!

Beatles

TITLE	LABEL & NO.	GOOD	VERY GOOD	NEAR MINT
BEATLES				
ABBEY ROAD	Apple (S) SO 383	1.50	3.00	4.50
AMERICAN TOUR WITH ED RUDY (#2)	Radio Pulsebeat News	8.00	16.00	24.00
Beatle Interviews.				
AMERICAN TOUR WITH ED RUDY (#3)	Radio Pulsebeat News	10.00	20.00	30.00
Beatle Interviews.				
BEATLES	Apple (S) SWBO 101	4.00	8.00	12.00
Also known as the "White Album" a two record set.				
BEATLES	Apple (S) SWBO 101	3.00	6.00	9.00
With number on cover.				
BEATLES	Apple (S) SW 385	3.50	5.25	7.00
Without number on cover.				
BEATLES AGAIN				
(Original title of "Hey Jude")				
BEATLES AND FRANK IFIELD (On Stage)	Vee Jay (M) LP 1085	80.00	160.00	240.00
Has a drawing of the four Beatles on cover-Mono.				
BEATLES AND FRANK IFIELD (On Stage)	Vee Jay (S) LPS 1085	170.00	340.00	510.00
Same-but Stereo.				
BEATLES—THE CHRISTMAS FAN CLUB ALBUM	Apple (S) SBC 100	18.00	36.00	54.00
Released only to Beatle fan club members . . . containing				

Christmas messages from the Beatles to their fans.
(Beware of a very convincing bootleg. The cover photos are slightly out of focus and less detailed.)

TITLE	LABEL & NO.	GOOD	VERY GOOD	NEAR MINT
BEATLES 1962-1966	Apple (S) SKBO 3403	4.00	8.00	12.00
Two record set-originals were with a red cover.				
BEATLES 1962-1966	Apple (S) SKBO 3403	3.00	6.00	9.00
With orange/Red cover.				
BEATLES 1967-1970	Apple (M) T 2080	3.00	6.00	9.00
BEATLES 1967-1970	Capitol (M) ST 2080	3.00	6.00	9.00
BEATLES SECOND ALBUM	Capitol (S) ST 2080	5.00	10.00	15.00
Black label.				
BEATLES SECOND ALBUM	Apple (S) ST 2080	3.00	6.00	9.00
Green label.				
BEATLES SECOND ALBUM	Apple (S) ST 2080	1.50	3.00	4.50
With Capitol logo.				
BEATLES SECOND ALBUM				
Without Capitol logo.				

Beach Boys

TITLE	LABEL & NO.	GOOD	VERY GOOD	NEAR MINT
PET SOUNDS	Capitol (M) T 2458	3.00	6.00	9.00
PET SOUNDS	Capitol (S) DT 2458	3.00	6.00	9.00
PET SOUNDS (RI of Capitol 2458)	Reprise (S) MS 2197	2.00	3.00	4.00
SHUT DOWN VOL. 2	Capitol (M) T 2027	4.00	8.00	12.00
SHUT DOWN VOL. 2	Capitol (S) ST 2027	3.00	6.00	9.00
SHUT DOWN VOL. 2 (Compact 33)	Capitol (S) SXA 2027	25.00	37.50	50.00
SMILEY SMILE (Capitol Record Club issue)	Capitol (S) DT8 2891	34.00	68.00	102.00
SMILEY SMILE	Brother (M) ST 9001	3.00	6.00	9.00
SMILEY SMILE	Brother (S) SVBB 11384	2.25	3.75	4.50
SPIRIT OF AMERICA	Capitol (S) DKAO 2893	25.00	50.00	75.00
SPIRIT OF AMERICA	Capitol (S) DKAO 2893	17.00	25.50	51.00
STACK-O-TRACKS (With Book)	Capitol (S) DT 2354	4.00	8.00	12.00
STACK-O-TRACKS (Without Book)	Capitol (S) DT 2354	2.00	3.00	4.00
SUMMER DAYS AND SUMMER NIGHTS	Reprise (S) 6382	2.00	3.00	4.00
SUMMER DAYS AND SUMMER NIGHTS	Capitol (S) SXA 1981	25.00	50.00	75.00
SUNFLOWER	Capitol (M) T 1981	4.00	8.00	12.00
SUNFLOWER	Capitol (S) ST 1981	4.00	6.00	9.00
SUPER GIRL (Compact 33)	Pickwick (S) SPC 3351	1.50	2.25	3.00
SURFER GIRL	Capitol (M) T 1808	4.00	8.00	12.00
SURFER GIRL	Capitol (S) DT 1808	3.00	6.00	9.00
SURFIN' SAFARI	Capitol (M) T 1890	4.00	8.00	12.00
SURFIN' SAFARI	Capitol (S) ST 1890	3.00	6.00	9.00
SURFIN' USA	Reprise (S) 6453	3.00	4.50	6.00
SURF'S UP	Capitol (EP) PRO 2186	70.00	140.00	210.00
10 LITTLE INDIANS	Capitol (S) SKAO 133	6.00	9.00	12.00
(The Beach Boys sing "10 Little Indians," and "Little Miss America" on one side, and Ray Anthony sings two songs on the flip side.				
20/20	Reprise (S) 2MS 2166	7.50	11.25	15.00
20/20 - WILD HONEY (RI of Capitol 133 & 2859) (2 records)	Capitol (M) T 2859	5.00	7.50	10.00
WILD HONEY	Capitol (S) ST 2859	5.00	7.50	10.00
WILD HONEY	Pickwick (S) SPC 3309	2.00	3.00	4.00
WOW! GREAT CONCERT				

(Many of the Capitol LP's have been reissued. These prices apply to original, black label, first issues)

TITLE	LABEL & NO.	GOOD	VERY GOOD	NEAR MINT
BEACON STREET UNION, THE				
CLOWN DIED IN MARVIN GARDENS, THE	MGM (M) SE 4568	2.50	3.75	5.00
EYES OF THE BEACON STREET UNION, THE	MGM (M) SE 4517	2.50	3.75	5.00
BEAN, Arnold				
COSMIC BEAM	SSS (S) SSS21	2.50	3.75	5.00
BEARCATS				
BEATLEMANIA	Somerset (M) 20800	4.00	8.00	12.00
RAMA LAMA DING DONG	Bravo (EP) 70-2	2.00	4.00	6.00
BEASLEY, Jimmy				
FABULOUS	Crown (M) CLP 5014	5.00	12.50	20.00
TWIST WITH JIMMY BEASLEY	Crown (M) CLP 5247	3.00	7.50	12.00
BEAST				
BEAST	Cotillion (S) 9012	2.50	3.75	5.00
BEATLE BUDDIES				
BEATLE BUDDIES	Diplomat (M) 2313	4.00	8.00	12.00

(M) Mono   (S) Stereo   (EP) Extended Play   (Q) Quad   (RI) Re-issued

This is a sample of an actual page reduced from 8½ x 11" from one of our price guides, *Record Albums 1948-1978, Second Edition*, Page 12.

PLEASE READ THIS INTRODUCTION
by Bruce Hamilton

When we decided to publish *A Guide to Record Collecting,* we sent notices to collectors whose help we were soliciting and we told them, first thing, that "this book is not for you!" But interest in it among those same serious collectors has been high, because many realize that out of the ranks of non-collectors, namely the general public, future collectors will come. This book, we feel—and most collectors we've talked to agree—can only benefit the hobby by introducing more people to it.

Unlike any of the other price guides in the Osborne-Hamilton Series, however, this book outlines what all of the others are all about. It represents an average of 3½% of the material in each section of every book currently in release or scheduled in our series. At that, there are several thousand listings falling under the general categories of the big dance bands, popular and rock albums, pop and rock singles, blues, and country/western, with such subcategories as rockabilly, rhythm and blues, comedy, soundtracks and musical shows.

This book goes into sufficient detail for anyone to determine their future interest in collecting. The options open include direct contact with any of the collectors, dealers or publications listed in our Directory, beginning on page XIII. All of our books have directories, some with as many as 1,300 names and addresses, worldwide.

There are some important things concerning prices that one should understand before assimilating the information in this guide. The prices dealers charge, or that collectors assess each other when buying, selling or trading among themselves, are those we have averaged from our sources before going to press. A dealer, in attempting to reach a customer who has an interest in any one given record, finds himself faced with all of the usual expenses of running a retail business. His overhead includes investment in stock he has bought but cannot sell and the costs of continuous advertising. What he charges for a record must absorb all of this, plus reimbursement for his time, which translates into his profit margin.

The Fireflies

A dealer must also charge a minimum amount for any record, regardless how common, to justify handling. Most records valued under $10.00 equally reflect the factors of handling, rarity and demand, whereas the more valuable they become, the more competitive demand alone drives up the prices. Paradoxically, however, rarity is one of the factors that contributes to demand in the eyes of many collectors!

The point is that it is unrealistic for a layman to expect to sell his used collection of common records to a dealer for what he considers a reasonable percentage of the guide. These types of records are too easily found at garage sales, swap meets or thrift stores.

Conversely, it's exciting to build a collection this way, by sifting through these same hunting grounds. Inevitably, an occasional jewel will surface among the rubble.

The reputable dealer must also guarantee his product; so, to compete, the layman who chooses to advertise directly to the consumer should be prepared to sell at set bargain prices or to auction off what he has for whatever the traffic will bear.

Grading accurately is very important and not particularly difficult. The most commonly accepted standards, detailed on page XI, can be learned with a minimum of effort. What is not so easy is retaining a fair perspective. To over-grade, or to represent a record as better than it is—a rampant problem in mail order—is much like rolling back the odometer on an automobile. It's interpreted by the buyer as an attempt to sell it for more than it's worth.

Collectors place very high values on perfect, unplayed, or near mint records, and have been known to willingly pay ten times as much for one in that pristine condition as compared to what they would have paid for an average, commonly available, used copy. The documented value spread between good and near mint in this book, however, only ranges from two to four times, which we discuss in the introductions to each section.

Collectors and laymen should both be aware that in the special cases of 78s or albums dating back to the mid-60's or earlier, the average selling price in this book for the average *best condition available* — in other words, those prices that set the standards — should be assumed to be halfway between the two prices shown! A 78 rpm record listed at $10.00 in good and $30.00 in near mint will normally sell for $20.00 in the top condition usually found.

Any guide to record collecting can never be all inclusive nor even definitive. Only a small percentage of the total output ever reaches record stores or receives radio station air play. And added information about known and documented records never stops coming in. The Beatles and Elvis Presley are exhaustively detailed in our books, yet what is known about their records is still being expanded. We've documented a proliferation of over 100 different authorized, bootleg or counterfeit Elvis Presley 45's, 78's, albums and EPs that have been released in the U.S. alone in the first 14 months after his death!

Even though we've chosen not to continue legitimizing bootlegs by documenting their existence, we do recognize some of the arguments that favor them. But we must warn the novice to beware of the counterfeit—the deliberate copying of a rare and valuable record with no attempt to identify it as such. Even though some of these are sold originally as copies, the unscrupulous sometimes palm them off at "bargain" prices to the unsuspecting. Anyone who gets a chance to buy a $600 album for $50, or even $250, *watch out*! It's not recommended that a newcomer jump into the purchase of very expensive records until he becomes familiar with the hobby, unless he confines his buys exclusively to dealers with established reputations to protect.

A bootleg is often taken from a live concert where someone smuggled a tape recorder and then illegally released a record of it, or they are sometimes outtakes from recording sessions which were never commercially released. This material is of little concern to the collector other than to decide if he's interested. The fake, though, is of a great deal of concern.

If you're a new collector—and especially if you're interested in Elvis—be very suspicious of bargains. If you encounter this situation and can examine the record, look and see if it appears brand new. If there's no wear on the record or the label, see if you can take it to an oldie record store for their opinion. Most dealers know a fake when they see one. If you're buying through the mail, be suspicious even if an Elvis fan is trying to sell you a mint Sun label record for full price. If it's in brand new condition, it's probably not real.

Get to know collectors in your area; call someone in the Collector's Directory who lives near you. They're usually glad to help you learn the in's and out's of the hobby, so you can begin to buy with confidence. The investment potential at this time, as the hobby is showing signs of healthy and rapid growth—and as the entire world's nostalgia-consciousness increases—is excellent.

Elvis Presley

CONDITION:
YOU NEED TO KNOW
WHAT SHAPE YOUR RECORDS ARE IN

Just because a record is old does not necessarily make it valuable. There *has* to be a demand for it. For the value to continue to rise, the demand must always be greater than the supply. Another factor is condition. The most accurate grading system and the easiest one to explain and understand is as follows:

M - MINT

Mint means the record must be in perfect condition. There can be no compromise. If you have two mint records, but can tell a slight difference between the two, one is not mint. It is for this reason that the term "near mint" appears as the highest grade listed in our books. Label defects—such as stickers, writing, rubbing, fading, or warping and wrinkling—will detract from its value. If a record is, indeed, perfect in every way, it will bring somewhat more than the near mint listing.

VG - VERY GOOD

The halfway mark between good and near mint. The disc should have only a minimum amount of foreign, or surface noise and it should not detract at all from the recorded sound. A VG record may show some label wear, but as with audio, it would be minimal.

G - GOOD

The most misunderstood of all grades. Good should not mean bad! A record in good condition will show signs of wear, with an audible amount of foreign noises. There may be scratches and it may be obvious it was never properly cared for (such as being stacked with other records not in sleeves). Nevertheless, it still plays "good" enough to enjoy.

F - FAIR

Fair is the beginning of bad. A fair record will play all the way through without skips, but will contain a distracting amount of noise.

P-POOR

Stepped on by an elephant and it sells for peanuts.

The more this system is used, the more widespread will be the satisfaction between buyers and sellers. More and more dealers are subscribing to it.

All reputable dealers offer a money-back guarantee if the record is not in the condition described.

WHAT WE'LL DO FOR YOU
IF YOU HELP US!

Had we known it couldn't be done, we wouldn't have tried, but we took on the task of documenting records and their worth on the collector's market, and we now have six books under our belt and several more in various stages of completion.

We had a few very vocal critics at the beginning who have now joined our team, and each book is, as a result, a dramatic improvement over the last. Just how good they will become in the future will depend to a great extent on the input we receive from every possible source. Every bit of information we get helps everyone when we are able to pass it along!

This is an open solicitation for that help.

By the time most people read this plea, there will be five titles in the Osborne-Hamilton series of price guides. Two are already in their second editions and two scheduled for 1979 release (check with your bookstore for availability dates). The important thing to realize is that each title will be expanded, corrected and updated every year or two, so our need for input, corrections, opinions, will continue.

To document every record every artist ever released would be impossible. Also—and equally important—we don't want any *one* book to become ponderously large and expensive, merely documenting thousands of records no one cares about. Do not confuse the samplings of this compendium with the completeness (as it is) of our full-sized books. But *do* give us your input on who or what you'd like to see that we don't already list. Would you like more photos and would you like to see the **Collectors Directory** expanded?

Any person who will take the time to drop us a note will be put on our mailing list to notify him of all upcoming projects! We really do want to hear from you!

Write to us directly at:

Jellyroll Productions, Inc.
Dept. G
Box 3017
Scottsdale, Arizona 85257

COLLECTORS DIRECTORY

The listings on these five pages have been accepted in good faith, and though many of the collectors and dealers are known to us and we can attest to their unquestioned integrity, neither the authors nor the publisher of this book can guarantee satisfaction in any or all dealings.

For information on how to get your name in the second edition of *A Guide to Record Collecting*, write:

Jellyroll Productions Inc.
Dept. A
Box 3017
Scottsdale, Arizona 85257.

DANCE BANDS AND BIG BANDS
of the '20s, '30s, and '40s

Dance bands came in all sizes, and, for that matter, not all "big" bands were all that big—it's the era and the sound that set them apart; the dance bands generally thought of as a product of the 1920s and early '30s and the big band sound as being from the mid '30s until just after World War II.

The actual perimeters of our forthcoming price guide on *Dance Bands and Big Bands of the '20s, '30s, and '40s,* (tentative title) reach back before WWI and forward into the '50s with a few 45s. However, it is primarily those three headlined decades of the great 78s that will be recalled, priced and arranged for examination.

The documentation in the first edition will total 20,000 records, 500 or more by Benny Goodman alone, listing discs he recorded by his orchestra, trio, quartet, quintet, sextet and all of the other groups he formed. Both sides of each release are indicated alphabetically by the "A" (or first) side, and all vocalists on each side are noted. Any other information of sufficient interest which affects the value of the record on the collector's market will be included.

Our book will put heavy emphasis on a written and photographic journey through these lively and chaotic times, taking a glance back to where the stars performed and how they looked at the peaks of their careers. One artist alone has 56 different cross-references of band names and pseudonyms he used to record , yet everything he did is listed together! This one feature alone makes it a must for any musician, collector or fan!

The examples we've chosen on the pages that follow typify the ranges of today's values according to labels or time periods. The 78s are standardized at a price spread according to condition of three times between the more common *"good"* and the rarely found *"near mint,"* the lower half of this range representing the average sale today.

Alphabetical Listing:
Records of Dance Bands & Big Bands

TITLE/Flip	LABEL & No.	GOOD	NEAR MINT	YR.

ARMSTRONG, Louis (1900 — 1971)

TITLE/Flip	LABEL & No.	GOOD	NEAR MINT	YR.
AFTER YOU'VE GONE/St. Louis Blues	Okeh 41350	4.00	12.00	29
Louis Armstrong vocals.				
IF WE NEVER MEET AGAIN (Louis Armstrong vocal)/Dipper Mouth Blues (Louis Armstrong with Jimmy Dorsey & His Orchestra)	Decca 906	2.50	7.50	36
LAUGHIN' Louie/Tomorrow Night	Bluebird B-5363	3.00	9.00	33
Louis Armstrong vocals.				
LEAP FROG/I Used To Love You	Decca 4106	1.00	3.00	41
THREE PENNY OPERA/Back O' Town Blues (45)	Columbia 40587	2.25	4.50	56
Louis Armstrong vocals.				

ARMSTRONG, Louis & His Hot Five

TITLE/Flip	LABEL & No.	GOOD	NEAR MINT	YR.
BIG FAT MA AND SKINNY PA (Louis Armstrong vocal)/Sweet Little Papa	Okeh 8379	25.00	75.00	26
WILLIE THE WEEPER/Alligator Crawl	Okeh 8482	15.00	45.00	27

BALLEW, Smith (1902 —)
Smith Ballew vocals on both sides of most listings.

TITLE/Flip	LABEL & No.	GOOD	NEAR MINT	YR.
FORBIDDEN LIPS/Foolin' With The Other Woman's Man (Kay Weber vocal)	Oriole 2904	5.00	15.00	34
I'M THROWIN' MY LOVE AWAY (Kay Weber vocal)/ Little Did I Dream	Melotone M-12970	3.50	10.50	34
SNUGGLED ON YOUR SHOULDER/ Dancing On The Ceiling	Conqueror 7928	5.00	15.00	32
TAKE THE ACHE FROM MY HEART/ Footloose And Fancy Free	Perfect 16129	4.00	12.00	35
THEME FOR BEN SELVIN'S RADIO SHOW	Private recording, Banner matrix number.	50.00	150.00	34
TIA JUANA/Isle of Capri	Banner 33273	5.00	15.00	34
WHOLE DARNED THING'S FOR YOU, THE/ Girl Trouble	Odeon ONY 36078	3.50	10.50	30
YOU WERE ONLY PASSING TIME WITH ME/ You're Simply Delish	Columbia 2320-D	5.00	15.00	30

BASIE, Count & His Orchestra (1904 —)

TITLE/Flip	LABEL & No.	GOOD	NEAR MINT	YR.
HONEYSUCKLE ROSE/Roseland Shuffle	Decca 1141	1.50	4.50	37
HOUSE RENT BOOGIE/Take A Little Off The Top (J. Rushing vocal)	RCA Victor 20-2435	1.00	3.00	47
RIDE ON (Earl Warren vocal)/It's Sand, Man!	Columbia 36647	1.00	3.00	42
TAXI WAR DANCE/If I Could Be With You	Okeh 4748	1.50	4.50	39
WHAT GOES UP MUST COME DOWN (J. Rushing vocal)/ Don't Worry 'Bout Me (Helen Humes vocal)	Conqueror 9214	2.00	6.00	39
WHAT GOES UP MUST COME DOWN (J. Rushing vocal)/ Don't Worry 'Bout Me (Helen Humes vocal)	Vocalion 4734	2.00	6.00	39

BEN'S BAD BOYS—see Pollack, Ben as Ben's Bad Boys

CALLOWAY, Cab (1907 —)
Cab Calloway vocals on one or both sides of all listings.

TITLE/Flip	LABEL & No.	GOOD	NEAR MINT	YR.
AT THE CLAMBAKE CARNIVAL/Jive (Page One Of The Hepster's Dictionary)	Vocalion 4437	5.00	15.00	38
BOOGIE-WOOGIE, THE/Shout, Shout, Shout	Conqueror 9091	4.50	13.50	38
COPPER-COLORED GAL/The Wedding Of Mr. And Mrs. Swing	Brunswick 7748	5.00	15.00	36
GEECHY JOE/St. James' Infirmary	V-Disc 259	4.50	13.50	41
GHOST OF SMOKY JOE, THE/Floogie Walk	Okeh 4807	5.00	15.00	39
MOOD INDIGO/Farewell Blues	Regal 10327	3.50	10.50	31
NOBODY'S SWEETHEART/St. James' Infirmary	Brunswick 6105	4.00	12.00	30
PECKIN'/Manhattan Jam	Vocalion 3830	3.50	10.50	38
STRANGE AS IT SEEMS/Beale Street Mama	Romeo 1980	4.00	12.00	32
YALLER/The Viper's Drag	Jewel 6285	4.00	12.00	30

All records are 78 rpm unless indicated as (45) 45 rpm.

TITLE/Flip	LABEL & No.	GOOD	NEAR MINT	YR.
CARTER, Benny (1907 —)				
ALL OF ME/The Very Thought Of You (Roy Felton vocal)	Bluebird B-10962	2.50	7.50	40
BIG BEN BLUES (Benny Carter vocal)/ When Day Is Done	Brunswick 7786	3.50	10.50	36
DEVIL'S HOLIDAY/Symphony In Riffs	Columbia 2898-D	3.00	9.00	33
EVERYBODY SHUFFLE/Synthetic Love	Vocalion 2870	3.50	10.50	34
FISH FRY (Roy Felton vocal)/Slow Freight	V-Disc 449	3.00	9.00	40
HURRY, HURRY! (Savannah Churchill vocal)/Poinciana	Capitol 144	3.00	9.00	44
I'M COMING, VIRGINIA/Blue Light Blues	Victor 26221	3.00	9.00	38
LAST KISS YOU GAVE ME, THE (Roy Felton vocal)/ Boogie Woogie Sugar Blues	Decca 3588	3.50	10.50	40
LONESOME NIGHTS/Blue Lou	Okeh 41567	3.00	9.00	33
NIGHT HOP/O.K. For Baby	Decca 3294	3.00	9.00	40
CASA LOMA ORCHESTRA—see Gray, Glen & The Casaloma Orchestra				
CUMMINS, Bernie				
GOODBYE, JONAH (vocal by Bernie Cummins and The Sophisticates)/ Dreams For Sale (Walter Cummins vocal)	Vocalion 3749	2.50	7.50	37
LADY IS A TRAMP, THE (Connie Barleau vocal)/ Getting Some Fun Out Of Life (Bernie Cummins vocal)	Conqueror 8959	2.00	6.00	37
SAILING HOME/In The Mission By the Sea	Vocalion 3759	2.00	6.00	37
Walter Cummins vocals.				
SEEMS LIKE A MONTH OF SUNDAYS (Bernie Cummins vocal)/ I'm Losing My Mind (Because Of You) (Connie Barleau vocal)	Bluebird B 10777	2.00	6.00	40
THERE'LL BE SOME CHANGES MADE/Basin Street Blues	Vocalion 4181	3.00	9.00	37
Bernie Cummins vocals.				
CUMMINS, Bernie & His Toadstool Inn Orchestra				
HOME FOLKS BLUES/Ida	Gennett 5395	5.00	15.00	24
DAVIS, Johnny (Scat) (1915 —) Vocals by Davis on all songs listed.				
COLLEGE RHYTHM/Take A Number From One To Ten	Decca 272	6.00	18.00	34
DON'T STOP ME IF YOU'VE HEARD IT BEFORE/ Were You Foolin'?	Decca 256	5.00	15.00	34
TRUCKIN'/Loafin' Time	Decca 573	3.50	10.50	35
DEAN & HIS KIDS—see Pollack, Ben as the Dean & His Kids				
DORSEY BROTHERS Jimmy Dorsey (1904 — 1957) Tommy Dorsey (1905 — 1956)				
COQUETTE/The Yale Blues	Okeh 41007	3.00	9.00	28
Bill Dutton vocals.				
DIPPER MOUTH/The Gentleman Obviously Doesn't Believe (Kay Weber vocal)	Decca 561	4.00	12.00	35
DOWN 'T UNCLE BILL'S (Skeets Herfurt vocal)/ Dream Man (Bob Crosby vocal)	Brunswick 01964	5.00	15.00	34
English release.				
DREAM MAN (Bob Crosby vocal)/Hands Across The Table (Kay Weber vocal)	Decca 291	3.50	10.50	34
HARLEM CHAPEL CHIMES/Weary Blues	Brunswick 02149	7.50	22.50	35
English release.				
HEAT WAVE/Stop, Look And Listen	Decca 208	4.00	12.00	34
I'VE GOT A SWEET SOMEBODY/ Dream A Little Dream Of Me	Embassy E 133	10.00	30.00	31
Vocals by Scrappy Lambert as The Joy Spreaders.				
JUDY/Annie's Cousin Fanny (vocal by Glenn Miller and chorus)	Brunswick 6938	6.00	18.00	34
MILENBERG JOYS/St. Louis Blues	Decca 119	6.00	18.00	34

Halfway between good and mint is the true value and the best condition usually available in old records. Mint is rare.

TITLE/Flip	LABEL & No.	GOOD	NEAR MINT	YR.
MOOD HOLLYWOOD/Shim Sham Shimmy		7.50	22.50	33
RHYTHM OF THE RAIN (Kay Weber vocal)/				
I Was Lucky (Bob Crosby vocal)	Decca 358	3.50	10.50	34
'ROUND EVENING/Out Of The Dawn	Okeh 41124	5.00	15.00	28
Smith Ballew vocals.				
SHE'S FUNNY THAT WAY (Jerry Cooper vocal)/				
But I Can't Make A Man (Mildred Bailey vocal)	Brunswick 7542	5.00	15.00	33
SO HELP ME/Easy Come, Easy Go		5.00	15.00	34
Chick Bullock vocals.				
SOLITUDE (Kay Weber vocal)/Weary Blues	Decca 15013	5.00	15.00	35
An oversize 12" record.				
SPELL OF THE BLUES, THE/Let's Do It	Okeh 41181	12.50	37.50	29
Bing Crosby vocals.				

ELLINGTON, Duke (1899 — 1974)

TITLE/Flip	LABEL & No.	GOOD	NEAR MINT	YR.
SOUVENIR OF DUKE ELLINGTON, A	Oriole, no number.	15.00	45.00	33
Accompanying himself on the piano, Ellington talks with Percy Brooks, editor of Melody Maker. This one-sided record was given free to customers of Messrs. Levy's of Aldgate, London, with the purchase of any six Duke Ellington records.				
WASHINGTON WOBBLE/Harlem River Quiver	Victor 21284	10.00	30.00	27
(YOU'VE GOT THOSE) WANNA-GO-BACK-AGAIN BLUES/				
If You Can't Hold The Man You Love	Gennett 3291	25.00	75.00	26
Jimmy Harrison vocals.				

ELLINGTON, Duke & His Cotton Club Orchestra

TITLE/Flip	LABEL & No.	GOOD	NEAR MINT	YR.
I CAN'T GIVE YOU ANYTHING BUT LOVE (vocal by Baby Cox, Irving Mills)/				
Diga Diga Doo (vocal by Irving Mills, Ozie Ware)	Victor V 38008	10.00	30.00	28
RED HOT BAND/Doin' The Frog	Vocalion 1155	12.50	37.50	27

ELLINGTON, Duke & His Famous Orchestra

TITLE/Flip	LABEL & No.	GOOD	NEAR MINT	YR.
JACK THE BEAR/Morning Glory	Victor 26536	5.00	15.00	40

ELLINGTON, Duke & His Kentucky Club Orchestra

TITLE/Flip	LABEL & No.	GOOD	NEAR MINT	YR.
NEW ORLEANS LOW-DOWN/Song Of The Cotton Field	Vocalion 1086	12.50	37.50	27

ELLINGTON, Duke as The Harlem Footwarmers

TITLE/Flip	LABEL & No.	GOOD	NEAR MINT	YR.
BIG HOUSE BLUES/Rocky Mountain Blues	Okeh 8836	12.50	37.50	30
JUNGLE JAMBOREE/Snake Hip Dance	Okeh 8720	12.50	37.50	29

ELLINGTON, Duke as Harlem Hot Chocolates

TITLE/Flip	LABEL & No.	GOOD	NEAR MINT	YR.
ST. JAMES INFIRMARY (Irving Mills vocal)	Hit Of The Week 1046	12.50	37.50	30

ELLINGTON, Duke as Joe Turner & His Memphis Men

TITLE/Flip	LABEL & No.	GOOD	NEAR MINT	YR.
FREEZE AND MELT/Mississippi Moan	Columbia 1813 D	10.00	30.00	29

ELLINGTON, Duke as The Jungle Band

TITLE/Flip	LABEL & No.	GOOD	NEAR MINT	YR.
SWEET MAMA/When You're Smiling				
(vocal by Irving Mills as Sunny Smith)	Brunswick 4760	7.50	22.50	30
WALL STREET WAIL/Cotton Club Stomp		10.00	30.00	30

ELLINGTON, Duke as Mills' Ten Black Berries

TITLE/Flip	LABEL & No.	GOOD	NEAR MINT	YR.
HOT AND BOTHERED/Black And Tan Fantasy	Diva 6056 G	15.00	45.00	30

ELLINGTON, Duke as The Washingtonians

TITLE/Flip	LABEL & No.	GOOD	NEAR MINT	YR.
I'M GONNA HANG AROUND MY SUGAR/				
Trombone Blues	Pathe Actuelle 36333	12.50	37.50	25
SWEET MAMA/Bugle Call Rag	Harmony 577 H	10.00	30.00	28

ELLINGTON, Duke as The Whoopee Makers

TITLE/Flip	LABEL & No.	GOOD	NEAR MINT	YR.
DOIN' THE VOOM VOOM/Saturday Night Function	Lincoln 3330	15.00	45.00	29
THEM THERE EYES/Rockin' Chair	Banner 32070	10.00	30.00	31
Chick Bullock vocals.				

TITLE/Flip	LABEL & No.	GOOD	NEAR MINT	YR.
GAILLARD, Slim (1916 —)				
CHITTLIN' SWITCH BLUES/Huh! Oh Huh!	Vocalion 5341	2.00	6.00	39
PUT YOUR ARMS AROUND ME, BABY/Hey! Chief	Okeh 6088	1.50	4.50	40
RHYTHM MAD/Bongo	Okeh 6015	2.00	6.00	40
THAT'S A BRINGER, THAT'S A HANGER/				
Early In The Morning	Vocalion 5220	1.50	4.50	39
GAILLARD, Slim as Slim & Slam				
DOPEY JOE/Buck Dancy Rhythm	Vocalion 4521	1.50	4.50	38
GARBER-DAVIS ORCHESTRA—see Garber, Jan as Garber-Davis Orchestra				
GARBER, Jan (1897 — 1977)				
AVALON/Stardust	Brunswick 8039	1.50	4.50	37
ALL I DO IS DREAM OF YOU (Fritz Heilbron vocal)/				
Grandfather's Clock (Lee Bennett vocal)	Victor 24629	1.50	4.50	34
DOING WHAT COMES NATUR'LLY (vocal by June Arthur & The Foursome)/				
The Gypsy (Tommy Traynor vocal)	Black & White 774	1.50	4.50	46
HOW COULD RED RIDING HOOD? (Harry Goldfield vocal)/	Victor 20322	5.00	15.00	26
This record was withdrawn three weeks after it was issued. The second side is unknown.				
LAZY LOU'SIANA MOON (unknown vocalist)	Hit Of The Week 1043	3.00	9.00	30
RHYTHM SAVED THE WORLD (Fritz Heilbron vocal)/				
Basin Street Blues (Lee Bennett vocal)	Decca 803	1.50	4.50	36
SINCE MY BEST GIRL TURNED ME DOWN (Harry Goldfield vocal)/				
I Wish I Could Shimmy Like My Sister Kate	Columbia 1306 D	1.50	4.50	28
GARBER, Jan as Garber-Davis Orchestra				
HAUNTING BLUES/If You Don't Think So You're Crazy	Columbia A 3781	2.00	6.00	22
TEASIN'/In My Heart, On My Mind All Day	Columbia A 3600	2.00	6.00	22
THAT BRAN' NEW GAL OF MINE/				
You're In Kentucky Sure As You're Born	Victor 19216	1.50	4.50	23
GARBER, Jan & His Greater Columbia Recording Orchestra				
PUTTIN' ON THE RITZ/When A Woman				
Loves A Man	Columbia 2115 D	3.00	9.00	30
Unknown vocalists.				
GOLDKETTE, Jean (1899 — 1962)				
I'M GONNA MEET MY SWEETIE NOW/Slow River	Victor 25354	3.50	10.50	27
IN MY MERRY OLDSMOBILE (waltz)/In My Merry Oldsmobile (foxtrot)				
(vocal by Fuzzy Farrar, Ray Lodwig, Doc Ryker				
and Howdy Quicksell)	Biltmore 1012	5.00	15.00	27
IN MY MERRY OLDSMOBILE (waltz)/In My Merry Oldsmobile (foxtrot)				
(vocal by Fuzzy Farrar, Ray Lodwig, Doc Ryker				
and Howdy Quicksell)	Victor Special issue, no number.	12.50	37.50	27
IN THE EVENING/Where The Lazy Daisies Grow	Victor 19308	4.00	12.00	24
MY OHIO HOME (Hoagy Carmichael vocal)/Here Comes The Showboat				
(vocal by Myron Schultz, Ray Porter, and Harold Stokes)	Victor 21166	1.50	4.50	28
PLAY ME SLOW/What's The Use Of Dreaming	Victor 19664	2.50	7.50	24
TAKE A GOOD LOOK AT MINE (Harold Stokes vocal)/				
Ya Comin' Up Tonight, Huh? (vocal by				
"Wynken-Blynken-Nod")	Victor 21889	2.50	7.50	29
GOODMAN, Benny (1909 —)				
GOODNIGHT, MY LOVE/Take Another Guess	Victor 25461	12.50	37.50	36
Ella Fitzgerald vocals. The record was withdrawn due to Decca's protest over Ella's presence.				
OOOOO-OH BOOM! (vocals by Benny Goodman and Martha Tilton)/				
Always And Always (Martha Tilton vocal)	Victor 25808	3.00	9.00	38
This was issued the same record number as "Pop-Corn Man" after it was withdrawn.				

Check with your bookstore on the availability date of the full price guide on the big bands era.

TITLE/Flip	LABEL & No.	GOOD	NEAR MINT	YR.
GOODMAN, Benny as Benny Goodman's Boys				
BLUE/Shirt Tail Stomp ....Brunswick 3975		7.50	22.50	28
GOODMAN, Benny as Benny Goodman's Boys with Jim & Glenn				
JAZZ HOLIDAY, A/Wolverine Blues .... Vocalion 15656		7.50	22.50	28
GOODMAN, Benny Quartet				
BLUES IN YOUR FLAT, THE/The Blues In My Flat .... Victor 26044		3.00	9.00	38
GOODMAN, Benny Quintet				
PICK-A-RIB/Pick-A-Rib Part 2........................... Victor 26166		4.00	12.00	38
GOODMAN, Benny Sextet				
SIX APPEAL (MY DADDY ROCKS ME)/				
These Foolish Things ....Columbia 35553		2.50	7.50	40
TILL TOM SPECIAL/Gone With "What" Wind ....Columbia 35404		3.00	9.00	40
GOODMAN, Benny Trio				
WHO?/Someday, Sweetheart .... Victor 25181		3.50	10.50	35
GRAY, Glen & The Casaloma Orchestra				
Glen Gray, leader (1906 — 1963)				
BLACK JAZZ/Maniac's Ball ....Brunswick 6242		4.00	12.00	31
BLUE JAZZ/Don't Tell A Soul (Kenny Sargent vocal) .... Brunswick 6358		3.50	10.50	32
CASA LOMA STOMP/Constantly .... Brunswick, no number.		10.00	30.00	32
A 7" publicity record which features a picture of the orchestra on one side, with advertising on the flip.				
CASA LOMA STOMP/Royal Garden Blues .... Harmony 1271 H		3.50	10.50	30
(As Roy Carroll and His Sands Point Orchestra)				
CHINA GIRL/San Sue Strut............................ Okeh 41403		3.50	10.50	30
COTTON (Pee Wee Hunt vocal)/Chant Of The Jungle .... Decca 463		2.50	7.50	35
LAZYBONES (Pee Wee Hunt vocal)/Sophisticated Lady .... Victor 24338		2.50	7.50	33
LIMEHOUSE BLUES ....Brunswick advertising record, no number.		7.50	22.50	32
TOO MARVELOUS FOR WORDS/Sentimental And Melancholy .... Decca 1158		1.50	4.50	37
Kenny Sargent vocals on both sides.				
WHEN I TAKE MY SUGAR TO TEA (Kenny Sargent vocal)/				
I Wanna Be Around My Baby All The Time				
(Pee Wee Hunt vocal) ....Brunswick 6085		3.00	9.00	31
WHERE THERE'S SMOKE THERE'S FIRE/Blue Moon................... Decca 312		2.00	6.00	35
Kenny Sargent vocals on both sides.				
GRAY, Kitty & Her Wampus Cats				
Kitty Gray vocals on most sides.				
DOING THE DOOGA/I'm Yours To Command..................... Vocalion 04629		4.50	13.50	37
I CAN'T DANCE (GOT ANTS IN MY PANTS)/				
Round And Round .... Vocalion 03992		5.00	15.00	37
MY BABY'S WAYS/Gettin' Away .... Vocalion 04121		5.00	15.00	37
SWINGOLOGY/Posin' .... Vocalion 03869		4.00	12.00	37
YOU'RE STANDING ON THE OUTSIDE NOW/				
Weeping Willow Swing .... Vocalion 04014		4.00	12.00	37
HAMPTON, Lionel (1909 —)				
DINAH/Singin The Blues...................................... Victor 26557		3.00	9.00	39
IT DON'T MEAN A THING (IF IT AIN'T GOT THAT SWING)				
(Lionel Hamption vocal)/Shufflin' At The Hollywood .... Victor 26254		2.50	7.50	39
JIVIN' THE VIBRES/Stomp .... Victor 25535		2.00	6.00	37
WIZZIN' THE WIZZ/Denison Swing .... Victor 26233		1.50	4.50	39
HAMPTON, Lionel & His Quartet				
HAMP'S SALTY BLUES (Lionel Hampton vocal)/				
Chord-A-Re-Bop .... Victor 27409		3.00	9.00	46

Samples chosen for each artist represent the range of high and low values that artist's records usually bring.

TITLE/Flip	LABEL & No.	GOOD	NEAR MINT	YR.

HAMPTON, Lionel & His Sextette

BOGO JO/Open House .... Victor 27341		2.00	6.00	40
GIVE ME SOME SKIN (Lionel Hampton vocal)/				
Three-Quarter Boogie		2.50	7.50	41
NOW THAT YOU'RE MINE (Rubel Blakey vocal)/				
Chasin' With Chase .... Victor 27529		1.50	4.50	41
SWEETHEARTS ON PARADE (Lionel Hampton vocal)/				
Shufflin' At The Hollywood .... Blue Ace 204		1.00	3.00	39

HARLEM FOOTWARMERS—see Ellington, Duke as the Harlem Footwarmers

HARLEM HOT CHOCOLATES—see Ellington, Duke as the Harlem Hot Chocolates

HAWKINS, Erskine (1914 —)

FINE AND MELLOW (Dolores Brown vocal)/Midnight ....Bluebird B 10709		2.00	6.00	40
GIN MILL SPECIAL/Tuxedo Junction ....Montgomery Ward M 8340		2.00	6.00	39
ROCKIN' ROLLERS' JUBILEE/Let This Be A Warning To You (Jimmy				
Mitchelle vocal) ....Bluebird B 7826		1.50	4.50	38
STRICTLY SWING/What Do You Know About Love? (Ida James				
vocal) ....Bluebird B 10012		1.00	3.00	38

HAWKINS, Erskine & His 'Bama State Collegians

IT WAS A SAD NIGHT IN HARLEM/				
Without A Shadow Of A Doubt .... Vocalion 3289		1.50	4.50	36
Jimmy Mitchelle vocals.				
SWINGING IN HARLEM/A Swingy Little Rhythm................... Vocalion 3336		2.50	7.50	36
UNTIL THE REAL THING COMES ALONG/				
I Can't Escape From You .... Vocalion 3280		2.00	6.00	36
Billy Daniels vocals.				

HERMAN, Woody (1913 —)
Vocals by Woody Herman on many sides.

AT THE WOODCHOPPER'S BALL .... V-Disc 29		2.00	6.00	39
DUPREE BLUES/It Happened Down In Dixieland .... Decca 1288		1.50	4.50	37

HERMAN, Woody & The New Third Herd

JUMP IN THE LINE/Stompin' At The Savoy .... Mars M 200		1.50	4.50	57
MESS AROUND/Castle Rock .... Mars M 1005		2.00	6.00	58

JAMES, Harry

B-19 .... V-Disc 493		1.50	4.50	41
FROM THE BOTTOM OF MY HEART/Melancholy Mood .... Brunswick 8443		1.50	4.50	39
Frank Sinatra vocals.				
HERE COMES THE NIGHT (Frank Sinatra vocal)/				
Feet Draggin' Blues ....Columbia 35227		1.50	4.50	39
HODGE PODGE/Four Or Five Times (vocal by orchestra) ....Philharmonic 71		1.50	4.50	40
MEMPHIS BLUES .... V-Disc 299		2.00	6.00	42
MISTER MEADOWLARK/The Nearness of You ....Varsity 8293		1.50	4.50	40
Dick Haymes vocals.				
SHEIK OF ARABY, THE/Exactly Like You ....Elite 5036		1.50	4.50	40
'TAIN'T WHAT YOU DO (Jack Palmer vocal)/				
Two O'Clock Jump .... Brunswick 8337		1.50	4.50	39
TUXEDO JUNCTION/Palms Of Paradise.................Montgomery Ward 10006		1.50	4.50	40
WHEN WE'RE ALONE/Life Goes To A Party .... Brunswick 8035		2.00	6.00	37

JONES, Spike & His City Slickers (1911 — 1964)

DER FUEHRER'S FACE (Carl Grayson vocal)/I Wanna Go Back				
To West Virginia (vocal by Del Porter and				
The Boys In The Back Room) ....Bluebird B 11586		2.00	6.00	42
LITTLE BO-PEEP HAS LOST HER JEEP/				
Pass The Biscuits Mirandy ....Bluebird B 11530		2.50	7.50	42
Del Porter vocals.				
RED WING/Behind Those Swinging Doors ....Bluebird B 11282		2.50	7.50	41
Del Porter vocals.				

TITLE/Flip	LABEL & No.	GOOD	NEAR MINT	YR.

JORDAN, Louis & His Tympany Five (1908 —)
Vocals on most listings are by Louis Jordan.

KEEP A-KNOCKIN/At The Swing Cat's Ball .... Decca 7609		1.50	4.50	39
RATION BLUES/Deacon Jones.................................... Decca 8654		1.00	3.00	42
SAM JONES DONE SNAGGED HIS BRITCHES/				
Swingin' In The Cocoanut Trees................................ Decca 7623		2.00	6.00	39

JUNGLE BAND—see Ellington, Duke as the Jungle Band

KRUPA, Gene (1909 — 1973)
Some listings with vocals by Irene Day.

BYE-BYE BLUES/After Looking At You .... Brunswick 8249		2.50	7.50	58
BLUE RHYTHM FANTASY/Blue Rhythm Fantasy Part 2 .... Okeh 5627		1.50	4.50	40
GRANDFATHER'S CLOCK/I Know That You Know .... Brunswick 8124		3.00	9.00	38
OLD BLACK JOE/My Old Kentucky Home .... Columbia 35205		1.50	4.50	39
SO LONG/Tuxedo Junction .... Columbia 35423		2.00	6.00	40
THANKS FOR THE BOOGIE RIDE (vocal by Anita O'Day and Roy Eldridge)/				
Keep 'Em Flying (Johnny Desmond vocal) .... Okeh 6506		1.50	4.50	41

KRUPA, Gene & His Chicagoans

LAST ROUND-UP, THE/Jazz Me Blues .... Parlophone 2268		6.00	18.00	35
THREE LITTLE WORDS/Blues Of Israel .... Parlophone 2224		6.00	18.00	35

KRUPA, Gene as Gene Krupa's Swing Band

MUTINY IN THE PARLOR/I'M Gonna Clap My Hands .... Victor 25263		4.00	12.00	36
Helen Ward vocals.				

LOMBARDO, Guy & His Royal Canadians (1902 — 1977)

COTTON PICKER'S BALL/Mama's Gone, Goodbye .... Gennett 5416		6.00	18.00	24
LAWD, YOU MADE THE NIGHT TOO LONG/				
A Moment In The Dark .... Brunswick 6300		2.00	6.00	32
Carmen Lombardo vocals.				
SHANGHAI LIL/Annie Doesn't Live Here Anymore .... Banner 33158		2.50	7.50	33
Carmen Lombardo vocals.				
TOO LATE/River, Stay 'Way From My Door .... Columbia 2578 D		3.00	9.00	31
Kate Smith vocals.				
UNDER THE MOON/Charmaine .... Columbia 1048 D		2.50	7.50	27
Unknown vocalists.				

LOUISVILLE RHYTHM KINGS—see Pollack, Ben as Louisville Rhythm Kings

LUNCEFORD, Jimmie (1902 — 1947)

I'M IN AN AWFUL MOOD (Trummy Young vocal)/				
Blues In The Groove .... Conqueror 9498		2.50	7.50	40
JAZZNOCRACY/Chillun, Get Up (Henry Wells vocal) .... Victor 24522		3.00	9.00	34
OKAY FOR BABY/Flight Of The Jitterbug....................... Columbia 35967		2.00	6.00	40
SOPHISTICATED LADY/Unsophisticated Sue (vocal by trio) .... Decca 129		2.00	6.00	34
WHITE HEAT .... V-Disc 355		4.00	12.00	34

LUNCEFORD, Jimmie & His Chickasaw Syncopators

IN DAT MORNIN'(preaching by Moses Allen)/				
Sweet Rhythm .... Victor V 38141		6.00	18.00	30
SOPHISTICATED LADY/Unsophisticated Sue (vocal by trio) .... Decca 129		2.00	6.00	34
WHITE HEAT .... V-Disc 355		4.00	12.00	34

LUNCEFORD, Jimmie & His Chickasaw Syncopators

IN DAT MORNIN'(preaching by Moses Allen)/				
Sweet Rhythm .... Victor V 38141		6.00	18.00	30

All records are 78 rpm unless indicated as (45) 45 rpm

Halfway between good and mint is the true value and the best condition usually available in old records. Mint is rare.

TITLE/Flip	LABEL & No.	GOOD	NEAR MINT	YR.

MILLER, Glenn (1904 — 1944)

AT THE PRESIDENT'S BALL (Vocal by Marion Hutton and the Modernaires)/
Angels of Mercy (Ray Eberle vocal and chorus) ....*Bluebird B 11429* — 5.00 — 15.00 — 42
This record was never re-issued. Angels Of Mercy was written for and dedicated to the American Red Cross.

BLUES SERENADE, A/Moonlight on The Ganges
(Smith Ballew vocals)...................................... *Columbia 3051 D* — 10.00 — 30.00 — 35

DEAR MOM (vocal by Ray Eberle and the Modernaires)/
Keep 'Em Flying...*Bluebird B 11443* — 4.00 — 12.00 — 42

DOIN' THE JIVE (Kathleen Lane vocal)/Dipper Mouth Blues ....*Conqueror 9489* — 1.00 — 30.00 — 38

GLENN MILLER AND HIS ORCHESTRA LIMITED EDITION, VOLUME ONE
(45 rpm boxed set of 10 records) ....*RCA Victor (M) SPD-18* — 10.00 — 20.00 — 55

I KNOW WHY (vocal by Paula Kelly and the Modernaires)/Chattanooga Choo Choo
(vocal by Tex Beneke, the Modernaires and Paula Kelly) ....*Bluebird B 11230* — 1.50 — 4.50 — 41
This was the first awarded "gold record." It was sprayed with gold by RCA Victor and presented to Glenn Miller on Feb. 10, 1942.

IT MUST BE JELLY ('CAUSE JAM DON'T SHAKE LIKE THAT) (vocal by the Modernaires)/
Rainbow Rhapsody .... *Victor 20 1546* — 2.00 — 6.00 — 42

JUKE BOX SATURDAY NIGHT (vocal by Marion Hutton, Tex Beneke and the Modernaires)/
Sleepy Town Train .... *Victor 20 1509* — 1.00 — 3.00 — 42

KNIT ONE, PURL TWO (vocal by Marion Hutton and the Modernaires)/Lullaby Of The Rain
(vocal by Ray Eberle and the Modernaires)...................... *Victor 27894* — 5.00 — 15.00 — 42
This record was never re-issued.

OH, YOU CRAZY MOON (Ray Eberle vocal)/Ain't Cha Comin' Out?
(vocal by Marion Hutton and Tex Beneke) ....*Montogomery Ward 8367* — 3.00 — 9.00 — 39

RENDEZVOUS TIME IN PAREE (Ray Eberle vocal)/We Can Live On Love (We Haven't Got
A Pot To Cook In) (Marion Hutton vocal) ....*Bluebird B 10309* — 5.00 — 15.00 — 39
This record was never re-issued.

TUXEDO JUNCTION/Danny Boy (Londonderry Air) ....*Bluebird B 106712* — 1.00 — 3.00 — 40

MILLS' TEN BLACK BERRIES—see Ellington, Duke as Mills' Ten Black Berries

NOBLE, Ray (1903 —)

BUGLE CALL RAG/Dinah .... *Victor 25223* — 3.00 — 9.00 — 35

COMANCHE WAR DANCE/Iroquois ....*Columbia 35258* — 1.50 — 4.50 — 39

EASY TO LOVE/I've Got You Under My Skin .... *Victor 25422* — 2.00 — 6.00 — 36
Al Bowlly vocals.

JUST LET ME LOOK AT YOU/You Couldn't Be Cuter .... *Brunswick 8076* — 1.50 — 4.50 — 38
Tony Martin vocals.

LET'S SWING IT (vocal by the Freshmen)/Chinatown, My Chinatown .... *Victor 25070* — 2.50 — 7.50 — 35

SLUMMING ON PARK AVENUE (vocals by the Merry Macs)/I've Got My Love
To Keep Me Warm (Howard Phillips vocal) .... *Victor 25507* — 1.50 — 4.50 — 37

TIGER RAG/Japanese Sandman .... *HMV B 6425* — 3.00 — 9.00 — 33
English release.

VILIA/Crazy Rhythm .... *Brunswick 8098* — 2.00 — 6.00 — 38

NORVO, Red (1908 —)
Many sides with vocals by Mildred Bailey.

CLAP HANDS, HERE COMES CHARLIE/Russian Lullaby............ *Brunswick 7975* — 3.00 — 9.00 — 37

GARDEN OF THE MOON/Jump Jump's Here...................... *Brunswick 8202* — 2.50 — 7.50 — 38

IT ALL BEGINS AND ENDS WITH YOU/Picture Me Without You ..... *Brunswick 7732* — 4.00 — 12.00 — 36

JERSEY BOUNCE/Arthur Murray Taught Me Dancing In A Hurry .....*Columbia 36557* — 1.50 — 4.50 — 39

KNOCKIN' ON WOOD/Hole In The Wall........................ *Brunswick 6562* — 5.00 — 15.00 — 33
Xylophone or marimba solos.

LET YOURSELF GO/If You Love............................. *Champion 40100* — 3.50 — 10.50 — 36
Unknown vocalists. First side recorded as Ken Kenny, second side as Len Herman.

PORTER'S LOVE SONG TO A CHAMBERMAID, A/I Know That
You Know .... *Brunswick 7744* — 4.00 — 12.00 — 36

SOME LIKE IT HOT/Have Mercy .... *Vocalion 5009* — 2.00 — 6.00 — 39

TOADIE TODDLE/There'll Never Be Another You .... *Vocalion 4738* — 3.00 — 9.00 — 39

NORVO, Red & His Swing Octet/Septet

BUGHOUSE/Blues In E Flat................................ *Columbia 3079 D* — 4.50 — 13.50 — 35

NIGHT IS BLUE, THE/With All My Heart And Soul .... *Columbia 3026 D* — 4.00 — 12.00 — 35

OLD FASHIONED LOVE/Honeysuckle Rose .... *Columbia 3059 D* — 4.00 — 12.00 — 35

TITLE/Flip	LABEL & No.	GOOD	NEAR MINT	YR.
NORVO, Red & His Swing Sextette				
I GOT RHYTHM/Oh! Lady Be Good	Decca 779	3.50	10.50	36
NORVO, Red as Mildred Bailey & Her Orchestra				
All with Mildred Bailey vocals.				
I LET A SONG GO OUT OF MY HEART/Rock It For Me	Vocalion 4083	2.50	7.50	38
LOVE IS WHERE YOU FIND IT/I Used To Be Color Blind	Conqueror 9106	2.50	7.50	38
POLLACK, Ben (1903 — 1971)				
DEEP ELM/The Moon Is Grinning At Me (Ben Pollack vocal)	Vocalion 3769	5.00	15.00	36
IF I COULD BE WITH YOU (ONE HOUR TONIGHT) (Jack Teagarden vocal)/				
There's A Wah-Wah Girl In Agua Caliente (vocal by trio)	Conqueror 7576	5.00	15.00	30
I'M FOLLOWING YOU (Ben Pollack vocal)	Hit Of The Week 1026	6.00	18.00	30
I'VE GOT FIVE DOLLARS (vocal by Ben Pollack as Ted Bancroft)/Sweet And Hot				
(vocal by Ben Pollack as Ted Bancroft with Jack Teagarden and				
Nappy Lamare)	Banner 32104	5.00	15.00	31
POLLACK, Ben & His Californians				
SINGAPORE SORROWS (Ben Pollack vocal)/Sweet Sue -- Just You				
(Franklyn Baur vocal)	Victor 21437	5.00	15.00	28
POLLACK, Ben & His Park Central Orchestra				
MY KINDA LOVE (vocal by Smith Ballew as Charles Roberts)/				
On With The Dance! (Ben Pollack vocal)	Victor 21944	4.00	12.00	29
POLLACK, Ben & His Pick-A-Rib Boys				
BOOGIE WOOGIE/California, Here I Come	Decca 1517	2.00	6.00	37
FIDGETY FEET/Stompin' At The Savoy	Two-Beat T.B. 8551	2.50	7.50	
POLLACK, Ben as Ben's Bad Boys				
WANG-WANG BLUES/Yellow Dog Blues (Ben Pollack vocal)	Victor 21971	5.00	15.00	29
POLLACK, Ben as Louisville Rhythm Kings				
LET'S SIT AND TALK ABOUT YOU (Smith Ballew vocal)/				
In A Great Big Way (vocal by trio)	Okeh 41189	3.50	10.50	
SPREADIN' KNOWLEDGE AROUND/Zoom Zoom Zoom				
(Harry James vocal)	Vocalion 3342	4.00	12.00	36
PRINCE'S BAND/ORCHESTRA				
BEN HUR CHARIOT RACE MARCH	Little Wonder 329	50.00	150.00	
Little Wonders were 5½", one-sided records issued in the 'teens and early 20's without				
performer credits. The labels simply stated dance band, baritone solo, etc. This label, how-				
ever, does show Prince's Band as performing artists, and is one of what is believed to be an				
extremely few, if not the only, Little Wonder issue released with performer identification on				
the label.				
DREAMY MELODY/Goodnight	Paramount 20225	2.50	7.50	23
LASSUS TROMBONE (DE CULLUD VALET TO MISS TROMBONE)/				
Miss Trombone (A Slippery Rag)	Columbia A 2825	2.00	6.00	18
MY HAWAIIAN SUNSHINE/I've Got The Army Blues	Columbia A 5951	1.00	3.00	17
YAH-DE-DAH/New Orleans Jazz	Columbia A 5983	1.50	4.50	17
RANDALL, Clark				
Each listing has a vocal by Clark Randall on one side and Nappy Lamare on the other.				
DRIFTING TIDE/Here Comes Your Pappy				
With The Wrong Kind Of Load	Brunswick 7435	6.00	18.00	35
TOUBLESOME TRUMPET/When Icky Morgan Plays The Organ	Brunswick 7415	5.00	15.00	35
RANDALL, Clark as Gil Rodin				
Vocals by Clark Randall on all sides.				
RIGHT ABOUT FACE/Love's Serenade	Melotone M 13376	4.00	12.00	35
WHAT'S THE REASON (I'M NOT PLEASIN' YOU)/Restless	Perfect 16107	4.50	13.50	35

The left hand price column represents the true value of the average, used record.

TITLE/Flip	LABEL & No.	GOOD	NEAR MINT	YR.

SHAW, Artie (1910 —)

TITLE/Flip	LABEL & No.	GOOD	NEAR MINT	YR.
ANY OLD TIME (Billie Holiday vocal)/Zigeuner	V-Disc 399	5.00	15.00	39
BACK BAY SHUFFLE/Any Old Time (Billie Holiday vocal)	Bluebird B 7759	2.50	7.50	38
BILL (Helen Forrest vocal)/Carioca	Bluebird B 10124	1.50	4.50	39
CHANTEZ-LEX BAS (SING 'EM LOW)/Danza Lucimi	Victor 27354	2.00	6.00	40
CONCERTO FOR CLARINET/Concerto For Clarinet Part 2	Victor 36383	3.00	9.00	40
This is an oversize 12" record.				
I'M COMING, VIRGINIA/Out Of Nowhere	Montgomery Ward M 8384	3.00	9.00	39
MAKE LOVE TO ME (Paula Kelly vocal)/Solid Sam	Victor 27705	1.50	4.50	41
SKELETON IN THE CLOSET/There's Frost On The Moon				
(Peg La Centra vocal)	Brunswick 7771	3.00	9.00	36
SOBBIN' BLUES/Cream Puff	Conqueror 9193	3.00	9.00	36
SOFTLY AS IN A MORNING SUNRISE/Copenhagen	Montgomery Ward M 7950	2.00	6.00	38
SUGAR FOOT STOMP/Thou Swell	Brunswick 7735	3.50	10.50	36

SHAW, Artie & His New Music

TITLE/Flip	LABEL & No.	GOOD	NEAR MINT	YR.
BLUES, THE/The Blues, Part 2	Vocalion 4401	2.50	7.50	37
BORN TO SWING (A long-play electrical transcription)	Thesaurus 395	12.50	37.50	
TWILIGHT IN TURKEY (A long play electrical transcription)	Thesaurus 388	12.50	37.50	
Seven songs, all specially recorded different versions, some with vocals by Dorothy Howe or Tony Pastor.				

SLIM & SLAM—see Gaillard, Slim as Slim & Slam

TEAGARDEN, Jack (1905–1964)
Most listings have one or both songs with vocal by Jack Teagarden.

TITLE/Flip	LABEL & No.	GOOD	NEAR MINT	YR.
CAN'T WE TALK IT OVER?/The Blues	Montgomery Ward 10012	3.00	9.00	40
DARK EYES/Chicks Is Wonderful	Decca 3701	1.50	4.50	41
IF I COULD BE WITH YOU (ONE HOUR TONIGHT)/The Blues	Philharmonic 83	3.00	9.00	40
I SWUNG THE ELECTION/Aunt Hagar's Blues	Columbia 35206	2.00	6.00	39
LOVE FOR SALE/Wham (Re-Bop-Boom-Bam)	Varsity 8202	1.50	4.50	40
Kitty Kallen vocals.				
ON REVIVAL DAY/Wolverine Blues	V-Disc 724	5.00	15.00	39
SHAKE YOUR HIPS/Somebody Stole Gabriel's Horn	Columbia 2802 D	2.50	7.50	33
YOU RASCAL, YOU/That's What I Like About You	Columbia 2588 D	4.00	12.00	31
Jack Teagarden and Fats Waller vocals.				

TEAGARDEN, Jack as Jack Teagarden's Big Eight

TITLE/Flip	LABEL & No.	GOOD	NEAR MINT	YR.
ST. JAMES INFIRMARY (Jack Teagarden vocal)/Shine	Hot Record Society 2006	5.00	15.00	40
An oversize 12" record.				

TRUMBAUER, Frankie (1901 — 1956)

TITLE/Flip	LABEL & No.	GOOD	NEAR MINT	YR.
BABY, WON'T YOU PLEASE COME HOME? (Frank Trumbauer vocal)/				
I Like That	Okeh 41286	6.50	19.50	29
BREAK IT DOWN/Juba Dance	Brunswick 6763	3.00	9.00	34
CLARINET MARMALADE/Singin' The Blues	Okeh 40772	7.50	22.50	27
GET HAPPY/Deep Harlem	Okeh 41431	4.00	12.00	30
Frank Trumbauer vocals.				
HAPPY FEET (Smith Ballew vocal)/I Like To Do Things For You				
(Jeannie Lang vocal)	Okeh 41421	3.50	10.50	30
JIMTOWN BLUES/The Laziest Gal In Town (vocal by Fredda Gibson,				
later known as Georgia Gibbs)	Varsity 8223	2.50	7.50	40
NOBODY BUT YOU/Got A Feelin' For You	Okeh 41252	5.00	15.00	29
Smith Ballew vocals.				
NOT ON THE FIRST NIGHT, BABY (vocal by Wayne Williams, Frank Trumbauer and				
Fredda Gibson)/Walkin' The Dog (vocal chorus	Varsity 8225	2.00	6.00	40
PLANTATION MOODS/Troubled	Victor 24834	3.50	10.50	34
THERE'LL COME A TIME/Mississippi Mud				
(vocal by Bing Crosby and Frank Trumbauer)	Okeh 40979	12.50	37.50	28

TURNER, Joe & His Memphis Men—see Ellington, Duke as Joe Turner & His Memphis Men

All records are 78 rpm unless indicated as (45) 45 rpm

TITLE/Flip	LABEL & No.	GOOD	NEAR MINT	YR.

VENUTI, Joe (1904 — 1978)
STOP, LOOK AND LISTEN/Yankee Doodle Never Went To Town ..... Columbia 3104 D — 3.00 — 9.00 — 35
Ruth Lee vocals.
YOU'RE MY PAST, PRESENT AND FUTURE/Doin' The Uptown Lowdown .. Domino 154 — 4.00 — 12.00 — 33

VENUTI, Joe & His Blue Five
HIAWATHA'S LULLABY/My Gypsy Rhapsody .... Columbia CB 637 — 7.50 — 22.50 — 33
Labelled as Joe Venuti and His Orchestra. English, not issued in the U.S.

VENUTI, Joe & His Blue Six
SWEET LORRAINE/Doin' The Uptown Lowdown .... Decca 18167 — 5.00 — 15.00 — 33

VENUTI, Joe & His New Yorkers
THAT'S THE GOOD OLD SUNNY SOUTH/Weary River .... Okeh 41192 — 5.00 — 15.00 — 29
Smith Ballew vocals.

VENUTI, Joe as Joe Venuti's Blue Four
CHEESE AND CRACKERS/A Mug Of Ale .... Okeh 40897 — 7.50 — 22.50 — 27
MAN FROM THE SOUTH, THE/Pretty Trix .... Okeh 41076 — 5.00 — 15.00 — 28

VENUTI, Joe as Joe Venuti's Rhythm Boys
THERE'S NO OTHER GIRL/Now That I Need You, You're Gone ...... Columbia 2535 D — 4.00 — 12.00 — 31
Harold Arlen vocals.

VENUTI, Joe - Eddie Land & Their All-Star Orchestra
BEALE STREET BLUES/After You've Gone .... Melotone M 12294 — 6.00 — 18.00 — 31
Jack Teagarden vocals.
FAREWELL BLUES/Someday, Sweetheart .... Vocalion 15858 — 7.50 — 22.50 — 31

VENUTI, Joe - Eddie Lang Blue Five
HEY! YOUNG FELLA/Pink Elephants .... Columbia CB 601 — 9.00 — 27.00 — 33
English release, not issued in the U.S.
JIG SAW PUZZLE BLUES/Vibraphonia (this side played by Joe Venuti and his
Blue Five) .... Columbia 2782 D — 7.50 — 22.50 — 33

WASHINGTONIANS—see Ellington, Duke as the Washingtonians

WHITEMAN, Paul (1890 — 1967)
BELL HOPPIN' BLUES/St. Louis Blues .... Victor 20092 — 1.50 — 4.50 — 26
CHINA BOY/Oh! Miss Hanna (Bing Crosby vocal) .... Columbia 1945 D — 6.00 — 18.00 — 29
C-O-N-S-T-A-N-T-I-N-O-P-L-E (vocal by Al Rinker, Harry Barris, Jack Fulton, Charles
Gaylord and Austin Young)/Get Out And Get Under The Moon
(vocal by Bing Crosby and trio) .... Columbia 1402 D — 3.50 — 10.50 — 28
DARKTOWN STRUTTER'S BALL (Jack Teagarden vocal)/Farewell Blues .. Victor 25192 — 2.00 — 6.00 — 35
DO I HEAR YOU SING (I LOVE YOU) (vocal by Bing Crosby, Al Rinker and Charles Gaylord)/
You Took Advantage Of Me (vocal by Bing Crosby, Jack Fulton, Charles Gaylord and
Austin Young) .... Victor 21398 — 5.00 — 15.00 — 28
I'M BRINGING A RED, RED ROSE (Jack Fulton vocal)/Makin' Whoopee
(vocal by Bing Crosby, Jack Fulton, Charles Gaylord &
Austin Young) .... Columbia 1683 D — 3.00 — 9.00 — 28
I'M COMING, VIRGINIA (vocal by Bing Crosby, Al Rinker and Harry Barris)/
Just Once Again (Austin Young vocal) .... Victor 20751 — 4.00 — 12.00 — 27
LONELY EYES (Wilbur Hall vocal)/Wistful And Blue
(vocal by Bing Crosby and Al Rinker) .... Victor 20418 — 3.00 — 9.00 — 26
SAN/Poor Butterfly (vocal by Bing Crosby, Al Rinker, Charles Gaylord and
Austin Young) .... Victor 24078 — 7.50 — 22.50 — 28
'TAIN'T SO, HONEY, 'TAIN'T SO (Bing Crosby vocal)/ That's My Weakness Now
(vocal by Bing Crosby, Al Rinker and Harry Barris) .... Columbia 1444 D — 4.00 — 12.00 — 28

WHITEMAN, Paul & His Convert Orchestra
RHAPSODY IN BLUE/Rhapsody In Blue Part 2 .... Victor 35822 — 3.00 — 9.00 — 27
This is an oversized 12" record featuring George Gershwin at the piano.
Samples chosen for each artist represent the range of high and low values that artist's records usually bring.

Check with your bookstore on the availability date of the full price guide on the big bands era.

TITLE/Flip	LABEL & No.	GOOD	NEAR MINT	YR.

WHITEMAN, Paul & His Swing Wing
I'M COMIN', VIRGINIA (vocal by The Four Modernaires)/Aunt Hagar's Blues
(vocal by Jack Teagarden and The Four Modernaires) .... *Decca 2145* 1.50 **4.50** *38*

WHITEMAN, Paul as Paul Whiteman's Sax Soctette
BLUE SKIES/What'll I Do? .... *Decca 2698* 1.50 **4.50** *39*
Vocals by Art Ryerson and Dave Barbour.

WHOOPEE MAKERS—see Ellington, Duke as the Whoopee Makers

WOLVERINE ORCHESTRA
BIX BEIDERBECKE (1903 — 1931)
FIDGETY FEET/Jazz Me Blues .... *Gennett 5408* 20.00 **60.00** *24*
OH BABY/Copenhagen .... *Gennett 5453* 17.50 **52.50** *24*

ZURKE, Bob & His Delta Rhythm Boys (1912 — 1944)
BETWEEN THE DEVIL AND THE DEEP BLUE SEA (Claire Martin vocal)/
I've Found A New Baby..................................... *Victor 26355* 2.00 **6.00** *39*
MELANCHOLY MOOD (Claire Martin vocal)/Honky Tonk Train Blues..... *Victor 26342* 1.50 **4.50** *39*
TOM CAT ON THE KEYS/Everybody Step .... *Victor 26526* 2.50 **7.50** *39*

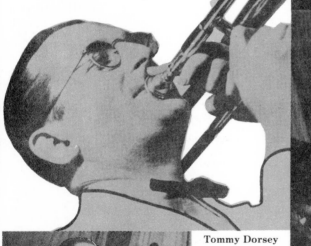

Tommy Dorsey

Cab Calloway

Glenn Miller

Ella Fitzgerald

Cugat

Benny Goodman

Ray Noble

The following section contains excerpts from our best seller:

Record Albums 1948-1978
Official Price Guide for Collectible Records

Now out in a greatly expanded 2nd edition, *Record Albums 1948-1978* is bursting with helpful information for the record collector. Over 28,000 listings that chronicle the values on today's market of the "big records with the little holes" — the 10" and 12" long play albums. Listings cover popular artists, rock, country/western, rockabilly, rhythm & blues and a special, "easy reference" section of original cast and movie soundtrack albums.

$7.95

Each of our price guides includes a special *Dealers and Collectors Directory* listing hundreds of buyers and sellers of collectible records!

Record Albums 1948-1978

Can be purchased at your local book or record store
or send check or money order to:
O'Sullivan Woodside & Company
2218 East Magnolia
Phoenix, Arizona 85034
please add 75¢ per book for postage and handling
(Hardcover edition available. See below.)

FIRST EDITIONS STILL AVAILABLE!
OUR BEST-SELLER FIRST EDITION, NOW OUT OF PRINT, HAS BECOME A COLLECTOR'S ITEM!

Complete your library with the *Record Album Price Guide, First Edition* while the limited supply lasts! No longer available in most bookstores. Order either the soft or hard cover edition directly from:

Jellyroll Productions
Box 3017 Scottsdale, Arizona 85257
**(Soft cover: $10.00 plus $1.00 postage.
Hard cover: $20.00 plus $1.00 postage.)**
ALSO
SPECIAL, LIMITED **SECOND EDITIONS**
OF HARD COVER COPIES ARE
AVAILABLE WHILE THE SUPPLY LASTS.

These are permanently bound, limited and numbered books!
If you wish to order direct, send **$18.95** to Jellyroll Productions.

Record Albums 1948-1978
Price Guide of Current
Collectible Records (8½" x 11" 264 pages)

THE LONG PLAY AND YOU

Popular music has worn many labels over the years, including "Tin Pan Alley," "The Hit Parade," "Top 40," and "Rock & Roll." During the mid-sixties, this mainstream of popular bestsellers became known as "Rock" music and carries that label to the present. *Popular and Rock Albums, 1948-1978* will be more accurately titled by exact contents in the future than it is now. The first and current editions were more broadly based.

In our first edition, we envisioned this book as the long play counterpart to all of our other singles price guides. The expansion of listings from the first to the second editions, however, altered that thinking. By the time the third edition comes out—probably in the spring of 1980—we will have dropped the rhythm and blues albums because they already will have been added to our *Blacks and Blues* price guide. In fact, the R&B albums listed under the *Blacks and Blues* prevue (see pages 78-109) of this compendium (the book you're holding) are actually all taken from the second edition of the *Record Albums* guide (the cover is pictured one page back), but with prices brought up-to-date as they will be reflected in the first edition of *Blacks and Blues*!

The *Record Albums* guide excerpts contained in this book do not reflect any Country/Western albums either, even though they, too, are in the book. Lack of room in the compendium mandated their exclusion, and they will also be moved to the second edition of our *Country/Western* price guide. Collector interest in country albums runs a distant third behind the old-time 78 singles and the contemporary 45s.

Collector interest in the popular field—or rock, if you wish—places a very high priority on the long play album, as is clearly shown by the number of them in the World's Top 50. Because newer collectors have brought this about (we figure a male, age 28, comes close to the average profile of the album buyer today) the selections we've chosen to highlight on the following pages represent a slightly disproportionate slant to the contemporary. The singles book section (see pages 51-77) shows a greater emphasis on vintage artists.

The important point to remember, however, to put *A Guide to Record Collecting* to its best and most effective use, is to keep in mind that almost all of the artists represented in each of these sections actually appear, and with listings in depth, in *both* of our pop and rock price guides for singles *and* albums. We felt this plan enabled us to most effectively cover as much ground in our prevue as possible. If an artist's albums tend to be more sought-after than his singles, for whatever reason, we chose to excerpt his albums in this section and we left his name out of the other.

There are, naturally, a very few exceptions, and, again, most notably, the Beatles and Elvis Presley. Readers of the compendium will discover that these giants' singles and LPs heavily dominte the World's Top 50, so to leave them out of either section would have been unthinkable.

Price structuring is more complicated in the *Record Albums* book, and might appear unfathomable to the layman with limited examples to examine. Basically, the average difference in value between a recent album in used, *"good"* condition and an almost perfect, *"near mint"* copy is double, mainly because—and this may come as a surprise—younger collectors tend to be less discriminating about condition. Their pocketbooks may be slimmer, too, and they are often only interested in the sound.

Of all recorded music, historically, the album has been the most fragile, the most abused, and, thusly, the most difficult to find in new, unplayed condition. The further back one goes, the more the problem magnifies, and so does the spread. LPs from the '50s are almost impossible to secure in that premium condition, and, therefore, will bring four times as much.

Where our problems took on nightmarish proportions were in the cases of albums we couldn't date. Structuring on this sliding scale became such an impossible task, in our newly-expanded Soundtrack and Original Cast section we had to set all albums at double (i.e. $20.00 to $40.00) between good and near mint, cautioning the collector that the information is, after all, only a guide, and that one must be prepared, for instance, if lucky enough to have the opportunity to bid on a rare, mint 10" LP from 1949, to go very high or risk being outbid.

If you're seriously interested in collecting records, you should know some basic facts:

Keep your records in paper sleeves and in as dust-free an area as possible. Store them standing on edge, not stacked flat like pancakes. Don't ever get them in direct sunlight! Keep them away from heat sources; even setting a record on top of your TV set or amplifier can warp it. Don't get your records wet, handle them only by the edges, and never put your fingers on anything except the label and the very edge of the disc. Even then, wipe the disc with a lint-free record cleaner before you play it, and make sure your needle is not worn.

When storing record albums, place the disc back in its (usually paper) inner sleeve and then slide it and the sleeve into the jacket, with the open side of the sleeve pointing up. As much as is possible, this prevents the record from getting dust on it because the record is sealed away from the outside air. If a record is valuable—and most albums are expensive enough when purchased new to justify the small expense—store the whole package in a heavy plastic bag to protect the jacket as well as the record. The condition of the jacket can be as important as the record when it comes time to consider resale potential.

Remember, when it comes to taking care of records, good habits—after they've become automatic— can be as hard to break as bad ones!

Alphabetical Listing of Record Albums, Original Casts & Soundtracks

This section represents a 3½% sampling of the artists and songs in *Record Albums 1948-1978*.

TITLE	LABEL & No.	GOOD	NEAR MINT
ABBA			
ARRIVAL	Atlantic (S) SD 18207	2.50	5.00
ADRIAN & THE SUNSETS			
BREAKTHROUGH	Sunset (M) SE 63-601	6.00	18.00
AEROSMITH			
TOYS IN THE ATTIC	Columbia (S) PC-33479	2.50	5.00
ALLEN, Woody			
WONDERFUL WACKY WORLD	Bell (S) 6008	5.00	15.00
WOODY ALLEN	Colpix (S) SCP-488	6.00	18.00
ALLMAN BROTHERS BAND			
EAT A PEACH	Capricorn (S) 2CP-0102	5.00	10.00
IDLEWILD SOUTH	Atco (S) SD 33-342	7.00	14.00
ALPERT, Herb, & The Tijuana Brass			
LONELY BULL (Orig.)	A&M (S) SP 101	4.00	12.00
WHIPPED CREAM & OTHER DELIGHTS	A&M (S) SP 4110	2.00	4.00
AMBOY DUKES			
AMBOY DUKES, THE	Mainstream (S) 6104	5.00	10.00
JOURNEY TO THE CENTER OF THE MIND	Mainstream (S) 6112	4.00	8.00
ANGELS			
AND THE ANGELS SING	Caprice (S) SLP 1001	7.00	21.00
MY BOYFRIEND'S BACK	Smash (S) SRS 67039	6.00	12.00
ANIMALS, THE			
ANIMALS, THE	MGM (S) SE-4264	3.00	6.00
IN THE BEGINNING	Wand (S) WDS 690	4.00	8.00
ASTRONAUTS			
ROCKIN' WITH TIE ASTRONAUTS	RCA Victor (M) PRM 183	6.00	18.00
SURFIN' WITH THE ASTRONAUTS	RCA Victor (S) LSP 2760	5.00	10.00
BACHELORS			
BACK AGAIN	London (S) PS 393	5.00	10.00
HITS OF THE 60's	London (S) PS 460	4.00	8.00
BEACH BOYS			
BEACH BOYS DELUXE SET	Capitol (M) TCL 2813	35.00	105.00
BRIAN WILSON INTRODUCES SELECTIONS FROM			
BEACH BOYS CONCERT	Capitol (EP) PRO 2754/2755	70.00	210.00
Flip side is "Brian Wilson Introduces Selections From Beach Boys Songbook." This EP contains "Little Old Lady," "Johnny B. Goode," "I Get Around," "The Warmth Of The Sun."			
SHUT DOWN VOL. 2 (Compact 33)	Capitol (S) SXA 2027	25.00	50.00
SMILEY SMILE (Capitol Record Club Issue)	Capitol (S) ST8 2891	34.00	102.00
STACK-O-TRACKS (With Book)	Capitol (S) DKAO 2893	25.00	75.00
10 LITTLE INDIANS	Capitol (EP) PRO 2186	70.00	210.00
The Beach Boys sing "10 Little Indians," and "Little Miss America" on one side, and Ray Anthony has two songs on the flip side.			
SUNFLOWER	Reprise (S) 6382	2.00	4.00
BEATLES			
BEATLES AND FRANK IFIELD (On Stage)	Vee Jay (S) LPS 1085	170.00	510.00
BEATLES VI	Capitol (S) ST 2358	3.00	9.00
Cover reads "See label for correct playing order" with black label.			
BEATLES '65	Capitol (M) T 2228	2.00	6.00
EARLY BEATLES	Capitol (S) ST 2309	2.00	6.00
HELP!	Capitol (M) MAS 2368	2.00	6.00

14

TITLE	LABEL & No.	GOOD	NEAR MINT
HEY JUDE ....Apple (S) SW 385		1.50	4.50
LET IT BE ....Apple (S) AR 34001		1.50	4.50
MEET THE BEATLES..............................Capitol (S) ST 2047		4.00	12.00
"Beatles" is in a light tan color on a black label.			
RUBBER SOUL ....Capitol (M) T 2442		1.50	4.50
YESTERDAY...AND TODAY			
(Original issue) ....Capitol (M) T 2553		80.00	240.00
YESTERDAY...AND TODAY			
(Original Issue)................................. Capitol (S) ST 2553		100.00	300.00 Tie
This album was first issued with a devastatingly controversial jacket photo showing the Beatles in butcher smocks sitting among pieces of meat and cut up toy dolls. Capitol shortly removed the now famous "Butcher Cover" from the record stores.			
YESTERDAY ...AND TODAY ....Capitol (S) ST 2553		3.00	9.00
Green label.			
YESTERDAY...AND TODAY .... Apple (S) ST 2553		1.50	4.50
With Capitol Logo.			
BEAU BRUMMELS			
BEST OF BEAU BRUMMELS............................ Vault (S) 114		11.00	33.00
INTRODUCING THE BEAU BRUMMELS .... Autumn (S) 103		6.00	18.00
BEE GEES			
BEE GEE'S 1ST....................................... Atco (S) 33-223		4.00	8.00
CHILDREN OF THE WORLD ....RSO (S) 3003		3.00	6.00
BELLUS, Tony			
ROBBIN' THE CRADLE................................. NRC (M) LPA 8		6.00	24.00
BIG BOPPER			
CHANTILLY LACE .... Mercury (M) MG-20402		15.00	60.00
CHANTILLY LACE .... Pickwick (M) 3365		3.00	6.00
BLACK OAK ARKANSAS			
IF AN ANGEL CAME TO YOU, WOULD YOU MAKE HER FEEL AT HOME?................................... Atco (S) SD 7008		3.00	6.00
X-RATED.. MCA (S) 2155		2.50	5.00
BLACK SABBATH			
MASTER OF REALITY ....Warner Bros. (S) BS 2562		3.00	6.00
PARANOID ....Warner Bros. (S) WS 1887		3.50	7.00
BLIND FAITH			
BLIND FAITH (WITH GROUP ON COVER) .... Atco (S) SD 33-304		3.00	6.00
BLIND FAITH (WITH GIRL ON COVER) .... Atco (S) SD 33-304		4.50	9.00
BLOOD, SWEAT & TEARS			
BLOOD, SWEAT & TEARS ....Columbia (S) CS 9720		3.00	6.00
BRAND NEW DAY .... ABC (S) 1015		2.00	4.00
BLUE OYSTER CULT			
BLUE OYSTER CULT.......................... Columbia (S) KC 31063		3.00	6.00
IN MY MOUTH OR ON THE GROUND (10 inch LP) ..... IMP (M) 11106		4.00	8.00

(M) Monaural, (S) Stereo, (EP) Extended Play.

TITLE	LABEL & No.	GOOD	NEAR MINT
BOOGIE KINGS			
BLUE-EYED SOUL	Montel-Michelle (M) LP 109	6.00	18.00
BOSTON			
BOSTON	Epic (S) PE 34188	2.00	4.00
BOWIE, David			
DAVID BOWIE	Deram (S) DES 18003	8.00	16.00
⑤⓪ MAN WHO SOLD THE WORLD	Mercury (S) SR 61246	125.00	250.00 Tie
(Original 'drag' cover)			
BROWNE, Jackson			
PRETENDER, THE	Asylum (S) 7E-1079	3.00	6.00
RUNNING ON EMPTY	Asylum (S) 6E-113	2.50	5.00
BRUCE, Lenny			
LENNY BRUCE IS OUT AGAIN	Philles (M) PHLP 4010	10.00	30.00
SICK HUMOR OF LENNY BRUCE, THE	Fantasy (M) LP7001	6.00	18.00
BUFFALO SPRINGFIELD			
BUFFALO SPRINGFIELD (Without "For What It's Worth")	Atco (S) SD 33-200	8.00	16.00
RETROSPECTIVE	Atco (S) SD 33-283	3.00	6.00
BYRDS			
MR. TAMBOURINE MAN	Columbia (S) CS 9172	4.00	8.00
PREFLYTE	Together (S) ST-T-1001	5.00	10.00
BYRNES, Edd			
EDD "KOOKIE" BYRNES	Warner Bros. (EP) EA 1309	2.50	10.00
KOOKIE	Warner Bros. (S) WS-1309	3.00	12.00
CALE, J.J.			
NATURALLY...J.J. CALE	Shelter (S) SW 8908	3.50	7.00
REALLY J.J. CALE	Shelter (S) SW 8912	3.50	7.00
CAMPBELL, Jo Ann			
ALL THE HITS BY JO ANN CAMPBELL	Cameo (M) C 1026	5.00	14.00
I'M NOBODY'S BABY	End (M) LP 306	5.00	20.00
CANNED HEAT			
BOOGIE WITH CANNED HEAT	Liberty (S) LST 7541	3.00	6.00
VINTAGE	Janus (S) JLS 3009	2.50	5.00
CANNON, Freddy			
ACTION!	Warner Bros. (M) W 1612	5.00	15.00
PALISADES PARK	Swan (M) LP 507	5.00	20.00

All artists shown in photos appear with listings in the guide these samples were taken from.

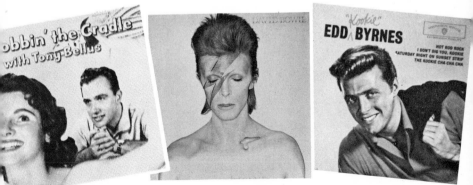

TITLE	LABEL & No.	GOOD	NEAR MINT
CASSIDY, Shaun			
BORN LATE	Warner Bros./Curb (S) BSK 3126	2.00	4.00
SHAUN CASSIDY	Warner Bros./Curb (S) BS 3067	2.00	4.00
CHAD & JEREMY			
BEFORE AND AFTER	Columbia (M) CL 2374	5.00	15.00
YESTERDAYS GONE	World Artists (M) WAM 2002	3.00	9.00
CHAPIN, Harry			
GREATEST STORIES -LIVE	Elektra (S) EKS 7E-2009	2.50	5.00
HEADS & TALES	Elektra (S) EKS 75023	3.00	6.00
CHEECH & CHONG			
BIG BAMBU	Ode (S) SP 77014	2.50	5.00
CHEECH & CHONG'S WEDDING ALBUM	Ode (S) SP 77025	2.50	5.00
CHICAGO			
CHICAGO	Columbia (S) KGP 24	3.00	6.00
CHICAGO AT CARNEGIE HALL	Columbia (S) C4X 30865	5.00	10.00
CHOCOLATE WATCH BAND			
THE INNER MYSTIQUE	Tower (S) ST 5106	12.00	36.00
NO WAY OUT	Tower (S) ST 5096	6.00	18.00
CLAPTON, Eric			
461 OCEAN BOULEVARD	RSO (S) 4801	3.50	7.00
HISTORY OF ERIC CLAPTON	Atco (S) 803	4.00	8.00
COCHRAN, Eddie			
EDDIE COCHRAN	Liberty (S) LST-7172	15.00	60.00
NEVER TO BE FORGOTTEN	Liberty (M) LRP3220	3.00	12.00
COLLINS, Judy			
IN MY LIFE	Elektra (S) EKS 7320	4.50	9.00
WILDFLOWERS	Elektra (S) EKS 74012	4.00	8.00
COOLIDGE, Rita			
ANYTIME...ANYWHERE	A&M (S) SP 4616	2.00	4.00
RITA COOLIDGE	A&M (S) SP 4291	2.00	4.00
COSTELLO, Elvis			
LIVE AT THE EL MOCAMBO (Canadian)	CBS (S)	15.00	30.00
MY AIM IS TRUE	Columbia (S) JC 35037	2.00	4.00
COUNTRY JOE & THE FISH			
COUNTRY JOE AND THE FISH	Rag Baby (M)	20.00	40.00
TOGETHER	Vanguard (S) VSD 79277	3.00	6.00
CRAWFORD, Johnny			
GREATEST HITS, VOL 2	Del Fi (M) DFLP 1248	6.00	18.00
RUMORS	Del Fi (M) DFLP 1224	4.00	12.00
CRICKETS			
CHIRPING CRICKETS	Brunswick (M) BL54038	16.00	64.00
SOUND OF THE CRICKETS	Brunswick (EP) EB 71038	6.00	18.00
CROCE, Jim			
FACES I'VE BEEN	Lifesong (S) 900	5.00	10.00
YOU DON'T MESS AROUND WITH JIM	ABC (S) 756	4.00	8.00
CROSBY, Bing			
BING CROSBY	Brunswick (M) BL58000-1	3.00	6.00
WHITE CHRISTMAS	Decca (M) DL8083	2.50	5.00
CROSBY, STILLS, NASH & YOUNG			
DEJA VU	Atlantic (S) SD 7200	3.00	6.00
SO FAR	Atlantic (S) 18100	2.50	5.00

Samples chosen for each artist represent the range of high and low values that artist's records usually bring.

TITLE	LABEL & No.	GOOD	NEAR MINT
DARIN, Bobby			
BOBBY DARIN .... Atco (M) 33-102		8.00	32.00
IF I WERE A CARPENTER .... Atlantic (S) SD 8135		5.00	15.00
DEEP PURPLE			
MACHINE HEAD.............................. Warner Bros. (S) BS 2607		3.00	6.00
SHADES OF DEEP PURPLE .... Tetragrammaton (S) T 104		4.00	8.00
DENVER, John			
JOHN DENVER SINGS .... HJD (S) 55		12.00	36.00
ROCKY MOUNTAIN HIGH .... RCA Victor (S) LSP 4731		3.00	6.00
DIAMOND, Neil			
FEEL OF NEIL DIAMOND .... Bang (S) BLPS 214		5.00	10.00
NEIL DIAMOND (Open End Radio			
Special with Neil Diamond) .... UNI (M) 1913		4.00	8.00
DONNER, Ral			
TAKIN CARE OF BUSINESS .... Gone (M) LP 5012		15.00	60.00
DOOBIE BROTHERS			
LIVIN' ON THE FAULT LINE ....Warner Bros. (S) BSK 3045		2.50	5.00
TOULOUSE STREET .... Warner Bros. (S) BS 2634		3.00	6.00
DYLAN, Bob			
BLONDE ON BLONDE .... Columbia (M) C2L 41		6.00	12.00
FREEWHEELIN (LP Containing 'Let Me Die In			
My Footsteps')............................... Columbia (M) CL 1936		40.00	160.00
EAGLES			
DESPERADO ....Asylum (S) 5068		3.50	7.00
HOTEL CALIFORNIA .... Asylum (S) 7E-1084		2.50	5.00
EDDY, Duane			
DUANE EDDY DOES BOB DYLAN ....Colpix (S) CPS 494		6.00	18.00
HAVE TWANGY GUITAR WILL TRAVEL ....Jamie (S) JLP 70 3025		8.00	32.00
ELECTRIC LIGHT ORCHESTRA			
ELDORADO ....United Artists (S) UA-LA339		2.50	5.00
OUT OF THE BLUE .... Jet (S) JT-LA 823		10.00	20.00
Promotional issue, pressed in blue vinyl.			
ENGLAND DAN & JOHN FORD COLEY			
FABLES...A&M (S) SP 4350		2.50	5.00
NIGHTS ARE FOREVER .... Big Tree (S) BT 89517		2.50	5.00
EVERLY BROTHERS			
DATE WITH THE EVERLY BROTHERS, A			
(Fold Out Cover) .... Warner Bros. (S) WS1395		9.00	27.00
SONGS OUR DADDY TAUGHT US .... Cadence (M) CLP 3016		9.00	36.00

Halfway between good and mint is the true value and the best condition usually available in old records. Mint is rare.

TITLE	LABEL & No.	GOOD	NEAR MINT
FANTASTIC BAGGYS (Phil Sloan & Steve Barri)			
TELL 'EM I'M SURFIN'	Imperial (S) LP 12270	11.00	33.00
FENDERMEN			
MULE SKINNER BLUES	Soma (M) MG 1240	14.00	56.00
FIREBALLS			
HERE ARE THE FIREBALLS	Warwick (M) W 2042	6.00	24.00
VAQUERO	Top Rank (S) RS-643	8.00	32.00
FIVE EMPREES			
FIVE EMPREES	Freeport (S)FRS 4001	9.00	27.00
FLAMIN GROOVIES			
SUPERSNAZZ	Epic (S) BN 26487	8.00	24.00
TEENAGE HEAD (Blue Label)	Kama Sutra (S) KSBS 2031	4.00	8.00
FLEETWOOD MAC			
ENGLISH ROSE	Epic (S) BN 26446	4.00	8.00
FLEETWOOD MAC	Reprise (S) MS 2225	2.50	5.00
FOREIGNER			
FOREIGNER	Atlantic (S) SD 19109	2.50	5.00
FOUR SEASONS			
BIG GIRLS DON'T CRY	Vee Jay (S) SR1056	10.00	20.00
DAWN (GO AWAY) & 11 OTHER GREAT HITS	Philips (S) PHS 600-124	6.00	10.00
FOUR SEASONS & The Beatles			
BEATLES VERSUS THE FOUR SEASONS	Vee Jay (S) DXS30	30.00	90.00
FRAMPTON, Peter			
FRAMPTON COMES ALIVE	A&M (S) SP 3703	3.50	7.00
I'M IN YOU	A&M (S) 4704	20.00	40.00

This is a special promotional disc A&M had made to give to the various companies that have helped them become successful. The record is made of clear vinyl, with a picture of Peter Frampton pressed in the plastic. The "picture record" came in a clear plastic bag which had a sticker on it saying, "From your friends at A&M."

FREBERG, Stan			
FREBERG UNDERGROUND SHOW #1	Capitol (S) ST2551	6.00	24.00
STAN FREBERG WITH THE ORIGINAL CAST	Capitol (S) SM1242	5.00	20.00

(M) Monaural, (S) Stereo, (EP) Extended Play.

TITLE	LABEL & No.	GOOD	NEAR MINT
GARLAND, Judy			
JUDY	Capitol (M) T 734	6.00	24.00
"LIVE" AT THE LONDON PALLADIUM (WITH LIZA MINNELLI)	Capitol (S) ST 2295	8.00	16.00
MISS SHOW BUSINESS	Capitol (M) T 676	6.00	24.00
GRAND FUNK RAILROAD			
E PLURIBUS FUNK	Capitol (S) SW 853	3.00	6.00
LIVE ALBUM	Capitol (S) SWBB 633	4.00	8.00
GRATEFUL DEAD			
EUROPE '72	Warner Bros. (S) 3WX2668	4.00	8.00
STEAL YOUR FACE	Grateful Dead GD-LA620	4.00	8.00
GUESS WHO			
AMERICAN WOMAN	RCA LSP 4266	3.50	7.00
SHAKIN' ALL OVER	Scepter (S) 533	3.00	6.00
HALL, Daryl & John Oates			
ABANDONED LUNCHEONETTE	Atlantic (S) SD 7269	2.50	5.00
PAST TIMES BEHIND	Chelsea (S) CHL 547	3.50	7.00
HARRISON, George			
ALL THINGS MUST PASS	Apple (S) STCH 639	6.00	12.00
PERSONAL MUSIC DIALOGUE WITH GEORGE HARRISON AT THIRTY-THREE AND A THIRD, A	Dark Horse (S) PRO 649	12.50	25.00
HAWKINS, Dale			
LET'S ALL TWIST (AT THE MIAMI BEACH PEPPERMINT LOUNGE)	Roulette (M) R-25175	4.00	16.00
SUZIE-Q	Chess (M) 1429	19.00	76.00
HEART			
LITTLE QUEEN	Portrait (S) PR 34799	2.50	5.00
MAGAZINE (Picture record)	Mushroom SP1	7.00	14.00
HENDRIX, Jimi			
AND A HAPPY NEW YEAR	Reprise (EP) PRO 595	22.50	45.00
ELECTRIC LADYLAND	Reprise (S) 6307	3.50	7.00
HOLLIES			
BUS STOP	Imperial (S) LP 12330	5.00	15.00
DEAR ELOISE/KING MIDAS IN REVERSE	Epic (S) BN 26344	3.50	7.00
HOLLY, Buddy			
BUDDY HOLLY STORY, THE VOL. 2	Coral (M) CRL 57326	6.00	24.00
All original first pressing Buddy Holly LP's are on the maroon Coral label.			
THAT'LL BE THE DAY	Decca (EP) ED 2575	40.00	120.00
Also see CRICKETS			
HOLLYWOOD ARGYLES			
ALLEY OOP	Lute (M) L-9001	12.00	48.00

TITLE	LABEL & No.	GOOD	NEAR MINT
HUMAN BEINZ			
EVOLUTIONS	Capitol (S) ST 2926	6.00	12.00
NOBODY BUT ME	Capitol (S) ST 2906	5.00	10.00
HUMPERDINCK, Engelbert			
AFTER THE LOVIN'	Epic/MAM (S) PE 34381	2.00	4.00
RELEASE ME	Parrot (S) PAS 71012	3.00	6.00
INTERNATIONAL SUBMARINE BAND			
SAFE AT HOME	LHI (M) 12,001	12.00	36.00
SAFE AT HOME	LHI (S) S-12,001	13.00	39.00
JACKSON, Wanda			
RIGHT OR WRONG	Capitol (S) ST 1596	6.00	18.00
ROCKIN' WITH WANDA!	Capitol (M) T 1384	9.00	36.00
JAN & DEAN			
LITTLE OLD LADY FROM PASADENA	Liberty (S) LST7377	4.00	12.00
SAVE FOR A RAINY DAY	Columbia (S) CS 9461	85.00	255.00
DJ copy only.			
JEFFERSON AIRPLANE			
RED OCTOPUS	Grunt (S) BFL1-0999	2.50	5.00
SURREALISTIC PILLOW	RCA (S) LSP 3766	4.00	8.00
JETHRO TULL			
AQUALUNG	Reprise (S) MS 2035	4.00	8.00
THICK AS A BRICK	Reprise (S) MS 2072	4.00	8.00
JOEL, Billy			
PIANO MAN	Columbia (S) KC 32544	2.50	5.00
STRANGER, THE	Columbia (S) JC 34987	2.00	4.00
JOHN, Elton			
BLUE MOVES	MCA/Rocket (S) 2-11004	3.00	6.00
ELTON JOHN	Uni (S) 73090	6.00	12.00
JOHNNY & THE HURRI			
BEATNICK FLY	5002	7.00	21.00
STORMSVILLE	2010	10.00	40.00
JOHNSTON, Bruce			
GOING PUBLIC	4459	2.50	5.00
SURFIN' ROUND THE WORL	8857	10.00	30.00
JONES, Spike			
NUTCRACKER SUITE	A143	2.00	6.00
SPIKE JONES PLAYS THE C	M 18	8.00	24.00
JOPLIN, Janis			
PEARL	0322	2.50	5.00
WICKED WOMAN	713	4.50	9.00

(49)

Most artists in this section [ ] & Rock Records 1948-1978.

TITLE	LABEL & No.	GOOD	NEAR MINT
KANSAS			
KANSAS	Kirshner (S) KZ-32817	2.50	5.00
POINT OF KNOW RETURN	Kirshner (S) JZ 34929	2.00	4.00
KINKS			
KINK KONTROVERSY	Reprise (S) RS6197	4.50	13.50
SLEEPWALKER	Arista (S) 4106	3.00	6.00
KISS			
HOTTER THAN HELL	Casablanca (S) NBLP 7006	2.50	5.00
KISS	Casablanca (S) 9001	3.50	7.00
KNICKERBOCKERS			
LIES	Challenge (S) CHS622	6.00	18.00
LLOYD THAXTON PRESENTS THE KNICKERBOCKERS	Challenge (M) LP 12664	10.00	30.00
LAWRENCE, Eddie			
EDDIE LAWRENCE, THE OLD PHILOSOPHER	Epic (S) BN26159	5.00	10.00
GARDEN OF EDDIE LAWRENCE	Signature (M) SM1003	7.50	30.00
LED ZEPPELIN			
LED ZEPPELIN II	Atlantic (S) SD 8236	3.50	7.00
PHYSICAL GRAFFITI	Swan Song (S) 2-200	4.00	8.00
LENNON, John			
JOHN LENNON SINGS THE ROCK & ROLL HITS (ROOTS)	Adam VIII Ltd. (S) A8018	15.00	30.00
Artists listed as "Plastic Ono Band."			
MIND GAMES	Apple (S) SW-3414	2.00	4.00
LENNON, John and Yoko Ono			
UNFINISHED MUSIC NO. 1 TWO VIRGINS (With Brown sleeve)	Apple (S) T 5001	15.00	30.00
WEDDING ALBUM	Apple (S) SMAX 3361	10.00	40.00

Johnny and the Hurricanes

TITLE	LABEL & No.	GOOD	NEAR MINT
LEWIS, Jerry Lee			
JERRY LEE LEWIS	Sun (M) LP1230	12.00	36.00
JERRY LEE LEWIS WHOLE LOT OF SHAKING	Sun (EP) 107	2.50	10.00
LIGHTFOOT, Gordon			
SUNDAY CONCERT	United Artists (S) UAS 6714	3.50	7.00
SUNDOWN	Reprise (S) MS 2177	3.00	6.00
LINDEN, Kathy			
THAT CERTAIN BOY	Felsted (M) FL7501	4.00	16.00
LOFGREN, Nils			
AUTHORIZED BOOTLEG	A&M (S) SP 8362	15.00	30.00
I CAME TO DANCE	A&M (S) SP 4628	2.00	4.00
LOGGINS & MESSINA			
FULL SAIL	Columbia (S) KC-32540	2.50	5.00
LOGGINS WITH MESSINA (LISTED AS KENNY LOGGINS & JIM MESSINA)	Columbia (S) KC 31748	4.00	8.00
LOVIN' SPOONFUL			
DAYDREAM	Kama Sutra (S) KLPS 8051	4.00	8.00
DO YOU BELIEVE IN MAGIC	Kama Sutra (S) KLPS 8050	4.00	8.00
LYNYRD SKYNYRD			
SECOND HELPING	MCA/Sounds of the South (S) 363	3.50	7.00
STREET SURVIVORS	MCA (S) 3029	2.50	5.00
MANILOW, Barry			
BARRY MANILOW	Bell (S) 1129	4.50	9.00
EVEN NOW	Arista (S) AB 4164	2.00	4.00
MANN, Carl			
LIKE, MANN	Phillips (M) PLP 1960	7.50	30.00
McCARTNEY, Paul & Wings			
OPEN END INTERVIEW	Capitol	20.00	40.00
RAM	Apple (S) SMAS 3375	2.00	4.00
McKUEN, Rod			
BETSVILLE	HIFI (S) SR-419	4.00	12.00
LISTEN TO THE WARM	RCA (S) LPS 3863	3.00	6.00
McLEAN, Don			
AMERICAN PIE	United Artists (S) UAS 5535	4.00	8.00
TAPESTRY	United Artists (S) UAS 5522	4.00	8.00
MIDLER, Bette			
DIVINE MISS M	Atlantic (S) SD7238	3.00	6.00
SINGS FOR THE NEW DEPRESSION	Atlantic (S) SD 18155	2.50	5.00

TITLE	LABEL & No.	GOOD	NEAR MINT
MILLER, Steve, Band			
CHILDREN OF THE FUTURE	Capitol SKAO-2920	4.00	8.00
FLY LIKE AN EAGLE	Capitol ST-11497	2.50	5.00
MITCHELL, Chad Trio			
BEST OF CHAD MITCHELL TRIO	Kapp (S) KS-3324	2.50	5.00
THAT'S THE WAY IT'S GONNA BE (FEATURING JOHN DENVER)	Mercury (S) SR 61049	5.00	10.00
MOODY BLUES			
GO NOW—MOODY BLUES #1	London (S) PS 428	6.00	18.00
ON THE THRESHOLD OF A DREAM	Deram (S) DES 18025	3.50	7.00
MOTHERS OF INVENTION			
FREAK OUT	Verve (S) V6-5005-2	7.00	14.00
LIVE, FILLMORE EAST-JUNE 1971	Bizarre (S) MS2042	4.00	8.00
NAZARETH			
HAIR OF THE DOG	A&M (S) SP 4511	2.00	4.00
NAZARETH	Warner Bros. (S) BS 2615	3.50	7.00
NELSON, Ricky			
GARDEN PARTY	Decca (S) DL 75391	3.00	6.00
TEEN TIME	Verve (M) MG V 2083	6.00	24.00
NELSON, Sandy			
LET THERE BE DRUMS	Imperial (M) LPP 9159	4.00	12.00
SANDY NELSON PLAYS TEEN BEAT	Imperial (M) LP 9044	4.00	12.00
NEWHART, Bob			
BOB NEWHART: DELUXE EDITION	Warner Bros. (M) 2N 1399	5.00	15.00
BUTTON-DOWN MIND OF BOB NEWHART	Warner Bros. (S) WS 1379	3.50	10.50
NEWTON-JOHN, Olivia			
IF NOT FOR YOU	Uni (S) 73117	5.00	10.00
LET ME BE THERE	MCA (S) 389	3.00	6.00
NITTY GRITTY DIRT BAND			
UNCLE CHARLIE AND HIS DOG TEDDY	Liberty (S) LST 7642	2.50	5.00
WILL THE CIRCLE BE UNBROKEN	United Artists (S) 9801	2.50	5.00
ORBISON, Roy			
CRYING	Monument (S) 14007	8.00	24.00
ROY ORBISON AT THE ROCK HOUSE	Sun (M) LP1260	8.00	32.00
ORLANDO, Tony			
BEFORE DAWN	Epic (S) BG-33785	2.00	4.00
BLESS YOU (& 11 OTHER GREAT HITS)	Epic (S) BN-611	12.00	36.00
PABLO CRUISE			
PABLO CRUISE	A&M (S) 4528	2.00	4.00
PAUL, Les & Mary Ford			
BYE BYE BLUES	Capitol (M) T 356	5.00	15.00
HITS OF LES & MARY	Capitol (M) T 1476	3.00	6.00
PETER & GORDON			
WORLD WITHOUT LOVE, A	Capitol (S) ST 2115	5.00	15.00
LADY GODIVA	Capitol (S) ST 2664	4.00	8.00
PINK FLOYD			
ATOM HEART MOTHER	Harvest (S) 382	3.00	6.00
PINK FLOYD	Tower (S) ST 5093	5.00	10.00

(M) Monaural, (S) Stereo, (EP) Extended Play.

Halfway between good and mint is the true value and the best condition usually available in old records. Mint is rare.

This section represents a 3½% sampling of the artists and songs in *Record Albums 1948-1978*.

TITLE	LABEL & No.	GOOD	NEAR MINT

PRESLEY, Elvis

BLUE HAWAII .... RCA Victor (M) LPM 2436 — 6.00 — 18.00
CHRISTMAS WITH ELVIS................... RCA Victor (EP) EPA 4340 — 6.00 — 18.00
DEALER'S PREVUE (EP)........................ RCA Victor SDS S7-39 — 60.00 — 180.00
Disc only.
Contains excerpts (not complete versions) of "Jailhouse Rock"
and "Treat Me Nice."

(18) DEALER'S PREVUE (WITH SPECIAL PICTURE
ENVELOPE) (EP)............................. RCA Victor SDS S7-39 — 150.00 — 450.00 Tie

(10) DEALER'S PREVUE (EP)........................ RCA Victor SDS-57-24 — 200.00 — 600.00 Tie
Contains complete version of "Teddy Bear" and edited version
of "Loving You."

DOUBLE TROUBLE .... RCA Victor PM-3787 — 11.00 — 33.00
Cover reads, "Special Bonus-Full Cover Photo of Elvis."

EASY COME, EASY GO .... RCA Victor (EP) EPA 4387 — 5.00 — 15.00
Black Dog on top

ELVIS, ALOHA FROM HAWAII VIA SATELLITE..... RCA Victor R-213736 — 5.00 — 15.00
Issued through RCA record club. Released in stereo instead of quad

ELVIS CHRISTMAS ALBUM.................... RCA Victor (S)LSP 1951 — 5.00 — 15.00
Black Dog on top

(38) ELVIS CHRISTMAS ALBUM.................... RCA Brazil (LOC 1035) — 100.00 — 300.00 Tie
Different picture cover than U.S. release.

ELVIS FOR EVERYONE .... RCA Victor (M) LPM 3450 — 6.00 — 15.00
ELVIS GOLDEN RECORDS .... RCA Victor (M) LPM-1707 — 20.00 — 60.00
LP title is printed in white...song titles appear on front cover.

ELVIS GOLDEN RECORDS .... RCA Victor (S) LSP-1707 — 5.00 — 15.00
ELVIS IN CONCERT .... RCA Victor APL 2-2587 — 3.00 — 9.00
2-record set double-pocket

(38) ELVIS IS BACK .... RCA Victor (M) LPM 2231 — 6.00 — 18.00
ELVIS PRESLEY .... RCA Victor (EP) SPD 23 — 100.00 — 300.00 Tie
Offered as a give-a-way bonus with RCA Victrola purchase–
Triple EP, same front cover as SPD 22, blank inside, liner notes on
back–contains 8 songs from LSP 1254 plus 4 songs from single
releases.

(18) ELVIS PRESLEY........................ RCA Chile (CML-3012) — 150.00 — 450.00 Tie
Issued in 1956 only–10" LP-10 songs.

(18) ELVIS PRESLEY-"THE MOST TALKED ABOUT
NEW PERSONALITY IN THE LAST
TEN YEARS OF MUSIC"... RCA Victor LPM-1254/EPB-1254/EPA-747 — 150.00 — 450.00 Tie
Two 45 RPM discs with six songs on each disc-(containing all 12
songs from LSP 1254) Issued with special paper sleeve.

ELVIS SAILS............................... RCA Victor (EP) EPA 4325 — 10.00 — 30.00
ELVIS SAILS............................... RCA Victor (EP) EPA 4325 — 4.00 — 12.00
Orange Label

ELVIS SINGS FLAMING STAR........ RCA Victor (S) Camden CAS 2304 — 2.00 — 4.00
Repackage of the Singer (PRS 279) LP.

ELVIS, THE SUN SESSIONS .... RCA Victor AMP-1-1675 — 2.00 — 6.00
50,000,000 ELVIS FANS CAN'T BE WRONG,
ELVIS GOLD RECORDS VOL. 2.............. RCA Victor (S) LSP 2075 — 5.00 — 15.00
FOLLOW THAT DREAM .... RCA Victor (EP) EPA 4368 — 4.00 — 12.00
FOR LP FANS ONLY .... RCA Victor (M) LPM 1990 — 11.00 — 33.00
FOR LP FANS ONLY .... RCA Victor (S) LSP 1990 — 5.00 — 15.00
GOLDEN BOY ELVIS .... Hor Zu Germany (SHZT 521) — 80.00 — 240.00
Available only for a few months in 1965, then removed from
the market.

(10) GOOD ROCKIN' TONIGHT .... RCA France (130-252) — 200.00 — 600.00 Tie
First issue-Has 1956 photo of Elvis from "Love Me Tender" on cover)

(38) GREAT COUNTRY/WESTERN HITS
Price including all ten discs and box .... RCA Victor (SPD-26) — 100.00 — 300.00 Tie

(18) INTERNATIONAL HOTEL PRESENTS ELVIS 1970 .... RCA Victor — 150.00 — 450.00 Tie
Limited edition box set issued by the International Hotel (now the
Las Vegas Hilton) to certain invited guests. Box contained: special
menu, Elvis calendar, Elvis record catalog, souvenir photo album.
Latest single "Kentucky Rain" and the double-LP "Vegas To
Memphis To Vegas" LSP-6020 (price includes box and contents)

JAILHOUSE ROCK .... RCA Victor (EP) EPA 4114 — 5.00 — 15.00
Black Dog on top.

Elvis Presley records are listed in all three of our guides on pop singles, albums and country/
western.

TITLE	LABEL & No.	GOOD	NEAR MINT	
(6) JANIS & ELVIS	*RCA South Africa (T-31-077)*	400.00	1200.00	
10" LP with four songs by Janis Martin on one side and four by Elvis on the other side.				
KING CREOLE	*RCA Victor (S) LSP 1884*	5.00	15.00	
KING CREOLE VOL. 1	*RCA Victor (EP) EPA 4319*	5.00	15.00	
Black Dog on top				
(18) KING OF THE WHOLE WIDE WORLD	*RCA South Africa (31-673)*	150.00	450.00	Tie
LOVE ME TENDER	*RCA Victor (EP) EPA 4006*	5.00	15.00	
Black Dog on top.				
LOVING YOU VOL. 1	*RCA Victor (EP) EPA 1-1515*	3.00	9.00	
Black Dog on side				
MOODY BLUE	*RCA Victor AFLI-2428*	2.00	6.00	
(Issued on blue vinyl)				
MOODY BLUE	*RCA Victor AFLI-2428*	40.00	80.00	
Black vinyl-Promotional copy. Foreign pressings are also black vinyl. Original "Moody Blue" album cover.				
PARADISE HAWAIIAN STYLE	*RCA Victor (M) LPM 3643*	5.00	15.00	
(38) PERFECT FOR PARTIES	*(RCA Germany) SPA 7-37*	100.00	300.00	Tie
Has one different cut-by Tony Cabot "Ring Out Then Your're Hoiahs" instead of "Anchors Away."				
POT LUCK	*RCA Victor (M) LPM 2523*	5.00	15.00	
(18) RCA Victor SPD 15 RCA ten record boxed set. Has one Elvis (EP-599-9089), the rest are by other RCA artists, and all the discs have gray labels. (56)		150.00	450.00	Tie
(10) RCA Victor SPD-19 RCA eight record EP boxed set, has one Elvis EP, the rest are by other artists.(56)		200.00	600.00	Tie
(18) SAVE-ON RECORDS EP	*RCA Victor SPA 7-27*	150.00	450.00	Tie
(This special EP was issued so that the record buyer could sample some of the songs and artists that RCA was releasing new product by, during the spring and early summer of 1956. This particular EP (for the month of June) offered an excerpt from Elvis' "I'm Gonna Sit Right Down And Cry." Issued with a special cover, which did not picture any of the artists...the above price range reflects both disc and cover. The cover is extremely rare, and without it the disc itself would be valued at 30%-50% of above prices.)				
SINGER PRESENTS ELVIS SINGING FLAMING STAR AND OTHERS	*RCA Victor (S) PRS 279*	10.00	30.00	
This album was sold only in Singer Sewing Machine Centers in conjunction with the '68 T.V. special.				
SPINOUT	*RCA Victor (S) LSP 3702*	9.00	27.00	
TICKLE ME	*RCA Victor (EP) EPA 4383*	4.00	12.00	
Black Dog on top				
TICKLE ME	*RCA South Africa (32-049)*	80.00	240.00	
A TOUCH OF GOLD VOL. 1	*RCA Victor (EP) EPA 5088*	11.00	33.00	
Maroon Label				
A TOUCH OF GOLD VOL. 1	*RCA Victor (EP) EPA 5088*	2.00	6.00	
Orange Label				
(18) ELVIS PRESLEY — Y SU CONJUNTO	*(Chile) Elvis Presley*	150.00	450.00	Tie
(2) TV GUIDE PRESENTS ELVIS PRESLEY	*RCA Victor Custom (EP) G8-MW-8705*	Est.	$3500	

This is a package containing a one-sided EP with four spoken responses by Elvis that were excerpted from an interview conducted by **TV Guide** reporter in Lakeland, Florida in 1956. These "answers" are only 19, 34, 54 and 44 seconds long, respectively. The estimated value listed is for the complete package (which we have never documented as having been sold) of the record and two paper inserts all in near mint condition. The value of any part of the package would be negotiable according to condition and assessment by the parties involved as to the desirability and relative worth of the record by itself, which is scarce; the "suggested continuity" insert, which is probably twice as rare (it was offered as a guide to anyone, such as a radio station disc jockey, who wanted to "ask" Elvis the questions he answered on the disc); and the second insert that tells the story behind the interview, which is much rarer than either of the other two.

(**Note:** the record has been bootlegged, but is easy to identify. The serial, or matrix number of the record has been scratched by hand lettering into the vinyl between the last band and the label, whereas on the original it has been pressed into the vinyl by a stamper. Also, the bootleg "tracks through," meaning that all four bands play one after the other with a pause between each. On the original, the bands are "locked," which means that after each response has been played, the needle has to be picked up and moved over by hand to the next track.)

Bill Haley and Elvis Presley

TITLE	LABEL & No.	GOOD	NEAR MINT
VIVA LAS VEGAS ....RCA Victor (EP) EPA 4382		4.00	12.00
Black Dog on side			
VIVA LAS VEGAS ....RCA Victor (EP) EPA 4382		2.00	6.00

PRESTON, Johnny
COME ROCK WITH ME .... Mercury (S) SR 60609		8.00	32.00
RUNNING BEAR............................... Mercury (S) SR-60250		10.00	40.00

PRETTY THINGS
PRETTY THINGS, THE .... Fontana (S) SRF 67544		7.00	14.00
SILK TORPEDO .... Swan Song (S) 8411		3.00	6.00

PROCOL HARUM
PROCOL HARUM LIVES (A CONSUMERS GUIDE TO PROCOL HARUM) Includes an Interview ....A&M (S) SP 8053		8.00	16.00
A SALTY DOG ....A&M (S) SP 4179		2.00	4.00

QUEEN
NIGHT AT THE OPERA...........................Elektra (S) 7E-1053		2.50	5.00
QUEEN .... Elektra (S) EKS 75064		3.50	7.00

RAFFERTY, Gerry
CAN I HAVE MY MONEY BACK ....Blue Thumb (S) BTS 58		4.00	9.00

RAINDROPS
RAINDROPS......................................Jubilee (S) SJ-5023		5.00	15.00

RARE EARTH
BAND TOGETHER ....Prodigal (S) P7-10025		2.00	4.00
GET READY ....Rare Earth (S) 507		3.50	7.00

REDDY, Helen
I AM WOMAN ....Capitol (S) ST 11068		2.50	5.00
LOVE SONG FOR JEFFREY .... Capitol (S) SO-11284		2.50	5.00

REED, Lou
LOU REED ....RCA Victor LSP-4701		5.00	10.00
WALK ON THE WILD SIDE (The Best of Lou Reed) .... RCA Victor (S) APL1-2001		2.50	5.00

Elvis Presley records are listed in all three of our guides on pop singles, albums and country/ western.

TITLE	LABEL & No.	GOOD	NEAR MINT
REVERE, Paul & The Raiders			
JUST LIKE US	Columbia (S) CS 9251	4.50	9.00
PAUL REVERE & THE RAIDERS	Sande (M) 1001	20.00	80.00
PAUL REVERE AND THE RAIDERS	Sears (S) SPS 493	16.00	32.00
RIGHTEOUS BROTHERS			
SOME BLUE EYED SOUL	Moonglow (M) 1002	5.00	10.00
YOU'VE LOST THAT LOVIN' FEELIN'	Philles (M) PHLP 4007	5.00	10.00
ROLLING STONES			
AN INTERVIEW WITH M. JAGGER BY TOM DONAHUE			
APRIL 1971	Rolling Stone ST-PR-B-164 PR	10.00	20.00
GOATSHEAD SOUP	Rolling Stones (S) 59101	3.00	6.00
IT'S HERE LUV!!! 1965 EXCLUSIVE TALK ALBUM			
ED RUDY INTERVIEW LP	INS Radio (M) LL-1003	8.00	24.00
OUT OF OUR HEADS	London (M) LL3429	5.00	15.00
RONETTES			
PRESENTING THE FABULOUS RONETTES			
FEATURING VERONICA	Philles (S) 4006	25.00	75.00
RONETTES FEATURING VERONICA	Colpix (M) CP 486	6.00	18.00
RONSTADT, Linda			
HEART LIKE A WHEEL	Capitol ST-11358	2.00	4.00
SIMPLE DREAMS	Asylum (S) 6E-104	2.00	4.00
ROXY MUSIC			
ROXY MUSIC	Reprise (S) 2114	4.00	8.00
SIREN	Atco (S) SD 36-127	3.50	7.00
RUNDGREN, Todd			
RUNT	Ampex (S) A10105	5.00	10.00
SOMETHING/ANYTHING?	Bearsville (S) 2066	3.00	6.00
RUSSELL, Leon			
CARNEY	Shelter SW-8911	4.00	8.00
LEON LIVE	Shelter (S) STCO 8917	5.00	10.00
SANTANA			
ABRAXAS	Columbia (S) KC-30130	2.50	5.00
SANTANA	Columbia (S) CS 9781	3.00	6.00
SAVAGE ROSE			
REFUGEE	Gregar (M) GG 104	4.00	8.00
SCAGGS, Boz			
BOZ SCAGGS & BAND	Columbia (S) 30796	3.50	7.00
SILK DEGREES	Columbia (S) JC 33920	2.00	4.00
SCOTT, Jack			
JACK SCOTT	Carlton (S) STLP 12/107	14.00	56.00
WHAT IN THE WORLD'S COME OVER YOU	Top Rank (S) RS-626	10.00	40.00
SEALS & CROFTS			
DOWN HOME	T.A. (S) 5004	5.00	10.00
TAKIN' IT EASY	Warner Bros. (S) BSK 3163	2.00	4.00
SEARCHERS			
MEET THE SEARCHERS	Kapp (S) KS 3363	3.50	10.50
SEARCHERS MEET THE RATTLES	Mercury (S) SR 60994	5.00	15.00
SEDAKA, Neil			
LITTLE DEVIL	RCA Victor (S) LSP 2421	6.00	18.00
NEIL SEDAKA (ROCK WITH SEDAKA)	RCA Victor (S) LSP-2035	10.00	30.00
SEGER, Bob System			
BACK IN '72	Palladium (S) MS 2126	4.00	8.00
NIGHT MOVES	Capitol (S) ST 11557	2.00	4.00
(With Silver Bullet Band)			

The left hand price column represents the true value of the average, used record.

TITLE	LABEL & No.	GOOD	NEAR MINT
SHADOWS OF KNIGHT			
BACK DOOR MEN	Dunwich (S) S 667	6.00	12.00
GLORIA	Dunwich (S) S 666	6.00	12.00
SHANGRI-LAS			
LEADER OF THE PACK	Red Bird (M) RB 20 101	5.00	10.00
SHANGRI-LAS '65	Red Bird (M) 20 104	9.00	18.00
SIMON, Carly			
ANTICIPATION	Elektra (S) 75016	3.00	6.00
BOYS IN THE TREES	Elektra (S) 6E-128	2.00	4.00
SKYLINERS			
SKY LINERS	Calico (M) LP 3000	12.00	36.00
SMALL FACES			
IMMEDIATE STORY	Sire (S) 3709	3.50	7.00
OGDEN'S NUT GONE FLAKE	Immediate (S) Z12 52 008	5.00	10.00
SMITH, Ray			
TRAVELIN' WITH RAY	Judd (M) JLPA 701	15.00	60.00
SMOTHERS BROTHERS			
CURB YOUR TONGUE, KNAVE!	Mercury (M) MG 20862	3.50	10.50
THINK ETHNIC!	Mercury (M) MG 20777	3.50	10.50
SONNY AND CHER			
BABY DON'T GO	Reprise (M) 6177	5.00	10.00
LOOK AT US	Atco (S) SD 33-177	4.00	8.00
SPIRIT			
SPIRIT	Ode (S) Z 12 44004	6.00	12.00
SPIRIT OF '76	Mercury (S) SRM-2-804	3.00	6.00
SPRINGFIELD, Dusty			
LOOK OF LOVE, THE	Philips (S) PHS 600-256	4.00	8.00
STAY AWHILE/I ONLY WANT TO BE WITH YOU	Philips (S) PHS 600-133	5.00	10.00
SPRINGSTEEN, Bruce			
BORN TO RUN	Columbia (S) PC-33795	2.00	4.00
GREETINGS FROM ASBURY PARK, N.J.	Columbia (S) KC-31903	2.50	5.00
STAFFORD, Terry			
SUSPICION!	Crusader (S) SC 1001	5.00	15.00
STANDELLS			
DIRTY WATER	Tower (S) ST 5027	6.00	12.00
STANDELLS IN PERSON AT P.J.'S	Liberty (S) LST 7384	5.00	15.00

Most artists in this section from the album book are also in *Popular & Rock Records 1948-1978.*

TITLE	LABEL & No.	GOOD	NEAR MINT
STEVENS, Cat			
FOREIGNER	A&M (S) 4391	2.00	4.00
MATTHEW AND SON/NEW MASTERS	Deram (S) 18005	4.00	8.00
STEWART, John			
CALIFORNIA BLOODLINES	Capitol (S) 203	5.00	10.00
PHOENIX CONCERTS	RCA Victor (S) CPL2-0265	3.50	7.00
STREISAND, Barbra			
COLOR ME BARBRA	Columbia (M) CL 2478	2.50	5.00
STONEY END	Columbia (S) 30378	2.00	4.00
STYX			
GRAND ILLUSION, THE	A&M (S) SP 4637	2.00	4.00
STYX 2	Wooden Nickel (S) 1012	3.50	7.00
SURFARIS			
FUN CITY U.S.A	Decca (M) DL 4560	3.00	9.00
WIPE OUT	DOT (S) DLP 25535	3.50	10.50
SURF STOMPERS			
ORIGINAL SURFER STOMP	Del Fi (S) DFS-1236	4.00	12.00
SYNDICATE OF SOUND			
LITTLE GIRL	Bell (S) SLP 6001	6.00	12.00
TAYLOR, James			
JAMES TAYLOR	Apple (S) SKAO 3352	4.50	9.00
JAMES TAYLOR & THE ORIGINAL FLYING MACHINE	Euphoria (S) 2	5.00	10.00
TEDDY BEARS (Featuring Phil Spector)			
TEDDY BEARS SING!	Imperial (S) LP-9067	19.00	76.00

TITLE	LABEL & No.	GOOD	NEAR MINT
10CC			
100 C.C.	53110	4.00	8.00
THIN LIZZY			
JAILBREAK	-1081	2.50	5.00
NIGHT LIFE	2002	3.50	7.00
13th FLOOR ELEVATO			
LIVE	ALP8	5.00	15.00
PSYCHEDELIC SOUNDS....	LP 1	7.00	28.00
TOKENS			
I HEAR TRUMPETS BLOW.................... BT Puppy (S) BTPS 1000		3.50	7.00
LION SLEEPS TONIGHT, THE................ RCA Victor (S) LSP 2514		7.00	21.00
TURTLES			
HAPPY TOGETHER .... White Whale (S) WWS 7114		3.50	7.00
IT AIN'T ME BABE....................... White Whale (S) WWS 7111		4.00	8.00
TWITTY, Conway			
CONWAY TWITTY SINGS .... MGM (S) SE 3744		9.00	36.00
LONELY BLE BOY .... MGM (M) E 3818		7.50	30.00
VALENS, Ritchie			
IN CONCERT AT POCOIMA JR. HIGH .... Del Fi (M) DFLP 1214		12.00	48.00
RITCHIE .... Del Fi (M) DFLP 1206		7.00	28.00
VANILLA FUDGE			
NEAR THE BEGINNING .... Atco (S) SD 33-278		3.00	6.00
VANILLA FUDGE .... Atco (S) SD 33-224		3.00	6.00
VINCENT, Gene			
BLUEJEAN BOP ....Capitol (M) T 764		20.00	80.00
GENE VINCENT AND THE BLUE CAPS .... Capitol (M) T 811		19.00	76.00
VINTON, Bobby			
DANCING AT THE HOP .... Epic (S) BN-579		4.00	8.00
MELODIES OF LOVE ....ABC (S) 851		2.50	5.00
WAR			
ALL DAY MUSIC........................... United Artists (S) UAS 5546		3.00	6.00
WORLD IS A GHETTO, THE................ United Artists (S) UAS 5652		3.00	6.00
WARREN, Rusty			
KNOCKERS UP! .... Jubilee (M) JGM 2029		5.00	15.00
SINSATIONAL .... Jubilee (M) JGM 2034		4.00	12.00

(M) Monaural, (S) Stereo, (EP) Extended Play.

TITLE	LABEL & No.	GOOD	NEAR MINT
WAYNE, Thomas			
TRAGEDY	Fernwood	6.00	24.00
WHO			
TOMMY (Original Cast)	Decca (S) DXSW 7205	3.50	7.00
WHO SELL OUT, THE	Decca (M) DL 4950	8.00	16.00
WINTER, Edgar, Group			
EDGAR WINTER'S WHITE TRASH	Epic (S) 30512	4.00	8.00
THEY ONLY CAME OUT AT NIGHT	Epic (S) KE-31584	2.50	5.00
WONDER, Stevie			
12 YEAR OLD GENIUS	Tamla (M) 240	8.00	16.00
UP-TIGHT	Tamla (S) 268	5.00	10.00
WRIGHT, Gary			
DREAM WEAVER	Warner Bros. (S) BS 2868	2.00	4.00
EXTRACTION	A&M (S) SP 4277	3.50	7.00
YARDBIRDS			
FOR YOUR LOVE	Epic (S) BN 26167	9.00	27.00
YARDBIRDS FEATURING PERFORMANCES BY E. CLAPTON, J. BECK, J. PAGE	Epic (S) EG 30135	15.00	30.00
YES			
CLOSE TO THE EDGE	Atlantic (S) 7244	3.00	6.00
YESSONGS	Atlantic (S) 3-100	4.50	9.00
YOUNG, Neil			
AFTER THE GOLD RUSH	Reprise 6383	3.00	6.00
EVERYONE KNOWS THIS IS NOWHERE (With Crazy Horse)	Reprise (S) 6349	3.00	6.00
ZACHERLEY, John			
MONSTER MASH	Parkway (M) P 7018	7.00	28.00
ZACKERLEY'S MONSTER GALLERY	Crestview (S) CRS7-803	7.00	28.00
ZOMBIES			
ODESSEY AND ORACLE	Date (S) TES 4013	5.00	10.00
ZOMBIES FEATURING SHE'S NOT THERE AND TELL HER NO	Parrot (M) PA 61001	4.00	8.00
ZZ TOP			
FIRST ALBUM	London (S) PS 584	2.50	5.00
TEJAS	London (S) PS 680	2.50	5.00

This section represents a 3½% sampling of the artists and songs in *Record Albums 1948-1978*.

Samples chosen for each artist represent the range of high and low values that artist's records usually bring.

ORIGINAL CASTS AND SOUNDTRACKS

In our **Record Albums** price guide, the 75 pages of Broadway original casts and motion picture soundtracks are disarmingly contagious reading, intriguing and interesting enough to provide long periods of diversion. This compendium gives a good tasty bite of that section. When we go back to press with our third edition of the price guide, probably in the spring of 1980, the additional information we seek primarily will be to fill in the significant artists, singers, narrators, or performers on soundtracks from movies that we've already listed. This area is one of the hottest in collectibility in the field.

If you do send us any information, send us all you can. Less information than we need is sometimes worse than none at all!

One of our biggest problems has been how to document the worth of the first pressings of big-hit shows that have never gone out of print and are still being issued with the original number. Even though we know these early pressings to be of significant value, until we can tell a collector how to identify them, we'll have to list them at a minimum price.

The minimum value attached to a single album release that is still in print is $4.00. A double is $6.00. A triple album is $8.00. It still might cost you more to go to a record store and ～～～～～～～～～ the retail prices of a record can vary ～～～～～～～～～～～～～～～～～ 's bought. But the min-
～～～～～～～～～～～～～～～～ dization only, plus the
～～～～～～～～～～～～～～～～ e would have to be less
～～～～～～～～～～～～～～～～ store.
～～～～～～～～～～～～～～～～ ns that is the date of the
～～～～～～～～～～～～～～～～ records were made or
～～～～～～～～～～～～～～～～ r record is when it was

TITLE/Flip	LABEL & No.	GOOD	NEAR MINT
ADDAMS FAMILY, THE (1964)			
TV Sondtrack .... *RCA Victor (S) LSP-3421*		10.00	20.00
ALEXANDER THE GREAT (1956)			
Soundtrack .... *Mercury (M) MG-20148*		40.00	80.00
ALICE IN WONDERLAND (1952)			
Soundtrack (1959) .... *Disneyland (M) DQ-1208*		6.00	12.00
AMERICAN IN PARIS, AN (1951)			
SOUNDTRACK (1951) (10") ....*MGM (M) E-93*		12.00	24.00
SOUNDTRACK (1959) .... *MGM (M) E-3767*		6.00	12.00
ANDY GRIFFITH SHOW, THE (1961)			
TV Soundtrack .... *Capitol (S) ST-1611*		6.00	12.00
ANNIE GET YOUR GUN (1946)			
Original Cast (1949) ....*Decca (M) DL 8001*		25.00	50.00
Ethel Merman, Ray Middleton, Robert Lenn.			
Original Cast (Re-issue) (1955) ....*Decca (M) DL 9018*		7.50	15.00
ATHENIAN TOUCH (1964)			
Original Cast .... *Broadway East (S) OCS 101*		70.00	140.00
Marion Marlowe, Butterfly McQueen, Robert Cosden.			
BAMBI (1942)			
Soundtrack (1957) ....*Disneyland (M) WDL-4009*		7.50	15.00
BAND OF ANGELS (1957)			
Soundtrack .... *RCA Victor (M) LPM-1557*		35.00	70.00
BIBLE, THE			
Soundtrack .... *20th Century Fox (S) 4184*		15.00	30.00
BLESS THE BEASTS AND CHILDREN (1971)			
Soundtrack ....*A&M (S) 4322*		10.00	20.00
BLOW UP			
Soundtrack ....*MGM (S) 4447*		10.00	20.00
BY THE BEAUTIFUL SEA (1954)			
Original Cast ....*Capitol (M) S 531*		50.00	100.00
Shirley Booth, Wilbur Evans, Cameron Prud'homme, Richard France, Mae Barnes, Libi Staiger, Thomas Gleason.			
Original Cast (Re-issue) .... *Capitol (M) T-11652*		2.00	4.00
❸ **CAINE MUTINY, THE (1954)**			
Soundtrack (With dialogue) (Limited release) (Value is estimated) .... *RCA Victor (M) LOC-1013*		1000.00	2000.00

TITLE/Flip	LABEL & No.	GOOD	NEAR MINT

CAN CAN (1953)

Original Cast . . . . Capitol (M) S 452 — 10.00 — 20.00
Lilo, Hans Conreid, Gwen Verdon, Erik Rhodes.
Soundtrack (From the 1960 film) . . . . Capitol (M) W1301 — 6.00 — 12.00
Frank Sinatra, Shirley MacLaine, Maurice Chevalier, Louis Jourdan.

CASINO ROYALE (1967)

Soundtrack . . . . Colgems (S) 5005 — 10.00 — 20.00

CLOWN AROUND (1972)

Original Cast (Not identified) . . . . RCA Victor (S) LSP 4741 — 75.00 — 150.00

DEEP THROAT, PART II (1974)

Soundtrack . . . . Bryan (S) BRS-101 — 3.00 — 6.00

DESTINATION MOON (1950)

Soundtrack (10") (Stevens Conducting) . . . . Columbia (M) CL-6151 — 15.00 — 30.00
Soundtrack (Sandauer Conducting) (1959) . . . . Omega (M) 1003 — 20.00 — 40.00
Soundtrack . . . . Omega (S) OSL-3 — 30.00 — 60.00

DRAGNET (1953)

TV Soundtrack (With Dialogue) (10") . . . . RCA Victor (M) LPM-3199 — 18.00 — 36.00

EASY RIDER (1969)

Soundtrack (Traditional Rock) . . . . Dunhill (S) 50063 — 6.00 — 12.00

FIDDLER ON THE ROOF (1964)

Original Cast (In Hebrew) . . . . Columbia (S) OS 6490 — 7.50 — 15.00

(M) Monaural, (S) Stereo, (EP) Extended Play.

TITLE/Flip	LABEL & No.	GOOD	NEAR MINT
FLAHOOLEY (1951)			
Original Cast .... Capitol (M) S 284		50.00	100.00
Yma Sumac, Barbara Cook, Jerome Courtland, Irwin Corey, Faye DeWitt, Marilyn Ross, Lulu Bates.			
FOR WHOM THE BELL TOLLS (1943)			
Soundtrack (Young Conducting) (1950) .... Decca (M) DL-8008		12.00	24.00
GLENN MILLER STORY, THE (1954)			
Soundtrack (10") (Traditional pop) .... Decca (M) DL-5519		12.00	24.00
Soundtrack (Re-channeled stereo) (1956)........... Decca (S) 78226		5.00	10.00
GONE WITH THE WIND (1939)			
Original London Cast (1973) .... Columbia (S) SCXA 9252		12.00	24.00
Harve Presnell, June Ritchie, Patricia Michael.			
Soundtrack (10") (1954) .... RCA Victor (M) LPM-3227		15.00	30.00
GOSPEL ACCORDING TO ST. MATTHEW, THE (1966)			
Soundtrack .... Mainstream (S) S-4000		30.00	60.00
HIGH TOR (1956)			
TV Soundtrack .... Decca (M) DL-8272		50.00	100.00
ISLAND IN THE SKY (1953)			
Soundtrack (10") (With Dialogue)................. Decca (M) DL-7029		50.00	100.00
IT'S A BIRD, IT'S A PLANE, IT'S SUPERMAN (1966)			
Original Cast .... Columbia (S) OS 2970		10.00	20.00
Jack Cassidy, Bob Holliday, Eric Mason, Patricia Marand.			
KING & I (1951)			
Original Cast .... Decca (M) DL 9008		10.00	20.00
Gertrude Lawrence, Yul Brynner.			
KISMET (1953)			
Original Cast .... Columbia (M) 4850		10.00	20.00
Alfred Drake, Doretta Morrow, Joan Diener, Richard Kiley.			
LOOK MA I'M DANCIN'! (1948)			
Original Cast (1950) (10") .... Decca (M) DL 5231		75.00	150.00
Nancy Walker, Harold Lang, Sandra Deel, Bill Shirley.			
LOVE ME OR LEAVE ME (1955)			
Soundtrack (Traditional pop) .... Columbia (M) CL-710		7.00	15.00
Doris Day sings the songs of Ruth Etting.			
MAKE A WISH (1951)			
Original Cast .... RCA Victor (M) LOC 1002		50.00	100.00
Nanette Fabray, Stephen Douglass, Helen Gallagher.			
Original Cast .... RCA Victor (M) CBM 1 2033		2.00	4.00

TITLE/Flip	LABEL & No.	GOOD	NEAR MINT

MARIA GOLOVIN (1958)
Original Cast (3 records) .... *RCA Victor (M) LM 6142*   75.00   150.00

MEXICAN HAYRIDE (1944)
Original Cast (1950) (10") .... *Decca (M) DL 5232*   75.00   150.00
   June Havoc, Wilbur Evans, Corinna Mura.

MIKADO, THE (1960)
TV Soundtrack .... *Columbia (S) OS-2022*   25.00   50.00
   Groucho Marx.

MRS. PATTERSON (1954)
Original Cast .... *RCA Victor (M) LOC 1017*   25.00   50.00
   Eartha Kitt, Enid Markey, Ruth Attaway.

MR. WONDERFUL (1956)
Original Cast ....*Decca (M) DL 9032*   20.00   40.00
   Sammy Davis, Jr., The Will Mastin Trio, Jack Carter.

NIGHT OF THE HUNTER (1955)
Soundtrack (With Dialogue) .... *RCA Victor (M) LPM-1136*   50.00   100.00

NO FOR AN ANSWER (1941)
Original Cast (With the composer, Blitzstein, at
   the piano) (1951, off Broadway) .... *Theme (M) TALP 103*   100.00   200.00
   Carol Channing, Olive Deering, Lloyd Gough.

OF THEE I SING (1952)
Original Revival Cast ....*Capitol (M) S 350*   75.00   150.00
   Jack Carson, Paul Hartman, Jack Whiting.
TV Soundtrack .... *Columbia (S) S 31763*   10.00   20.00
   Carroll O'Conner, Jack Gilford, Cloris Leachman, Michelle Lee.

OKLAHOMA (1943)
Original Cast The first Broadway show to be recorded and released in
   its entirety on 78's. The re-release of the LP's are all excerpts.
   (1949) ....*Decca (M) DL 8000*   15.00   30.00
   Alfred Drake, Joan Roberts, Howard daSylva, Celeste Holm, Lee Dixon.

PETER PAN (Bernstein) (1950)
Original Cast ....*Columbia (M) OL 4312*   7.50   15.00
   Jean Arthur, Boris Karloff, Marcia Henderson.

PEYTON PLACE (1957)
Soundtrack .... *RCA Victor (S) LSO-1042*   18.00   36.00

PORGY & BESS (1935)
Original Cast (10") (1950) .... *Decca (M) DL 7006*   20.00   40.00
   Excerpts from the original 1930's cast with Todd Duncan
   and Anne Brown, taken from 78's recorded in 1940.

TITLE/Flip	LABEL & No.	GOOD	NEAR MINT
RAINTREE COUNTY (1957)			
Soundtrack (2 Record Set) .... RCA Victor (M) LOC-6000		50.00	100.00
ROAD TO SINGAPORE (1940)			
Soundtrack (10") (1951) .... Decca (M) DL-6015		12.00	24.00
Soundtrack (1962) .... Decca (M) DL-4254		6.00	12.00
ROCKY HORROR SHOW (1974)			
Original London Cast .... U.K. (S) UKAL 1006		10.00	20.00
Tim Curry, Jonathan Adams, Richard O'Brien.			
Soundtrack .... Ode (S) 78332		7.50	15.00
Tim Curry, Susan Sarandon, Barry Bostwick, Richard O'Brien.			
SATCHMO THE GREAT (1958)			
TV Soundtrack .... Columbia (M) CL-1077		10.00	20.00
SEVENTEEN (1951)			
Original Cast .... RCA Victor (M) LOC 1003		50.00	100.00
Ann Crowley, Kenneth Nelson, Doris Dalton, Frank Albertson.			
"1776" (1969)			
Original Cast .... Columbia (S) SCX 6424		12.00	24.00
Lewis Fiander, Bernard Lloyd, David Kernan.			
7TH VOYAGE OF SINBAD, THE (1959)			
Soundtrack .... Colpix (M) CP-504		36.00	72.00
SMILING THE BOY FELL DEAD (1961)			
Original Cast .... Sunbeam (M) LB 549		100.00	200.00
Charles Goff, Danny Meehan, Ted Beniades, Warren Wade.			
SNOW WHITE AND THE 7 DWARFS (1937)			
Soundtrack (10") (1949) .... Decca (M) DL-5015		15.00	30.00
Soundtrack (1957) .... Disneyland (M) WDL-4005		7.50	15.00
SODOM & GOMORRAH (1963)			
Soundtrack .... RCA Victor (S) LSO-1076		36.00	72.00
SONG OF BERNADETTE, THE (1943)			
Soundtrack (10") (1952) .... Decca (M) DL-5358		50.00	100.00
STAR IS BORN, A (1954)			
Soundtrack (Boxed) .... Columbia (M) BL-1201		18.00	36.00
SWAN, THE (1956)			
Soundtrack .... MGM (M) E-3300		25.00	50.00

This section represents a 3½% sampling of the artists and songs in *Record Albums 1948-1978.*

TITLE/Flip	LABEL & No.	GOOD	NEAR MINT

THIS IS THE ARMY (1942)
Original Cast (All soldier) (10")
(1950) .... Decca (M) DL 5108 **45.00** 90.00
Earl Oxford, Ezra Stone, Philip Truex, Irving Berlin.

THREE LITTLE WORDS (1950)
Soundtrack (10") .... MGM (M) E-516 12.00 24.00
Soundtrack (1953) .... MGM (M) E-3229 7.50 15.00
Soundtrack (1960) .... MGM (M) E-3768 6.00 12.00
Soundtrack (1967) .... Metro (M) M-615 5.00 10.00
Soundtrack (Re-channeled stereo) .... Metro (S) MS-615 4.00 8.00

⑤⓪ THREE WISHES FOR JAMIE (1952)
Original Cast .... Capitol (M) S 317 125.00 250.00 Tie
Bert Wheeler, Anne Jeffreys, John Raitt, Charlotte Rae.

TOP BANANA (1951)
Original Cast .... Capitol (M) S308 50.00 100.00
Phil Silvers, Rose Marie, Judy Lynn, Jack Albertson.

TWO'S COMPANY (1952)
Original Cast .... RCA Victor (M) LOC 1009 50.00 100.00
Bette Davis, Hiram Sherman, David Burns, George S. Irving.

VERTIGO (1958)
Soundtrack .... Mercury (M) MG-20384 36.00 72.00

WHITE CHRISTMAS (1954)
Soundtrack (10") .... Columbia (M) CL-6338 15.00 30.00

WIZARD OF OZ, THE (1939)
Soundtrack (With Dialogue) (1956) .... MGM (M) E-3464 15.00 30.00

ZIEGFELD FOLLIES (1907)
Radio Soundtrack (The first program of the series, "The Ziegfeld Follies
On The Air," 1/27/36) .... Nostalgia Special Release (M) 001 5.00 10.00
Fanny Brice, James Melton, Patty Chafin and chorus.

All artists shown in photos appear with listings in the guide these samples were taken from.

The following section contains excerpts from:

Popular & Rock Records 1948-1978

Official Price Guide for Collectible Records

The second edition of the "daddy" of all our price guides, the **Popular & Rock Records 1948-1978**, spans the entire history of the "little record with the big hole"—from Elvis, the Beatles, and Bill Haley's Comets on up to Fleetwood Mac. All the current collector prices and year of release dates on over 30,000 45s and 78s are listed.

$7.95

Each of our price guides includes a special *Dealers and Collectors Directory* listing hundreds of buyers and sellers of collectible records!

Popular & Rock Records 1948-1978
can be purchased at your local book or record store
or send check or money order to:
O'Sullivan Woodside & Company
2218 East Magnolia
Phoenix, Arizona 85034
please add 75¢ per book for postage and handling

ALSO A SPECIAL, VERY LIMITED EDITION OF HARD COVER COPIES ARE AVAILABLE WHILE THEY LAST
These are permanently bound, limited and numbered books!
Available only from Jellyroll Productions
(address below) for $18.95. Order direct.

FIRST EDITION
THIS IS THE BOOK THAT STARTED IT ALL! THE BEST-SELLING
FIRST EDITION, NOW OUT OF PRINT, HAS BECOME
A COLLECTOR'S ITEM!

Complete your library with
Record Collectors Price Guide, 1st Edition
while the remaining limited supplies last!
The hard-bound copies have long since sold out,
and the soft covers are no longer available
in most bookstores, so order directly from:

Jellyroll Productions
Box 3017 Scottsdale, Arizona 85257
(Price: $10.00 plus $1.00 postage.)

Popular & Rock Records 1948-1978
Price Guide of Current
Collectible Records (8½" x 11" 264 pages)

ROCKING WITH THE POP SINGLES

Our two price guides, *Popular and Rock Records 1948-1978* and *Record Albums 1948-1978* are companion volumes. To the reader who is skip-reading and has chanced on this section first, please refer to page 16 for an explanation of the cross-over of artists and the interplay between the singles and album sections of this guide.

It is important for the newcomer to collecting to notice the labels that an artist's records come out on. He may recognize the name of a big hit listed as being worth $15, but he can't automatically assume that's the record he has in his closet, because chances are he bought it when it was a hit and his copy was actually the second label to have released the record. Take the case of Captain and Tennille's,*"The Way I Want to Touch You."* The hit version was on *A&M Records* and is worth only a couple of dollars today, but a $40 version was released earlier on another label called *Butterscotch* and a $15 version on *Joyce Records.* The label makes the difference!

Picture sleeves that come with 45 singles are being collected more and more these days, so it's wise to try and keep them in as perfect condition as possible. They invariably prove to be much rarer than the records. It's best to remove the record from the picture sleeve and put it in a plain white sleeve (they can be purchased inexpensively). This is wise, because a record will often wear the sleeve to the point of breaking through on the bottom or sides, or, without a collector's even knowing it, the record inside can cause rubbing wear on the side of the sleeve because of the raised portion of the label. Many collectors today also place their sleeves in protective plastic bags so nothing will happen to them.

Handle them with care, store them with care, and —above all!— never stack your 45s on an automatic record player. If they're worth collecting, they're worth playing one at a time!

The Overwhelming Popularity of Rock

by Greg Shaw

Rock & roll, once laughed off as a silly fad, has become the dominant popular music form of our century, while the record business has surpassed films and every other form of entertainment.

At this point, there's little risk in predicting that posterity will look back on the early years of rock & roll as one of the greatest cultural phenomena of modern history. Already, young scholars who sucked their thumbs to *"Heartbreak Hotel"* are earning doctorates in rock & roll from major universities. What even now may seem frivolous is sure to be surpassed by subsequent extremes of academic recognition. And yet, the general awareness of rock & roll's importance in our society has been held back or lost amid the overall "future shock" condition of our age.

The time has now arrived for the public, or at least that portion of it which listens to and consumes popular music (upwards of 10 million regular buyers, by conservative estimate), to acknowledge and pay heed to the unique characteristics of the idiom. What we're dealing with is a vast multi-billion-dollar industry, whose function it is to develop, mass-produce and market a product that, in addition to being a tangible commodity, is also a work of art in a genre, rock music, that holds a very important place in the minds and lives of its fans.

Because records are an industry as well as an art form, there is intense competition for successful new products, resulting in a situation where, in addition to the dozen or so major labels, there have always been hundreds of adolescents for whom it was made and its subsequent nostalgic attachments, and its following has been all the more devout.

Thus we find ourselves, midway into the third decade of rock, witnessing a most remarkable event: the beginning of the ascension of rock & roll collecting into the first rank of national hobby interests.

The Four Aces

Alphabetical Listing of Popular & Rock Records

This section represents a 3½% sampling of the artists and songs in *Popular & Rock Records 1948-1978*.

TITLE/Flip	LABEL & No.	GOOD	NEAR MINT	YR.
ACADEMICS				
HEAVENLY LOVE/Too Good To Be True .... (Ancho 101)		6.50	13.00	
ADDRISI BROTHERS				
CHERRYSTONE/Lilies Grow High .... (Del Fi 4116)		1.25	2.50	59
ADMIRATIONS				
TO THE AISLE/Hey Senorita .... (Mercury 71883)		12.50	25.00	61
ADVENTURERS				
ROCK & ROLL UPRISING/My Mama Done Told Me				
(Compact 33 single) .... (Columbia 3-42227)		12.50	25.00	61
ALAIMO, Steve				
EVERY DAY I HAVE TO CRY/Little Girl .... (Checker 1032)		1.25	2.50	63
I WANT YOU TO LOVE ME/Blue Skies (With the Red Coats) ..... (Marlin 6064)		5.00	10.00	59
ALDA, Alex (Nick Massi of 4 Seasons)				
LITTLE PONY/ .... (Topix 6007)		17.50	35.00	
(In all probability this record was never released commercially. Only promotional copies have been found and this accounts for the lack of a "flip" side.)				
ALICE COOPER				
I NEVER CRY/Go to Hell .... (Warner Bros. 8228)		1.00	2.00	76
LIVING/Reflected .... (Straight 101)		10.00	20.00	69
ALLEN, Chad (Later of Guess Who)				
LITTLE LONELY/Domino .... (Lama 7779)		2.50	5.00	61
ALLEN, Jimmy & The Two Jays				
MY GIRL IS A PEACH/				
Forgive Me My Darling .... (Al-Brite 1200)		37.50	75.00	
ALLENS, Arvee (Richie Valens)				
FAST FREIGHT/Big Baby Blues .... (Del-Fi 4111)		3.00	6.00	59
ALLEN, Steve				
WHAT IS A WIFE/What Is a Husband .... (Coral 61554)		1.25	2.50	55
ALLMAN JOYS (ALLMAN BROTHERS)				
SPOONFUL/You Deserve Each Other .... (Dial 4046)		4.00	8.00	66
(This was the first record by the Allman Brothers)				
AMERICA				
VENTURA HIGHWAY/Saturn Nights .... (Warner Bros. 7641)		1.00	2.00	72
AMES BROTHERS				
NAUGHTY LADY OF SHADY LANE/Addio..................... (RCA 5897)		1.25	2.50	54
ANGELS (The 'Safaris')				
A LOVER'S POEM (TO HER)/A Lover's Poem (To Him).......... (Tawny 101)		5.00	10.00	59
ANGIE & THE CHICKLETTES				
TREAT HIM TENDER, MAUREEN (NOW THAT RINGO				
BELONGS TO YOU)/Tommy .... (Apt 25080)		4.00	8.00	65
ANKA, Paul				
I CONFESS/Blau-Wile Deveest Fontaine....................... (RPM 499)		10.00	20.00	56
(With Backing by the Jacks)				
LONELY BOY/Your Love....................... (ABC-Paramount 10022)		1.75	3.50	59

TITLE/Flip	LABEL & No.	GOOD	NEAR MINT	YR.
ANNETTE (Funicello)				
MONKEYS UNCLE, THE (Vocal Backing by The Beach Boys)/				
How Will I Know My Love ....(Vista 440)		3.00	6.00	65
TALL PAUL/Ma He's Makin' Eyes at Me ....(Disneyland 118)		2.00	4.00	59
ANN-MARGRET				
I JUST DON'T UNDERSTAND/I Don't Hurt Anymore .... (RCA 7894)		1.50	3.00	61
ANTHONY & THE SOPHMORES				
PLAY THOSE OLDIES MR. D.J./Clap Your Hands ....(Mercury 72103)		3.50	7.00	63
ANTHONY, Paul				
HELLO TEARDROPS, GOODBYE LOVE/Angel Face ....(Gambit 1103)		9.00	18.00	
AQUA-NITES				
CARIOCA/Lover Don't You Weep.....................(Astra 1000)		12.50	25.00	
CHRISTIE/Lover Don't You Weep..........................(Astra 2001)		10.00	20.00	
ARCHIES				
SUGAR SUGAR/Melody Hill ....(Calendar 1008)		1.00	2.00	69
ARROGANTS (Featuring Ray Morrow)				
MIRROR MIRROR/Canadian Sunset.........................(Lute 6226)		4.00	8.00	
ASSOCIATION				
CHERRISH/Don't Blame the Rain ....(Valiant 747)		1.00	2.00	66
AUDREY 78				
DEAR ELVIS (PAGE 1)/				
Dear Elvis (Page 2) ....(Plus 104)		7.50	15.00	56
(Elvis Novelty/Break-in)				
AVALON, Frankie				
TEACHER'S PET/Shy Guy ....(Chancellor 1006)		4.00	8.00	57
TRUMPET SORRENTO/The Book .... ("X" 0006)		5.00	10.00	54
VENUS/I'm Broke.................................(Chancellor 1031)		1.25	2.50	59
BABY RAY & THE FERNS (Frank Zappa)				
HOW'S YOUR BIRD/World's Greatest Sinner ....(Donna 1378)		5.00	10.00	63
BACHMAN-TURNER OVERDRIVE				
YOU AIN'T SEEN NOTHIN' YET/Free Wheelin' ....(Mercury 73662)		1.00	2.00	74
BAEZ, Joan				
NIGHT THEY DROVE OLD DIXIE DOWN/				
When Tie is Stolen .... (Vanguard 35138)		1.00	2.00	71
BAKER, Kenny				
GOODBYE LITTLE STAR/I'm Gonna Love You .... (Orbit 541)		5.00	10.00	
(Song about the starlet who was killed while filming an Elvis Presley show.)				
BALIN, Marty (Later of Jefferson Starship)				
I SPECIALIZE IN LOVE/				
You Alive With Love .... (Challenge 9156)		8.50	17.00	62
BAND (Formerly the HAWKS)				
UP ON CRIPPLE CREEK/				
The Night They Drove Old Dixie Down .... (Capitol 2635)		1.00	2.00	69
BARBARA & THE BELIEVERS				
WHEN YOU WISH UPON A STAR/				
What Can Happen to Me Now .... (Capitol 5866)		5.00	10.00	67

The left hand price column represents the true value of the average, used record.

TITLE/Flip	LABEL & No.	GOOD	NEAR MINT	YR.
BARBARIANS				
ARE YOU A BOY OR A GIRL/Take It Or Leave It .... (Laurie 3308)		2.00	4.00	65
YOU'VE GOT TO UNDERSTAND/				
Hey Little Bird .... (Joy 290)		3.00	6.00	64
BARD, Annette (of the Teddy Bears)				
ALIBI/What Difference Does It Make.....................(Imperial 5643)		6.00	12.00	60
BARITONES				
AFTER SCHOOL ROCK/Sentimental Baby..................... (Dore 501)		10.00	20.00	58
BARONS				
REMEMBER RITA/Lucky Star.............................(Epic 9747)		5.00	10.00	64
(This group featured Larry Chance-of the Earls-as 2nd Tenor)				
BARRI, Steve (Later of the Fantastic Baggies)				
STORY OF THE RING/I Want Your Love..................... (Rona 1004)		3.50	7.00	61
BARRY & THE TAMERLANES				
(Featuring Barry De Vorzon)				
I WONDER WHAT SHE'S DOING TONIGHT/Don't Go ....(Valiant 6034)		1.75	3.50	63
BARRY, Jan (Of Jan & Dean)				
TOMORROWS TEARDROPS/				
My Midsummer Nights Dream .... (Ripple 6101)		12.50	25.00	61
UNIVERSAL COWARD, THE/				
I Can't Wait To Love You ....(Liberty 55845)		1.75	3.50	66
BARRY, Jeff (Of the Raindrops)				
IT'S CALLED ROCK & ROLL/Hip Couples.....................(RCA 7477)		10.00	20.00	59
BASH, Otto				
ELVIS BLUES, THE/Later ....(RCA 6585)		5.00	10.00	56
BAY CITY ROLLERS				
SATURDAY NIGHT/Marlina ....(Arista 0149)		1.00	2.00	75
BEACH BOYS				
BARBARA ANN/Girl Don't Tell Me ....(Capitol 5561)		2.00	4.00	65
(Lead Vocal on "Barbara Ann" shared by Dean Torrence)				
SAIL ON SAILOR/The Traitor ....(Reprise DJ 45)		7.50	15.00	73
(Special Promotional release)				
SALT LAKE CITY/Amusement Parks U.S.A. .... (Capitol Pro 2936)		50.00	200.00	65
(Special giveaway item - produced for Salt Lake City (Utah)				
downtown merchants to distribute free during one of their				
promotions)				
(Prices may vary widely on this record)				
SPIRIT OF AMERICA/				
Boogie Woogie (Instrumental) .... (Capitol Custom)		30.00	120.00	63
(Special giveaway item - produced in conjunction with				
KFWB radio & Wallichs Music City to enhance a record				
store grand opening.)				
SURFIN'/Luau ....(Candix 301)		25.00	50.00	61
(Doesn't show "Distributed by Era")				
SURFIN'/Luau ....(Candix 301)		20.00	40.00	61
(Shows "Distributed by Era")				
SURFIN'/Luau... ("X" 301)		30.00	60.00	62
SURFIN'/Luau...(Candix 331)		20.00	40.00	62
SURFIN SAFARI/409....................................(Capitol 4777)		2.00	4.00	62
TEN LITTLE INDIANS/County Fair ....(Capitol 4880)		4.50	9.00	62
WOULDN'T IT BE NICE/				
The Times They are A-Changin' (By Merry Clayton) .... (Ode 66016)		4.00	8.00	71
BEATLES				
A HARD DAY'S NIGHT/I Should Have Known Better.........(Capitol 5222)		2.00	4.00	64
A HARD DAY'S NIGHT/				
I Should Have Known Better (With Picture Sleeve) ....(Capitol 5222)		6.00	12.00	64

Halfway between good and mint is the true value and the best condition usually available in old records. Mint is rare.

TITLE/Flip	LABEL & No.	GOOD	NEAR MINT	YR
ALL YOU NEED IS LOVE/				
Baby You're a Rich Man ....(Capitol 5964)		1.00	2.00	67
CAN'T BUY ME LOVE/You Can't Do That ....(Capitol 5150)		2.00	4.00	64
CAN'T BUY ME LOVE/				
You Can't Do That (With Picture Sleeve) ....(Capitol 5150)		30.00	60.00	64
CAN'T BUY ME LOVE/				
You Can't Do That (Red Target) ....(Capitol 5150)		2.50	5.00	64
HELTER SKELTER/Helter Skelter (Promotional copy - same song on both sides...released in conjunction with the T.V. Showing of "Helter Skelter") ....(Capitol 4274)		5.00	10.00	76
LADY MADONNA/				
(With Picture Sleeve and Fan Club Flyer)				
The Inner Light (Red Target) ....(Capitol 2138)		2.00	4.00	68
LADY MADONNA/				
The Inner Light (Promotional Copy) ....(Capitol 2138)		25.00	50.00	68
LOVE ME DO/P.S. I Love You ....(Tollie 9008)		1.50	3.00	64
LOVE ME DO/P.S. I Love You (Promotional Copy) ....(Tollie 9008)		25.00	50.00	64

	TITLE/Flip	LABEL & No.	GOOD	NEAR MINT	YR
28	**MY BONNIE (WITH TONY SHERIDAN)**/				
	The Saints (Pink Label-Promotional Copy) ....(Decca 31382)		200.00	400.00	62
	(Actually released as Tony Sheridan & The Beat Brothers. This was the first American release featuring The Beatles.)				
7	**MY BONNIE**/The Saints (Black label, silver writing, red and yellow color.) ....(Decca 31382)		500.00	1000.00	62
4	**MY BONNIE**/The Saints (Promotional Copy).................(MGM 13213)		25.00	50.00	64
	MY BONNIE/The Saints (With Picture Sleeve) ....(Polydor 24 673)		500.00	1500.00	62
	An intro in German, "Mein Herz ist bei dir nur," appears in parenthesis under the title on the record and under the title on the back of the picture sleeve. The front of the sleeve has a small black and white photo of Tony Sheridan at a microphone; the back has the same photo enlarged. The record credits Tony Sheridan and the Beat Brothers, but only Sheridan's name is on the sleeve.				
8	**MY BONNIE**/The Saints (With picture Sleeve) ....(Polydor 24 673)		275.00	800.00	62
	This record is the same as the German, except that instead of the German words under the title, the word "Twist" appears on the record label. The picture sleeves are the same, except that the German phrase is gone from the back, and the word "Twist" is written across the bottom left of the photo on the front of the English Sleeve.				

	LABEL & No.	GOOD	NEAR MINT	YR	
PENNY LANE/					
Strawberry Fields Forever (Red Target) ....(Capitol 5810)		2.00	4.00	67	
PENNY LANE/					
Strawberry Fields Forever.........................(Capitol 5810)		25.00	50.00	67	
(Promotional Copy - With 3 seconds of music at ending that was not on commercial copies.)					
50 PLEASE PLEASE ME/Ask Me Why (Promotional Copy) .... Vee Jay 498)		125.00	250.00	64	Tie
SHE LOVES YOU/I'll Get You ....(Swan 4152)		50.00	100.00	63	
First pressing — white label with red printing — doesn't have "Don't Drop Out". Thicker lettering.					
SHE LOVES YOU/I'll Get You ....(Swan 4152)		7.50	15.00	64	
2nd pressing — white label and red printing with "Don't Drop Out". Thin lettering.					
SHE LOVES YOU/I'll Get You ....(Swan 4152)		1.00	2.00	64	
3rd Press — black label-silver printing.					
SIE LIEBT DICH (She Loves You)/I'll Get You ....(Swan 4182)		12.50	25.00	64	
1st pressing with (She Loves You) on the same line as title.					

TITLE/Flip	LABEL & No.	GOOD	NEAR MINT	YR.
SIE LIEBT DICH (SHE LOVES YOU)/I'll Get You .... (Swan 4182)		5.00	10.00	64

2nd pressing with (She Loves You) under title. So many reissue and
bootleg copies of the above Swan releases have flooded the market that
it has become very difficult to arrive at accurate prices. Only the most
advanced collector can now distinguish between original and reissue/
bootleg copies and therefore would be willing to pay the above prices.
Most Collectors are content to have one of the millions of copies available for 1-2 dollars. This does not detract from the fact that the original
pressings are just as rare as ever and a few collectors will still pay the
above prices, it's just that the values have been greatly deflated.

TITLE/Flip	LABEL & No.	GOOD	NEAR MINT	YR.
TICKET TO RIDE/Yes It Is (With Picture Sleeve) ....(Capitol 5407)		4.00	8.00	65
WHY (WITH TONY SHERIDAN)/				
Cry For A Shadow.......................... (MGM 13227)		5.00	10.00	64
WHY/Cry for a Shadow (With Picture Sleeve) .... (MGM 13227)		20.00	40.00	64

BEEFEATERS (Early BYRDS)
PLEASE LET ME LOVE YOU/Don't Be Long ....(Elektra 45013)		15.00	30.00	65

BEE GEES
HOW CAN YOU MEND A BROKEN HEART/				
Country Woman ....(Atco 6824)		1.00	2.00	71
JIVE TALKIN'/Wind of Change................................(RSO 510)		1.00	2.00	75

BELL NOTES
I'VE HAD IT/Be Mine (Blue) .... (Time 1004)		2.00	4.00	59

BELMONTS
COME ON LITTLE ANGEL/How About Me................... (Sabrina 505)		1.50	3.00	62
NOTHING IN RETURN/Summertime....................... (Sabrina 521)		11.25	22.50	64

BENNETT, Boyd
SEVENTEEN/Little Old You All (Maroon)..................... (King 1470)		5.00	10.00	55

BENNETT, Jerry
REPORT FROM OUTER-SPACE/............................ (Arch 1617)		7.50	15.00	
(Novelty/Break-in)				

BENNETT, Tony
COLD, COLD HEART/While We're Young ....(Columbia 39449)		1.50	3.00	51
I LEFT MY HEART IN SAN FRANCISCO/				
Once Upon A Time ....(Columbia 42332)		1.00	2.00	62

BERNARD, Rod
THIS SHOULD GO ON FOREVER/				
Pardon, Mr. Gordon (With the Twisters) ....(Jin 105)		5.00	10.00	59

TITLE/Flip	LABEL & No.	GOOD	NEAR MINT	YR.
BOYS/Kansas City (With Picture Sleeve) ....(Cameo 391)		15.00	30.00	66
(I'LL TRY) ANYWAY/I Wanna Be There ....(Beatles 800)		6.00	12.00	64

BIG BOPPER (Jape Richardson)
BIG BOPPER'S WEDDING/ Little Red Riding Hood .... (Mercury 71375)		1.25	2.50	58
CHANTILLY LACE/				
The Purple People Eater Meets The Witch Doctor ....(D 1008)		15.00	30.00	58

BILLY & EDDIE
KING IS COMING BACK, THE/Come Back, Baby...........(Top Rank 2017)		5.00	10.00	59
Song about Elvis' release from the U.S. Army.				

BLACK, Bill, Combo
SMOKIE PART II/Smokie Part I........................... (Hi 2018)		1.00	2.00	59

BLANC, Mel
I TAN'T WAIT 'TILL QUITHMUTH/Xmas Chopsticks ....(Capitol 1853)		3.25	6.50	51
I TAUT I TAW A PUDDY TAT/Yosemite Sam ....(Capitol 1360)		2.50	5.00	51

BLANDERS
JITTERBUG/Desert Sands .... (Smash 2005)		7.50	15.00	65

Samples chosen for each artist represent the range of high and low values that artist's records
usually bring.

TITLE/Flip	LABEL & No.	GOOD	NEAR MINT	YR.
BLOCKBUSTERS (50's Group)				
HI HON/Boogie Bop .... (Crystalette 725)		5.00	10.00	59
(Elvis Novelty)				
BLUE CHEER				
FEATHERS FROM YOUR TREE/Sun Cycle .... (Philips 40561)		5.00	10.00	68
(With Picture Sleeve)				
SUMMERTIME BLUES/Out of Focus..................... (Philips 40516)		1.00	2.00	68
BLUE EYED SOUL (Billy Vera)				
SHADOW OF YOUR LOVE, THE/				
Look Gently at the Rain .... (Cameo 401)		2.00	4.00	66
BLUES MAGOOS				
(WE AIN'T GOT) NOTHING YET/Gotta Get Away .... (Mercury 72622)		1.00	2.00	66
WHO DO YOU LOVE/Let Your Love Ride .... (Ganim 1000)		5.00	10.00	66
BLUESOLOGY (Featuring Elton John)				
MR. FRANTIC/Everyday I Have the Blues .... (Fontana 668)		12.50	25.00	66
BLUES PROJECT				
CATCH THE WIND/I Wanna Be Your Driver .... (Verve Folkways 5013)		1.50	3.00	66
BOB & SHERI (Featuring Brian Wilson)				
SURFER MOON, THE/				
Humpty Dumpty (Promo-White) .... (Safari 101)		125.00	500.00	61
SURFER MOON, THE/				
Humpty Dumpty (Commercial-Blue Label) .... (Safari 101)		200.00	600.00	61	Tie

Prices may vary widely on this record. Opinions still vary as to exactly how much Brian Wilson was involved with this record. Many are now of the opinion that Brian sings on Humpty Dumpty while others feel that his voice is heard on Surfer Moon. All agree, however, that it is the most sought after BEACH BOY collectable.

BOBOLINKS				
ELVIS PRESLEY'S SERGEANT/Your Cotton Pickin' Heart .... (Key 573)		5.00	10.00	59
BOONE, Pat				
APRIL LOVE/When The Swallows Come Back To Capistrano ..... (Dot 15660)		1.00	2.00	57
I NEED SOMEONE/Loving You Madly .... (Republic 7084)		4.00	8.00	54
BOP-CHORDS				
CASTLE IN THE SKY/My Darling To You .... (Holiday 2601)		6.00	12.00	57
WHEN I WAKE UP THIS MORNING/				
I Really Love Her .... (Holiday 2603)		7.50	15.00	57
BOWEN, Jimmy (Of the Rhythm Orchids)				
I'M STICKIN' WITH YOU/Party Doll (By Buddy Knox) .... (Triple D 797)		17.50	35.00	57
BOWIE, David				
CAN'T HELP THINKING ABOUT ME/				
And I Say to Myself .... (Warner Bros. 5815)		15.00	30.00	66
FAME/Right .... (RCA 10320)		1.00	2.00	75
SPACE ODDITY/Zig Zag Festival (Promo) .... (Mercury SRD 2-29)		12.50	25.00	69
BOYD, William (Hopalong Cassidy)				
HOPALONG CASSIDY & THE HAUNTED GOLD MINE/.........(Capitol 3166)		4.00	8.00	55
BREAD (Featuring David Gates)				
MAKE IT WITH YOU/				
Why Do You Keep Me Waiting .... (Elektra 45686)		1.00	2.00	70
BRENNAN, Walter				
DUTCHMAN'S GOLD/Back To The Farm .... (Dot 16066)		1.50	3.00	60
BREWER & SHIPLEY				
ONE TOKE OVER THE LINE/Oh Mommy .... (Kama Sutra 516)		1.00	2.00	71

TITLE/Flip	LABEL & No.	GOOD	NEAR MINT	YR.
BREWER, Teresa				
MUSIC! MUSIC! MUSIC!/Copenhagen	(London 604)	2.00	4.00	50
RICOCHET/Too Young To Tango	(Coral 61043)	1.50	3.00	53
BRITISH WALKERS				
WATCH YOURSELF/Bad Lightin'	(Manchester 651120)	3.00	6.00	
BROGUES (Early Quicksilver)				
BUT NOW I'M FINE/Someday	(Twilight 408)	5.00	10.00	
BROOKLYN BRIDGE (Featuring Johnny Maestro)				
WORST THAT COULD HAPPEN/Your Kite, My Kite	(Buddah 75)	1.00	2.00	68
BROOKS, Donnie				
MISSION BELL/Do It For Me	(Era 3018)	1.25	2.50	60
BROTHERS FOUR				
GREENFIELDS/Angelique O	(Columbia 41571)	1.00	2.00	60
RATMAN AND BOBIN IN THE CLIPPER CAPER/ Muleskinner	(Columbia 43547)	2.50	5.00	66
BRUCE & TERRY (Bruce Johnston & Terry Melcher)				
FOUR STRONG WINDS/Raining in My Heart	(Columbia 43378)	2.00	4.00	
BRYANT, Anita				
PAPER ROSES/Mixed Emotions	(Carlton 528)	1.25	2.50	60
BUCHANAN & ANCELL (Bill Buchanan & Bob Ancell)				
CREATURE, THE/Meet the Creature	(Flying Saucer 501)	5.00	10.00	57
(Novelty/Break-in)				
BUCHANAN & GOODMAN (Bill Buchanan & Dickie Goodman)				
BACK TO EARTH/Back to Earth (Pt. II)	(Luniverse 101x)	30.00	60.00	
(Original Title of "Flying Saucers")				
PUBLIC OPINION/Public Opinion (Pt. II)	(Luniverse 102X)	100.00	200.00	56
Only one known copy to exist!				
BUCKINGHAMS				
KIND OF A DRAG/You Make Me Feel So Good	(U.S.A. 860)	1.50	3.00	66
SWEETS FOR MY SWEET/Beginners Love	(Spectra-Sound 4618)	5.00	10.00	66
BURNETTE, Dorsey				
BE A NAVY MAN/ (Special Public Service song, aimed at recruiting for the Navy. Released with special picture sleeve)	(No Label or Number)	10.00	20.00	
HEY LITTLE ONE/Big Rock Candy Mountain	(Era 3019)	1.25	2.50	60
BURNETTE, Johnny Trio				
TEAR IT UP/You're Undecided	(Coral 61651)	15.00	30.00	56
In the beginning Johnny, Dorsey & Paul were known as the ROCK & ROLL TRIO. Then they became JOHNNY BURNETTE & THE ROCK & ROLL TRIO and finally they were called the JOHNNY BURNETTE TRIO.				
CABOTT, Johnny (Frankie Valli & The Four Seasons)				
NIGHT & DAY/On My Own Again	(Columbia 42283)	7.50	15.00	62
NIGHT & DAY/On My Own Again	(Columbia 3-42283)	15.00	30.00	62
(33 Compact Single)				
CALENDARS				
I'M GONNA LAUGH AT YOU/You're Too Fast	(Coed 564)	12.50	25.00	61
CAMEOS				
MERRY CHRISTMAS/New Years Eve	(Cameo 123)	12.50	25.00	58
(Group Sound)				

TITLE/Flip	LABEL & No.	GOOD	NEAR MINT	YR.
CAMPBELL, Glen				
GUESS I'M DUMB/That's All Right .... (Capitol 5441)		4.00	16.00	65
(Prices may vary widely on this record)				
Written, arranged, produced & conducted by Brian Wilson.				
Brian is probably singing harmony on this one too. Glen Camp-				
bell was once the "Traveling Beach Boy" - doing Brian's vocal				
chores when the Beach Boys were on tour.				
WICHITA LINEMAN/Fate of Man .... (Capitol 2302)		1.00	2.00	68
CAMPERS (Sonny Curtis & The Crickets)				
BALLAD OF BATMAN/Batmobile .... (Parkway 974)		4.00	8.00	65
CANADIAN SQUIRES (Later to be the Hawks-Then the Band)				
LEAVE ME ALONE/Uh-Uh-Uh .... (Ware 6002)		4.50	9.00	
CANNON, Freddy				
JUMP OVER/The Urge .... (Swan 4053)		1.50	3.00	60
CAPRIS				
THERE'S A MOON OUT TONIGHT/Indian Girl .... (Planet 1010)		25.00	50.00	60
WHERE I FELL IN LOVE/Some People Think .... (Old Town 1099)		3.00	6.00	61
CAPTAIN & TENNILLE				
LOVE WILL KEEP US TOGETHER/				
Gentle Stranger .... (A&M 1672)		1.00	2.00	
THE WAY I WANT TO TOUCH YOU .... (A&M)		1.00	2.00	
THE WAY I WANT TO TOUCH YOU .... (Butterscotch Castle)		20.00	40.00	
THE WAY I WANT TO TOUCH YOU .... (Joyce)		7.50	15.00	
CARPENTERS				
CLOSE TO YOU/I Kept On Loving You .... (A&M 1183)		1.00	2.00	70
CARR, Vikki				
HE'S A REBEL/Be My Love .... (Liberty 55493)		1.50	3.00	62
(Original-Released Before Crystals)				
CASCADES				
FLYING ON THE GROUND/Main Street .... (Smash 2101)		2.00	4.00	67
(Neil Young on Guitar)				
RHYTHM OF THE RAIN/Let Me Be .... (Valiant 6026)		1.25	2.50	62
CASSIDY, David				
CHERISH/All I Wanna Do is Touch You .... (Bell 45150)		1.00	2.00	71
CASTELLS (Featuring Chuck Girard)				
I DO/Teardrops .... (Warner Bros. 5421)		5.00	10.00	64
"I Do" was arranged, produced & written by Brian Wilson and				
he is probably singing in the backup vocals. Brian simply re-				
wrote new lyrics to "County Fair". (Flip side of "Ten Little				
Indians" Capitol 4880)				
SO THIS IS LOVE/On The Street Of Tears .... (Era 3073)		1.75	3.50	62
CHAMPS				
TEQUILA/Train To Nowhere .... (Challenge 1016)		1.25	2.50	58
CHANNEL, Bruce				
HEY! BABY/Dream Girl .... (Le Cam 953)		2.50	5.00	62
CHANTAYS				
PIPELINE/Move It .... (Downey 104)		2.25	4.50	63
CHER				
ALL I REALLY WANT TO DO/I'm Gonna Love You .... (Imperial 66114)		1.00	2.00	65
DREAM BABY/Stan Quetzal (Recorded as CHERILYN) .... (Imperial 66081)		3.00	6.00	64
CHIPMUNKS (With David Seville)				
(Staring Alvin, Theodore & Simon)				
CHIPMUNK SONG, THE/Almost Good .... (Liberty 55168)		1.25	2.50	58

TITLE/Flip	LABEL & No.	GOOD	NEAR MINT	YR.
CHOIR (Early RASPERRIES With Eric Carmen)				
IT'S COLD OUTSIDE/I'm Going Home .... *(Canadian American 203)*		10.00	20.00	67
CHORDETTES				
MR. SANDMAN/I Don't Wanna See You Crying............ *(Cadence 1247)*		1.50	3.00	54
CHRISTIE, Lou				
GYPSY CRIED, THE/Red Sails in the Sunset .... *(CO & CE 102)*		12.50	25.00	63
LIGHTNIN' STRIKES/Cryin' In The Streets.................. *(MGM 13412)*		1.25	2.50	65
CLANTON, Jimmy				
JUST A DREAM/You Aim To Please........................ *(Ace 546)*		1.25	2.50	58
VENUS IN BLUE JEANS/Highway Bound				
(Promotional Copy Only) .... *(Ace 644)*		3.00	6.00	62
CLARK, Dave, Five				
CHAQUITA/In Your Heart .... *(Jubilee 5476)*		4.00	8.00	64
GLAD ALL OVER/I Know You.............................*(Epic 9656)*		1.25	2.50	64
CLARK, Dick				
SEASON'S GREETINGS FROM DICK CLARK/........ *(Dick Clark No Number)*		7.50	15.00	
CLARK, Petula				
DOWNTOWN/You'd Better Love Me ....*(Warner Bros. 5494)*		1.00	2.00	64
WHERE DID MY SNOWMAN GO/3 Little Kittens ....*(Coral 61077*		1.75	3.50	54
CLARK, Sanford				
A CHEAT/Usta Be My Baby........................... *(Dot 15516)*		2.00	4.00	56
FOOL, THE/Lonesome For A Letter....................... *(MCI 1003)*		12.50	25.00	55
CLAY, Cassius (Muhammed Ali)				
STAND BY ME (Vocal)/				
I Am The Greatest (Poem-spoken) .... *(Columbia 43007)*		3.50	7.00	64
WILL THE REAL SONNY LISTON PLEASE FALL DOWN/				
The Prediction (Promotion Only).................. *(Columbia 75717*		5.00	10.00	64
(Shown as Cassius Marcellus Clay Jr.)				
(Comedy)				
CLIFFORD, Buzz				
BABY SITTER BOOGIE/Driftwood ....*(Columbia 41876)*		5.00	10.00	60
(Original Title)				
MORE DEAD THAN ALIVE/				
No One Loves Me Like You Do......................*(Roulette 4451)*		3.00	6.00	
CLOONEY, Rosemary				
TOO OLD TO CUT THE MUSTARD (With Marlene Dietrich)/				
Good For Nothing............................*(Columbia 39812)*		1.25	2.50	52
COCHRAN BROTHERS (Eddie & Hank)				
TIRED AND SLEEPY/Fool's Paradise .... *(Ekko 3001)*		50.00	100.00	
COCHRAN, Eddie				
SKINNY JIM/Half Loved .... *(Crest 1026)*		25.00	50.00	56
SUMMERTIME BLUES/Love Again ....*(Liberty 55144)*		2.00	4.00	58
COLE, Nat King				
MONA LISA/Greatest Inventor ....*(Capitol 1010)*		1.25	2.50	50
RAMBLIN' ROSE/The Good Times ....*(Capitol 4804)*		1.25	2.50	62
WHEN I FALL IN LOVE/Love Letters .... *(Capitol - No Number)*		4.00	8.00	
(Promotional Only)				
COMO, Perry				
CATCH A FALLING STAR/Magic Moments...................*(RCA 7128)*		1.25	2.50	57
(I LOVE YOU) DON'T YOU FORGET IT/				
One More Mountain ....*(RCA 8186)*		1.00	2.00	63
COMSTOCK, Bobby (With The Counts)				
G⁻ .DEN OF EDEN, THE/Just A Piece Of Paper........... *(Festival 25000)*		1.50	3.00	

TITLE/Flip	LABEL & No.	GOOD	NEAR MINT	YR.
CREEDENCE CLEARWATER REVIVAL (Formerly the Golliwogs)				
45 REVOLUTIONS PER MINUTE (Interview Disc) .... (Fantasy 2838)		5.00	10.00	69
PORTERVILLE/Call it Pretending .... (Scorpio 412)		4.00	8.00	67
PROUD MARY/Born On the Bayou .... (Fantasy 619)		1.00	2.00	69
CRESTS (Featuring Johnny Maestro)				
NO ONE TO LOVE/Wish She Was Mine .... (Joyce 105)		11.00	22.00	57
16 CANDLES/Beside You................................ (Coed 506)		1.50	3.00	58
CREW CUTS				
SH-BOOM/I Spoke Too Soon .... (Mercury 70404)		1.50	3.00	54
CRICKETS				
LOVE'S MADE A FOOL OF YOU/Someone, Someone ...... (Brunswick 55124)		2.00	4.00	59
PEGGY SUE GOT MARRIED/Don't Cha Know .... (Coral 62238)		5.00	10.00	60
CROCE, Jim				
BAD, BAD LEROY BROWN/				
Good Time Man Like Me Ain't Got No Business .... (ABC 11359)		1.00	2.00	73
CROSBY, Bing				
TRUE LOVE (with Grace Kelly)/				
Well Did You Evah? (With Frank Sinatra) .... (Capitol 3507)		1.00	2.00	56
DALE, Dick (With the Del-tones)				
JESSIE PEARL/St. Louis Blues........................ (Deltone 5014)		6.00	12.00	60
MR. ELIMINATOR/Victor .... (Capitol 5140)		1.25	2.50	64
DAMONE, Vic				
ON THE STREET WHERE YOU LIVE/				
We All Need Love .... (Columbia 40654)		1.25	2.50	56
DANA, Vic				
MORE/That's Why I'm Sorry .... (Dolton 81)		1.00	2.00	63
DANNY & THE JUNIORS				
AT THE HOP/Sometimes .... (Singular 711)		11.00	22.00	57
ROCK AND ROLL IS HERE TO STAY/				
School Boy Romance .... (ABC Paramount 9888)		1.75	3.50	58
DARREN, James				
GOODBYE CRUEL WORLD/Valerie .... (Colpix 609)		1.25	2.50	61
DAWN (Featuring Tony Orlando)				
CANDIDA/Look At .... (Bell 903)		1.00	2.00	70
WHAT ARE YOU DOING SUNDAY/				
Sweet Soft Sounds of Love (Price includes sleeve) .... (Bell 1169)		3.00	6.00	
(Issued in Europe prior to "Candida"-although this same song became the groups fifth U.S. hit. Also the backup group-"Dawn" was male instead of the two girls who later became "Dawn").				
DAY, Doris				
EVERYBODY LOVES A LOVER/Instant Love .... (Columbia 41195)		1.25	2.50	58
SECRET LOVE/Deadwood Stage .... (Columbia 40108)		1.50	3.00	53
DEAN, James				
JUNGLE RHYTHM/Dean's Lament .... (Romeo 100)		5.00	10.00	
(James Dean On Bongos)				
DEE, Joey & The Starliters				
PEPPERMINT TWIST/				
(Special Product-Price Includes Cover and Insert) .... (Vaseline Hair Tonic R-12)		6.00	12.00	
SHOUT (PART I)/Shout (Part II) .... (Roulette 4416)		1.25	2.50	62
DENNY & THE LP'S				
WHY NOT GIVE ME YOUR HEART/Slide-cha-lypso............ (Rock-it 001)		10.00	20.00	

Most artists in this section from the singles pop & rock book are also in *Record Albums 1948-1978.*

TITLE/Flip	LABEL & No.	GOOD	NEAR MINT	YR.
DeSHANNON, Jackie				
I WANNA GO HOME/So Warm .... (Edison International 416)		1.50	3.00	60
DETERGENTS				
LEADER OF THE LAUNDROMAT/Ulcers ....(Roulette 4590)		1.50	3.00	64
DIAMOND, Neil				
CLOWN TOWN/At Night ....(Columbia 42809)		7.50	15.00	63
SWEET CAROLINE/Dig In................................ (UNI 55136)		1.00	2.00	69
DIAMONDS				
LITTLE DARLIN'/Faithful And True .... (Mercury 71060)		1.25	2.50	57
DICK AND DEEDEE				
MOUNTAIN'S HIGH, THE/I Want Someone ....(Lama 7778)		4.00	8.00	61
THOU SHALT NOT STEAL/				
Just 'Round The River Bend...................(Warner Bros. 5482)		1.25	2.50	64
DINNING, Mark				
TEEN ANGEL/Bye Now Baby .... (MGM 1284)		1.25	2.50	59
DION & THE BELMONTS				
A TEENAGER IN LOVE/I've Cried Before .... (Laurie 3027)		1.25	2.50	59
WE WENT AWAY/Tag Along ....(Mohawk 107)		7.50	15.00	57
DR. WEST'S MEDICINE SHOW & JUNK BAND (With Norman Greenbaum)				
EGGPLANT THAT ATE CHICAGO, THE/				
You Can't Fight City Hall Blues......................... (Go Go 100)		1.50	3.00	66
DONEGAN, Lonnie				
DOES YOUR CHEWING GUM LOSE IT'S FLAVOR/				
Aunt Rhody .... (Dot 15911)		1.25	2.50	59
"Does Your Chewing Gum" was originally released in 1959, unsuccessfully. When re-issued (Same label number & flip) in '61 it became a very big hit.				
DONOVAN (Donovan Leitch)				
CATCH THE WIND/Why Do You Treat Me Like You Do .... (Hickory 1309)		1.25	2.50	65
DOO, Dickey & The Don'ts (With Gerry Granahan)				
NEE NEE NA NA NA NA NU NU/Flip Top Box ....(Swan 4006)		2.00	4.00	58
DOORS (Featuring Jim Morrison)				
LIGHT MY FIRE/Crystal Ship.........................(Elektra 45615)		1.00	2.00	67
DOUG & FREDDY & THE PYRAMIDS				
TAKE A CHANCE ON LOVE/				
I Know You're Lyin' .... (Finer Arts 1001)		15.00	30.00	
DOVELLS (Featuring Len Barry)				
YOU CAN'T SIT DOWN/Stompin' Everywhere .... (Parkway 867)		1.25	2.50	63
DUKE, Patty				
DON'T JUST STAND THERE/Everything But Love .... (United Artists 875)		1.25	2.50	65
DUPREES				
YOU BELONG TO ME/Take Me As I Am .... (Coed 569)		1.25	2.50	62
EARLS (Featuring Larry Chance)				
ALL THROUGH OUR TEENS/Whoever You Are ....(Rome 114)		5.00	10.00	76
(Multi-colored wax)				
REMEMBER THEN/Let's Waddle ....(Old Town 1230)		1.50	3.00	63
EDWARDS, Tommy				
IT'S ALL IN THE GAME/All Over Again .... (MGM 11035)		4.50	9.00	51
PLEASE MR. SUN/				
The Morning Side Of The Mountain .... (MGM 12757)		1.25	2.50	59

TITLE/Flip	LABEL & No.	GOOD	NEAR MINT	YR.
ELEGANTS (Featuring Vito Picone)				
LITTLE STAR/Getting Dizzy .... (Apt 25005)		6.00	12.00	58
(Black label - silver letters)				
LITTLE STAR/Getting Dizzy .... (Apt 25005)		2.00	4.00	58
(Multi-colored label)				
EVANS, Paul				
MIDNITE SPECIAL/Since I Met You Baby .... (Guaranteed 205)		1.25	2.50	59
EVERETT, Vince				
BABY LET'S PLAY HOUSE/Livin' High .... (ABC Paramount 10472)		6.00	12.00	63
SUCH A NIGHT/Don't Go .... (ABC Paramount 10313)		5.00	10.00	62
FABARES, Shelley				
JOHNNY ANGEL/Where's It Gonna Get Me .... (Colpix 621)		1.25	2.50	62
FABIAN				
HOUND DOG MAN/This Friendly World .... (Chancellor 1044)		1.25	2.50	59
FAITHFULL, Marianne				
AS TEARS GO BY/Green Sleeves .... (London 9697)		1.00	2.00	64
FAITH, Percy				
(THEME FROM) A SUMMER PLACE/				
Go-Go-Po-Go .... (Columbia 41490)		1.00	2.00	60
FERRANTE & TEICHER				
EXODUS/Twilight .... (United Artists 274)		1.00	2.00	60
FIFTH DIMENSION				
(Featuring Marilyn McCoo & Billy Davis Jr.)				
UP, UP & AWAY/Which Way to Nowhere .... (Soul City 756)		1.00	2.00	67
FIREFLIES (Featuring Richie Adams)				
YOU WERE MINE FOR AWHILE/				
One O'Clock Twist................................(Taurus 355)		4.00	8.00	62
YOU WERE MINE/Stella Got A Fella...................... (Ribbon 6901)		1.50	3.00	59
FISHER, Eddie				
LADY OF SPAIN/Outside Of Heaven .... (RCA 4963)		1.25	2.50	52
FIVE AMERICANS				
I SEE THE LIGHT/The Outcast............................ (Abnak 109)		2.50	5.00	65
WESTERN UNION/Now That It's Over .... (Abnak 118)		1.25	2.50	67
FLASH CADILLAC & THE CONTINENTAL KIDS				
AT THE HOP/She's So Fine ....(Epic 11043)		1.25	2.50	73
FLEETWOODS (Gary, Barbara & Gretchen)				
COME SOFTLY TO ME/I Care So Much .... (Liberty 55188)		2.25	4.50	59
MR. BLUE/You Mean Everything To Me .... (Dolton 5)		1.00	2.00	59
FONTANE SISTERS				
SEVENTEEN/If I Could Be With You........................ (Dot 15386)		1.25	2.50	55
FOUR ACES (Featuring Al Alberts)				
THREE COINS IN THE FOUNTAIN/				
Wedding Bells (Are Breaking Up				
That Old Gang Of Mine) .... (Decca 29123)		1.50	3.00	54
FOUR-EVERS				
BE MY GIRL/If I Were A Magician....................... (Smash 1887)		1.25	2.50	64
YOU BELONG TO ME/				
Such a Good Night For Dreaming................. (Columbia 42303)		12.50	25.00	62

This section represents a 3½% sampling of the artists and songs in *Popular & Rock Records 1948-1978*.

TITLE/Flip	LABEL & No.	GOOD	NEAR MINT	YR.
FOUR LADS				
MOCKING BIRD, THE/				
I May Hate Myself in the Morning .... (Okeh 6885)		2.50	5.00	52
MOMENTS TO REMEMBER/Dream On Love, Dream .... (Columbia 40539)		1.25	2.50	55
FOUR LOVERS (Early Four Seasons)				
MY LIFE FOR YOUR LOVE/Pucker Up .... (Epic 9255)		37.50	75.00	57
YOU'RE THE APPLE OF MY EYE/The Girl In My Dreams .... (RCA 6518)		5.00	10.00	56
FOUR PREPS				
A LETTER TO THE BEATLES/Collage Cannonball .... (Capitol 5143)		2.25	4.50	64
26 MILES/It's You .... (Capitol 3845)		1.25	2.50	57
FRANCIS, Connie				
MY HAPPINESS/Never Before .... (MGM 12738)		1.25	2.50	58
FREDDIE & THE DREAMERS				
I'M TELLING YOU NOW/What Have I Done To You .... (Capitol 5053)		3.00	6.00	63
YOU WERE MADE FOR ME/Send a Letter to Me .... (Capitol 5137)		4.00	8.00	64
FULLER, Bobby, Four				
I FOUGHT THE LAW/Little Annie Lou .... (Mustang 3014)		1.00	2.00	65
SATURDAY NIGHT/Stinger .... (Todd 1090)		5.00	10.00	
GAYLORDS (Featuring Ronnie Gaylord)				
FROM THE VINE CAME THE GRAPE/				
Stolen Moments .... (Mercury 70296)		1.25	2.50	54
GENTRYS				
KEEP ON DANCING/Make Up Your Mind .... (Youngstown 601)		4.00	8.00	65
SPREAD IT ON THICK/Brown Paper Sack .... (MGM 13432)		1.25	2.50	65
GERRY & THE PACEMAKERS				
DON'T LET THE SUN CATCH YOU CRYING/				
I'm The One .... (Laurie 3251)		1.50	3.00	64
GIBBS, Georgia				
HULA HOOP SONG, THE/Keep In Touch .... (Roulette 4106)		1.25	2.50	58
GILMER, Jimmy (And The Fireballs)				
SUGAR SHACK/My Heart Is Free .... (Dot 16487)		1.00	2.00	63
GIORDANO, Lou				
STAY CLOSE TO ME/Don't Cha Know .... (Brunswick 55115)		50.00	150.00	58
(Features Buddy Holly on Guitar)				
(Prices may vary widely on this record)				
GOLDSBORO, Bobby				
MOLLY/Honey Baby .... (Laurie 3148)		1.50	3.00	62
GORE, Lesley				
IT'S MY PARTY/Danny .... (Mercury 72119)		1.25	2.50	63
GORME, Eydie				
BLAME IT ON THE BOSSA NOVA/				
Guess I Should Have Loved Him More .... (Columbia 42661)		1.00	2.00	62
GRASS ROOTS				
MR. JONES/You're A Lonely Girl .... (Dunhill 4013)		1.25	2.50	65
GREAT SOCIETY (Featuring Grace Slick)				
SALLY GO 'ROUND THE ROSES/Did'nt Think So .... (Columbia 44583)		2.50	5.00	68
SOMEONE TO LOVE/Free Advice .... (Northbeach 1001)		12.50	25.00	
(This song was later recorded by the Jefferson Airplane as "Somebody To Love")				

The left hand price column represents the true value of the average, used record.

The Beach Boys

The Beatles

TITLE/Flip	LABEL & No.	GOOD	NEAR MINT	YR.
HALEY, Bill & His Comets				
*A YEAR AGO THIS CHRISTMAS/				
Don't Want To Be Alone This Christmas	(Holiday 111)	50.00	100.00	51
CRAZY, MAN, CRAZY/Whatcha Gonna Do	(Essex 321)	6.00	12.00	53
ROCK AROUND THE CLOCK (WE'RE GONNA)/				
Thirteen Women (And Only One Man In Town)	(Decca 29124)	2.00	4.00	55
ROCK THE JOINT/Icy Heart	(Essex 303)	10.00	20.00	52
HARPER'S BIZARRE				
59TH STREET BRIDGE SONG/Lost My Love Today	(Warner Bros. 5890)	1.00	2.00	67
HAWKINS, Ronnie & The Hawks				
FORTY DAYS/One Of These Days	(Roulette 4154)	1.75	3.50	59
HERMAN'S HERMITS				
I'M HENRY VIII, I AM/The End Of The World	(MGM 13367)	1.00	2.00	65
HIBBLER, Al				
HE/Breeze	(Decca 29660)	1.25	2.50	55
HIGH NUMBERS (Early "WHO")				
ZOOT SUIT/	(Fontana)	75.00	150.00	
(British Release)				
HIGHWAYMEN				
MICHAEL/Santiano	(United Artists 258)	1.25	2.50	61
HOLLY, Buddy				
BLUE DAYS, BLACK NIGHTS/Love Me	(Decca 29854)	15.00	30.00	56
GIRL ON MY MIND/Ting-A-Ling	(Decca 30650)	11.00	22.00	58
LOVE IS STRANGE/You're The One	(Coral 62558)	5.00	10.00	69
(With Picture sleeve)				
MAYBE BABY/Not Fade Away	(Coral 62407)	5.00	10.00	64
PEGGY SUE/Everyday	(Coral 61885)	1.75	3.50	57
SLIPPIN' AND SLIDIN'/What To Do	(Coral 62448)	6.00	12.00	65
HOLLYWOOD TORNADOES (A.K.A. TORNADOES)				
INEBRIATED SURFER, THE/Moon Dawg	(Aertaun 102)	1.50	3.00	64

The Champs

The Beau Marks

The Chocolate Watch Band

Teresa Brewer

Creedence Clearwater Revival

Johnny Burnette Trio

Lonnie Donegan

Ral Donner

TITLE/Flip	LABEL & No.	GOOD	NEAR MINT	YR.

HONEYS
SURFIN DOWN THE SWANEE RIVER/Shoot The Curl .... (Capitol 4952)   10.00   30.00   63

HYLAND, Brian
ITSY BITSY TEENIE WEENIE YELLOW POLKADOT BIKINI/
   Don't Dilly Dally Sally .... (Leader 805)   2.50   5.00   60
SEALED WITH A KISS/Summer Job .... (ABC Paramount 10336)   1.25   2.50   62

IDLE RACE (Features Jeff Lynne)
HERE WE GO AROUND THE LEMON TREE/
   My Fathers Son .... (Liberty 55997)   6.00   12.00   67
(Jeff Lynne-later of "Move" and more recently of the "Electric Light Orchestra")

IFIELD, Frank
I REMEMBER YOU/I Listen To My Heart .... (Vee Jay 457)   1.00   2.00   62

IRON BUTTERFLY
IN-A-GADDA-DA-VIDA/Iron Butterfly Theme .... (Atco 6606)   1.00   2.00   68

IVAN (Jerry IVAN Allison of the Crickets)
REAL WILD CHILD/Oh You Beautiful Doll .... (Coral 62017)   5.00   10.00   59
(Featuring Buddy Holly on guitar)

JAMES, Joni
HOW IMPORTANT CAN IT BE/This Is My Confession .... (MGM 11919)   1.25   2.50   55

JAMES, Tommy & Shondells
HANKY PANKY/Thunderbold .... (Red Fox 110)   5.00   10.00   66

JAN & DEAN (Jan Barry & Dean Torrence)
BABY TALK/Jeanette Get Your Hair Done .... (Dore 522)   1.50   3.00   59
HAWAII/Tijuana .... (Jan & Dean 10)   25.00   50.00   66
IN THE STILL OF THE NIGHT/
   Girl, You're Blowing My Mind (Promo Only) .... (Warner Bros. 7240)   20.00   40.00   68
SURF CITY/She's My Summer Girl .... (Liberty 55580)   1.00   2.00   63

JAY & THE AMERICANS
SHE CRIED/Dawning .... (United Artists 415)   1.25   2.50   62

JOHN, Elton
BORDER SONG/Bad Side of the Moon .... (Congress 6022)   4.00   8.00
GOODBYE YELLOW BRICK ROAD/
   Young Man's Blues .... (MCA 40148)   1.00   2.00   73
LADY SAMANTHA/It's Me That You Need .... (Congress 6017)   7.00   14.00   69
PINBALL WIZARD/Acid Queen (By Tina Turner) .... (Polydor 002)   10.00   20.00   75
   (Promotional issued only - for "Tommy")

JONES, Jack
WIVES AND LOVERS/Toys In The Attic .... (Kapp 551)   1.00   2.00   63

JONES, Tom
IT'S NOT UNUSUAL/To Wait For Love .... (Parrot 9737)   1.00   2.00   65

KALLEN, Kitty
LITTLE THINGS MEAN A LOT/
   I Don't Think You Love Me Anymore .... (Decca 29037)   1.25   2.50   54

KANE, Paul (Paul Simon)
CARLOS DOMINGUEZ/He Was My Brother .... (Tribute 128)   20.00   40.00

KENNY & THE CADETS (Beach Boys)
BARBIE/What Is a Young Girl Made Of .... (Randy 422)   100.00   200.00   61
(Half red & half yellow wax)
BARBIE/What Is A Young Girl Made Of .... (Randy 422)   62.50   125.00   61
(Pink Label)
BARBIE/What Is a Young Girl Made Of .... (Randy 422)   1.25   2.50
(Bootleg-White label/Black letters)
Both sides were later released on Beach Boys PICKWICK (Budget label) album.

TITLE/Flip	LABEL & No.	GOOD	NEAR MINT	YR.
KIDD, Johnny & The Pirates				
I'LL NEVER GET OVER YOU/Then I Got Everything .... (Capitol 5065)		1.25	2.50	63
KING, Carole				
IT MIGHT AS WELL RAIN UNTIL SEPTEMBER/				
Nobody's Perfect .... (Companion 2000)		10.00	20.00	62
OH NEAL/A Very Special Boy .... (Alpine 57)		15.00	30.00	60
KINGSMEN				
JOLLY GREEN GIANT, THE/Long Green .... (Wand 172)		1.25	2.50	
LOUIE LOUIE/Haunted Castle .... (Jerden 712)		4.00	8.00	
KINGSTON TRIO				
TOM DOOLEY/Ruby Red .... (Capitol 4049)		1.25	2.50	58
KITTENS				
COUNT EVERY STAR/I'm Worried .... (Chestnut 203)		6.00	12.00	
KNIGHTLY, John				
GREAT SPACE FLIGHT/Great Space Flight (Pt. 2) .... (Spar 103)		7.00	14.00	
KNIGHT, Terry & The Pack				
I (Who Have Nothing)/Numbers .... (Lucky Eleven 230)		1.25	2.50	66
KNOX, Buddy				
LOVEY DOVEY/I Got You .... (Liberty 55290)		1.25	2.50	60
PARTY DOLL/				
I'm Stickin' With You (by Jimmy Bowen) .... (Triple D 797)		17.50	35.00	57
LAINE, Frankie				
CRY OF THE WILD GOOSE, THE/Black Lace .... (Mercury 5363)		2.00	4.00	50
I BELIEVE/Your Cheating Heart .... (Columbia 39938)		1.50	3.00	53
LANDIS, Jerry (Paul Simon)				
LONE TEEN RANGER/Lisa .... (Amy 875)		5.00	10.00	62
LANZA, Mario				
ARRIVEDERCI ROMA/Younger Than Springtime .... (RCA 7164)		1.25	2.50	58
LAWRENCE, Steve				
GO AWAY LITTLE GIRL/If You Love Her Tell Her So .... (Columbia 42601)		1.25	2.50	62
LEE, Brenda				
I'M SORRY/That's All You Gotta Do .... (Decca 31093)		1.25	2.50	60
JAMBALAYA/Bigelow 6-200 (with The Jordanaires) .... (Decca 30050)		2.00	4.00	56
SWEET NOTHIN'S/Weep No More My Baby .... (Decca 30967)		1.50	3.00	59
LEE, Dickie				
PATCHES/More Or Less .... (Smash 1758)		1.25	2.50	62
STAY TRUE BABY/Dream Boy .... (Tampa 131)		7.50	15.00	
LEE, Peggy				
FEVER/You Don't Know .... (Capitol 3998)		1.00	2.00	58
LESLEY, Tom				
NASHVILLE REPORTER/Rockin' Banjo .... (Enola 314)		5.00	10.00	
LETTERMEN				
WAY YOU LOOK TONIGHT, THE/				
That's My Desire .... (Capitol 4586)		1.00	2.00	61
LEWIS, Gary & The Playboys				
I SAW ELVIS PRESLEY LAST NIGHT/				
Something Is Wrong .... (Liberty 56144)		2.00	4.00	69
THIS DIAMOND RING/Hard to Find .... (Liberty 55756)		1.00	2.00	64

TITLE/Flip	LABEL & No.	GOOD	NEAR MINT	YR.
LONDON, Julie				
CRY ME A RIVER/S'Wonderful ....(Liberty 55006)		1.25	2.50	55
LUKE, Robin				
EVERLOVIN'/Well Oh, Well Oh .... (Dot 16096)		1.25	2.50	60
SUSIE DARLIN'/Living's Loving You .... (International 206)		10.00	20.00	58
LUMAN, Bob				
LET'S THINK ABOUT LIVING/				
You've Got Everything ....(Warner Bros. 5172)		1.25	2.50	60
RED HOT/Whenever You're Ready......................(Imperial 8313)		15.00	30.00	55
LYNDON, Frank (Of The Belmonts)				
EARTH ANGEL/Don't Look at Me ....(Sabina 520)		7.50	15.00	
MADISON, Ronnie				
LINDA/Here I Stand .... (Storm 987)		10.00	20.00	
MAESTRO, Johnny (Johnny Mastroangelo)				
BESAME BABY/It Must Be Love .... (Coed 562)		20.00	40.00	61
MODEL GIRL/We've Got To Tell Them .... (Coed 545)		1.50	3.00	61
MAMAS & PAPAS (Formerly the Mugwumps) *PS*				
MONDAY MONDAY/Got A Feelin' .... (Dunhill 4026)		1.00	2.00	66
MANFRED MANN				
DO WAH DIDDY DIDDY/What You Gonna Do ....(Ascot 2157)		1.25	2.50	64
PRETTY FLAMINGO/You're Standing By .... (United Artists 50040)		1.00	2.00	66
MANILOW, Barry				
COULD IT BE MAGIC/Cloudburst........................ (Bell 45422)		1.25	2.50	74
MANN, Carl				
GONNA ROCK & ROLL TONIGHT/Rockin' Love .... (Jaxon 502)		7.50	15.00	
MARTIN, Dean				
MEMORIES ARE MADE OF THIS/				
Change Of Heart....................(Capitol 3295)		1.25	2.50	55
SANTA LUCIA/Hold Me .... (Apollo 1116)		2.00	4.00	

Jan Barry, Jim Pewter & Dean Torrence (Jan and Dean)

All artists shown in photos appear with listings in the guide these samples were taken from.

TITLE/Flip	LABEL & No.	GOOD	NEAR MINT	YR.
MARTINO, Al				
HERE IN MY HEART/I Cried Myself To Sleep .... (BBS 101)		2.25	4.50	52
I LOVE YOU BECAUSE/Merry-Go-Round .... (Capitol 4930)		1.00	2.00	63
MATHIS, Johnny				
CHANCES ARE/The Twelfth Of Never .... (Columbia 40993)		1.00	2.00	57
MC5 (Motor City Five)				
KICK OUT THE JAMS/				
Motor City is Burning (Uncensored) .... (Elektra)		3.00	6.00	
LOOKING AT YOU/Borderline........................... (A-Square 333)		25.00	50.00	
(With Picture Sleeve)				
McGUIRE SISTERS				
SUGARTIME/Banana Split .... (Coral 61924)		1.00	2.00	57
MINDBENDERS				
UM, UM, UM/First Taste Of Love........................ (Fontana 1945)		2.50	5.00	
MOJO MEN				
SHE'S MY BABY/Fire In My Heart .... (Autumn 27)		5.00	10.00	
MONKEES				
DAYDREAM BELIEVER/Goin' Down .... (Colgems 1012)		1.25	2.50	67
MONTEZ, Chris				
LET'S DANCE/You're The One .... (Monogram 505)		1.25	2.50	62
MOONSHINE				
(The Americans of Jay & The Americans)				
WHISTLING IN THE WIND/Out A Hand .... (United Artists 50658)		2.50	5.00	70
MOORE, Harv				
INTERVIEW OF THE FAB FOUR/I Feel So Fine .... (American Arts 20)		15.00	30.00	64
(Beatles)				
MOVE, THE (Featuring Jeff Lynne & Roy Wood)				
DISTURBANCE, THE/Night of Fear...................... (Deram 7604)		5.00	10.00	67
FIRE BRIGADE/Walk Upon The Water .... (A&M 914)		1.00	2.00	68
MRS. MILLER				
DOWNTOWN/A Lover's Concerto .... (Capitol 5640)		1.25	2.50	66
NAPOLEON XIV				
THEY'RE COMING TO TAKE ME AWAY, HA-HAAA/ ...... (Warner Bros. 5831)		2.00	4.00	66
Same title with label printed in reverse and song playing backwards				
NEWBEATS (Formerly Dean & Marc)				
BREAD AND BUTTER/Tough Little Buggy .... (Hickory 1269)		1.25	2.50	54
RUN, BABY, RUN/Mean Wolly Willie .... (Hickory 1332)		1.25	2.50	65
NEW COLONY SIX				
I CONFESS/Dawn Is Breaking .... (Centaur 1201)		1.50	3.00	66
NEWTON, Wayne				
COMING ON TOO STRONG/Looking Through A Tear .... (Capitol 5338)		7.50	15.00	65
With Terry Melcher & Bruce Johnson)				
DANKE SCHOEN/Better Now Than Later .... (Capitol 4989)		1.00	2.00	63
NILSSON(Harry Nilsson)				
EVERYBODY'S TALKIN'/Don't Leave Me .... (RCA 9544)		1.25	2.50	68
YOU CAN'T DO THAT/Ten Little Indians .... (RCA 9298)		3.00	6.00	67
(Beatle Novelty)				
NINO & THE EBB TIDES				
JUKE BOX SATURDAY NIGHT/				
(Someday) I'll Fall In Love .... (Madison 166)		2.50	5.00	61
REAL MEANING OF CHRISTMAS, THE/Purple Shadows .... (Recorte 408)		19.00	38.00	

TITLE/Flip	LABEL & No.	GOOD	NEAR MINT	YR.
NIX, Ford & The Moonshiners				
NINE TIMES OUT OF TEN/ .... *(Clix 813)*		30.00	60.00	
ORLANDO, Tony & The Millos				
DING DONG/You And Only You .... *(Milo 101)*		14.00	28.00	59
OSMOND BROTHERS				
MARY ELIZABETH/Speak Like A Child .... *(Barnaby 2002)*		1.00	2.00	68
OUR GANG (Jan & Dean)				
SUMMERTIME SUMMERTIME/				
Theme From Leon's Garage .... *(Br'er Bird 001)*		25.00	50.00	66
OUTSIDERS				
TIME WON'T LET ME/Was It Really Real .... *(Capitol 5573)*		1.00	2.00	66
PAGE, Jimmy				
SHE JUST SATISFIES/Keep Moving .... *(Fontana 533)*		50.00	100.00	65
(English Release)				
PAGE, Patti				
DOGGIE IN THE WINDOW, THE/				
My Jealous Eyes .... *(Mercury 70070)*		1.50	3.00	53
HUSH, HUSH, SWEET CHARLOTTE/				
Longing To Hold You Again .... *(Columbia 43251)*		1.00	2.00	65
PETER, PAUL & MARY				
(Peter Yarrow, Paul Stookey & Mary Travers)				
PUFF (THE MAGIC DRAGON)/Pretty Mary .... *(Warner Bros. 5348)*		1.00	2.00	63
PETTY, Norman, Trio				
MOONDREAMS/ .... *(Columbia 41039)*		5.00	10.00	57
(Features Buddy Holly on Guitar)				
PICKETT, Bobby (Boris) & The Crypt-Kickers				
MONSTER MASH/Monster Mash Party .... *(Garpax 44167)*		1.00	2.00	62
This was re-released in 1970 on Parrot (348).				
PITNEY, Gene				
PLEASE COME BACK/I'll Find You .... *(Festival 25002)*		2.00	4.00	61
TOWN WITHOUT PITY/				
Air. Mail Special Delivery .... *(Musicor 1009)*		1.25	2.50	61
PLAYMATES				
BEEP BEEP/Your Love .... *(Roulette 4115)*		1.25	2.50	58

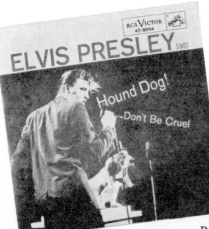

TITLE/Flip	LABEL & No.	GOOD	NEAR MINT	YR.
PRESLEY, Elvis				
ARE YOU LONESOME TONIGHT/I Gotta Know				
(Stereo) . . . . (RCA 61-7810)		30.00	60.00	60
50 BLUE CHRISTMAS/ . . . . (RCA HO-0808)		125.00	250.00	57 Tie
(promotional 45 release of this song from Elvis' Christmas Album)				
BLUE CHRISTMAS/Santa Claus Is Back In Town . . . . (RCA 447-0647)		2.50	5.00	65
BLUE CHRISTMAS/Santa Claus Is Back In Town				
(Gold Standard Picture Sleeve) . . . . (RCA 447-0647)		6.00	12.00	
DON'T BE CRUEL/Hound Dog				
(Gold Standard Picture Sleeve) . . . . (RCA 447-0608)		5.00	10.00	64
(MARIE'S THE NAME) HIS LATEST FLAME/				
Little Sister . . . . (RCA 37-7908)		50.00	100.00	61
(compact 33 single)				
HOUND DOG/Don't Be Cruel (78 rpm) . . . . (RCA 6604)		8.00	24.00	56
50 I FEEL SO BAD/Wild In The Country . . . . (RCA 68-7880)		125.00	250.00	61 Tie
(stereo compact 33 single: second and last issued)				
KING OF THE WHOLE WIDE WORLD/				
Home Is Where The Heart Is . . . . (RCA SP-45-118)		50.00	100.00	62
50 KING OF THE WHOLE WIDE WORLD/				
Home Is Where The Heart Is . . . . (RCA SP-45-118)		125.00	250.00	62 Tie
(with picture sleeve)				
(Air play special featuring two songs from the "Kid Galahad" EP, issued with a picture sleeve listing the titles of the songs, but no photo of Elvis.)				
MY BOY/Loving Arms . . . . (RCA 2458EX)		25.00	50.00	74
MY BOY/Loving Arms . . . . (RCA 2458EX)		50.00	100.00	74
(With Insert Sleeve)				
(Both songs were taken from the "Good Times" LP. This was an unusual release in that it was issued on the gray RCA label and appears to have been earmarked as a new single release, except that instead of a regular picture sleeve this disc came with a special insert which resembled a sleeve but didn't hold the record (it was just a single piece of paper). The commercial release of "My Boy" actually came out in January of 1975, but with a different flip side and a standard, full color sleeve. The sleeve on this special issue was green and white.)				
WEAR MY RING AROUND YOUR NECK/				
Doncha Think It's Time . . . . (RCA 7240)		1.50	3.00	58
WEAR MY RING AROUND YOUR NECK/				
Doncha Think It's Time . . . . (RCA 7240)		8.00	24.00	58
(78 rpm)				
WEAR MY RING AROUND YOUR NECK/Don't . . . . (RCA SP-45-76)		62.50	125.00	60
50 WEAR MY RING AROUND YOUR NECK/Don't . . . . (RCA SP-45-76)		125.00	250.00	60 Tie
(With picture sleeve)				
(Special promotinal release. RCA chose two selections from the "Elvis Gold Records Vol. 2" album and coupled them for this release.)				
? (QUESTION MARK) & THE MYSTERIANS				
96 TEARS/Midnight Hour . . . . (Pagogo 102)		20.00	40.00	
QUICKSILVER MESSENGER SERVICE				
WHAT ABOUT ME/Good Old Rock And Roll . . . . (Capitol 3046)		1.50	3.00	
RACHEL & THE REVOLVERS				
(Produced by Brian Wilson)				
REVOLUTION, THE/Number One . . . . (Dot 16392)		6.00	12.00	62
RAIDERS				
CASTLE OF LOVE, THE/Raiders From Outer Space . . . . (Atco 6125)		12.50	25.00	
RAINDROPS (Jeff Barry-Ellie Greenwich)				
WHAT A GUY/It's So Wonderful . . . . (Jubilee 5444)		1.25	2.50	63
RANDY & THE RAINBOWS				
DENISE/Come Back . . . . (Rust 5059)		3.00	6.00	63
(Blue Label)				
RASCALS (Formerly Young Rascals)				
GOOD LOVIN'/Mustang Sally . . . . (Atlantic 2321)		1.00	2.00	66
RASPBERRIES				
GO ALL THE WAY/With You In My Life . . . . (Capitol 3348)		1.00	2.00	72

Elvis Presley records are listed in all three of our guides on pop singles, albums and country/western.

The Jamies

Jerry Lee Lewis

Bob Luman

The Monkeys

Ricky Nelson

The Nortones

Del Shannon

The Skyliners

The Safaris

Terry Tigre

Bobby Vee

The Standels

Gene Vincent

PAGE 72

TITLE/Flip	LABEL & No.	GOOD	NEAR MINT	YR.
RAY, Johnnie				
CRY/Little White Cloud That Cried . . . . (Okeh 6840)		2.00	4.00	51
REFLECTIONS				
IN THE STILL OF THE NIGHT/Tic Toc . . . . (Tigre 602)		5.00	10.00	
(JUST LIKE) ROMEO & JULIET/				
Can't You Tell By The Look In My Eyes . . . . (Golden World 8)		1.25	2.50	64
REGENTS				
BARBARA-ANN/I'm So Lonely . . . . (Cousins 1002)		15.00	30.00	61
REVERE, Paul & The Raiders				
INDIAN RESERVATION/Terry's Tune . . . . (Columbia 45332)		1.00	2.00	71
LIKE LONG HAIR/Sharon . . . . (Gardena 116)		4.00	8.00	61
REYNOLDS, Debbie				
TAMMY/French Heels . . . . (Coral 61851)		1.25	2.50	57
RICHARD, Cliff				
LIVING DOLL/Apron Strings . . . . (ABC Paramount 10042)		1.50	3.00	59
RIVERS, Johnny				
POOR SIDE OF TOWN/A Man Can Cry . . . . (Imperial 66205)		1.00	2.00	66
THAT'S MY BABY/ . . . . (Coral 62425)		5.00	10.00	64
ROCK-A-TEENS				
WOO-HOO/Untrue . . . . (Doran 3515)		7.50	15.00	
ROE, Tommy				
DIZZY/You I Need . . . . (ABC 11164)		1.00	2.00	68
SHEILA/Pretty Girl . . . . (Judd 1022)		10.00	20.00	62
ROLLING STONES				
HONKY TONK WOMAN/				
You Can't Always Get What You Want . . . . (London 910)		1.00	2.00	69
I WANNA BE YOUR MAN/Stoned . . . . (London 9641)		5.00	10.00	64
IT'S ALL OVER NOW/Good Times Bad Times . . . . (London 9687)		2.50	5.00	64
RONNY & THE DAYTONAS				
G.T.O./Hot Rod Baby . . . . (Mala 481)		1.25	2.50	64
ROYAL, Billy Joe				
DOWN IN THE BOONDOCKS/Oh What A Night . . . . (Columbia 43305)		1.25	2.50	65
ROYAL GUARDSMEN				
SNOOPY VS. THE RED BARON/I Need You . . . . (Laurie 3366)		1.00	2.00	66
ROYAL TEENS				
(With Bob Gaudio & Al Kooper)				
BELIEVE ME/Little Cricket . . . . (Capitol 4261)		2.00	4.00	59
SHORT SHORTS/Planet Rock . . . . (Power 215)		6.00	12.00	57
RUMBLERS				
BOSS/I Don't Need You No More . . . . (Downey 103)		2.50	5.00	63
RYDELL, Bobby				
ALL I WANT IS YOU/For You, For You . . . . (Cameo 164)		6.00	12.00	59
WILD ONE/Little Bitty Girl . . . . (Cameo 171)		1.25	2.50	59
RYDER, Mitch & The Detroit Wheels				
DEVIL WITH THE BLUE DRESS ON & GOOD GOLLY MISS MOLLY/				
I Had It Made . . . . (New Voice 817)		1.25	2.50	66
SAM THE SHAM & THE PHARAOHS				
RING DANG DOO/Don't Try It . . . . (MGM 13397)		1.00	2.00	65
WOLLY BULLY/Ain't Gonna Move . . . . (XL 105)		5.00	10.00	65

All artists shown in photos appear with listings in the guide these samples were taken from.

TITLE/Flip	LABEL & No.	GOOD	NEAR MINT	YR.
SANDS, Tommy				
TEEN-AGE CRUSH/Hep Dee Hootie . . . . (Capitol 3639)		1.50	3.00	57
SANTO & JOHNNY				
SLEEP WALK/All Night Diner . . . . (Canadian-American 103)		1.50	3.00	59
SCOTT, Jack				
BABY, SHE'S GONE/				
You Can Bet Your Bottom Dollar . . . . (ABC Paramount 9818)		12.50	25.00	57
WHAT IN THE WORLD'S COME OVER YOU/				
Baby, Baby. . . . . (Top Rank 2028)		1.50	3.00	60
SEARCHERS				
LOVE POTION NUMBER NINE/				
Hi-Heel Sneakers . . . . (Kapp 27)		1.25	2.50	64
SEDAKA, Neil				
BREAKING UP IS HARD TO DO/As Long As I Live . . . . (RCA 8046)		1.25	2.50	62
LAURA LEE/Snowtime . . . . (Decca 30520)		10.00	20.00	58
SERENDIPITY SINGERS				
DON'T LET THE RAIN COME DOWN (CROOKED LITTLE MAN)/				
Freedom's Star . . . . (Philips 40175)		1.25	2.50	64
SHANNON, Del				
FROM ME TO YOU/Two Silouettes . . . . (Big Top 3152)		2.00	4.00	63
Released before the Beatles version of their own song (In U.S.)				
RUNAWAY/Jody. . . . . (Big Top 3067)		1.25	2.50	61
SHANTONS				
LUCILLE/To be in Love With You. . . . . (Jay-Mar 241/241)		35.00	70.00	
SHERIDAN, Mike & The Nightriders				
PLEASE MR. POSTMAN/ . . . . (Liberpool Sound 902)		20.00	40.00	
(Some members of this group later joined "The Move".)				
SHERIDAN, TONY & THE BEAT BROTHERS				
See Beatles				
SHERMAN, Bobby				
IT HURTS ME/Give Me Your Word. . . . . (Decca 31741)		1.50	3.00	65
SHERWOODS				
COLD AND FROSTY MORNING/				
True Love Was Born (With Our Last Goodbye) . . . . (Dot 16540)		7.50	15.00	63
SHONDELL, Troy				
THIS TIME/Girl After Girl. . . . . (Goldcrest 161)		3.25	6.50	61
SIMON & GARFUNKEL				
MRS. ROBINSON/Old Friends-Bookends . . . . (Columbia 44511)		1.00	2.00	68
SIMON SISTERS (Lucy & Carly Simon)				
WINKIN' BLINKIN' AND NOD/				
So Glad I'm Here . . . . (Kapp 586)		1.50	3.00	64
SINATRA, Frank				
HEY JEALOUS LOVER/You Forgot All The Words . . . . (Capitol 3552)		1.25	2.50	56
LOVE AND MARRIAGE/Impatient Years . . . . (Capitol 3260)		1.25	2.50	55
SKYLINERS (Featuring Jimmy Beaumont)				
PENNIES FROM HEAVEN/I'll Be Seeing You . . . . (Calico 117)		1.50	3.00	60
SINCE I DON'T HAVE YOU/One Night, One Night . . . . (Calico 103/104)		1.50	3.00	59
SMALL FACES				
ITCHYCOO PARK/I'm Only Dreaming. . . . . (Immediate 501)		1.00	2.00	67
WHATCHA' GONNA DO ABOUT IT/				
What's A Matter Baby. . . . . (Press 9794)		3.50	7.00	65

TITLE/Flip	LABEL & No.	GOOD	NEAR MINT	YR.
SOUTH, Joe				
GAMES PEOPLE PLAY/Mirror of Your Mind...............(Capitol 2248)		1.00	2.00	68
PURPLE PEOPLE EATER MEETS THE WITCH DOCTOR, THE/				
My Fondest Memories ....(NRC 5000)		2.00	4.00	58
SPANKY & OUR GANG				
SUNDAY WILL NEVER BE THE SAME/Distance .... (Mercury 72679)		1.00	2.00	67
SPARROWS (Early Steppenwolf)				
HARD TIMES WITH THE LAW/				
Meet Me After Four .... (Capitol of Canada 72257)		7.50	15.00	
SPIDERS (Alice Cooper)				
DON'T BLOW YOUR MIND/No Price Tag .... (Santa Cruz 003)		25.00	50.00	67
STANDELLS				
DIRTY WATER/Rari .... (Tower 185)		1.00	2.00	66
ZEBRA IN THE KITCHEN/Someday You'll Cry .... (MGM 13350)		4.50	9.00	
STARR, Kay				
WHEEL OF FORTUNE/I Wanna Love You..................(Capitol 1964)		1.25	2.50	52
STARR, Ringo				
A DOSE OF ROCK AND ROLL/Cryin' .... (Atlantic 3361)		1.00	2.00	76
BEAUCOUPS OF BLUES/Coochy Coochy ....(Capitol-Apple 2969)		2.50	5.00	70
IT DON'T COME EASY/Early 1970........................(Apple 1831)		2.50	5.00	71
(With Picture Sleeve)				
STEVENS, Connie				
SIXTEEN REASONS/Little Sister....................(Warner Bros. 5137)		1.25	2.50	60
STEVENS, Ray				
AHAB, THE ARAB/It's Been So Long.................. (Mercury 71966)		1.25	2.50	62
UNWIND/For He's A Jolly Good Fellow ....(Monument 1048)		1.00	2.00	68
STOMPERS				
STOMPIN' ROUND THE CHRISTMAS TREE/				
Stompin' Round the Christmas Tree (Pt. II) .... (Gone 5120)		12.50	25.00	61
STORM, Gale				
DARK MOON/A Little Too Late........................... (Dot 15558)		1.25	2.50	57
STRAWBERRY ALARM CLOCK (Formerly Sixpence)				
INCENSE & PEPPERMINTS/				
Birdman of Alkatrash .... (All American 373)		2.75	4.50	67
STREISAND, Barbara				
PEOPLE/I Am Woman ....(Columbia 42965)		1.00	2.00	64
SUMMERS, Gene				
SCHOOL OF ROCK 'N ROLL/Straight Skirt .... (Jan 100)		10.00	20.00	
SURFARIS				
SCATTER SHIELD/				
I Wanna Take A Trip To The Islands................. (Decca 31581)		2.50	5.00	64
With the Honeys				
WIPE OUT/Surfer Joe (Containing two additional verses-				
not on the Dot & Princess issues) ....(DFS)		10.00	20.00	63
SURVIVORS (Beach Boys)				
PAMELA JEAN/After The Game........................(Capitol 5120)		20.00	40.00	63

"Pamela Jean" was actually "Car Crazy Cutie" with different lyrics. Probably released as The Survivors so as not to conflict with the success of the regular Beach Boy releases of that time.

The left hand price column represents the true value of the average, used record.

This section represents a 3½% sampling of the artists and songs in *Popular & Rock Records 1948-1978*.

TITLE/Flip	LABEL & No.	GOOD	NEAR MINT	YR.
SUZY & THE RED STRIPES (Linda McCartney)				
SEASIDE WOMAN/B-Side to Seaside ....(Epic 50403)		7.50	15.00	77
12" Disco pressing				
SWINGIN' MEDALLIONS				
DOUBLE SHOT/Here it Comes Again .... (4 Sale 002)		4.00	8.00	66
TAYLOR, True (Paul Simon)				
TEENAGE FOOL/True or False .... (Big 614)		10.00	20.00	58
(Pink Label)				
TEEN KINGS (Featuring Roy Orbison)				
OOBY DOOBY/Trying to Get to You ....(Jewel 101)		75.00	150.00	56
This is a completely different version than the Sun issue of "Ooby Dooby". The Sun (242) release is shown as "Roy Orbison & The Teen Kings" and had a different flip side. The Jewel issue is the original.				
TEMPO, Nino & April Stevens				
DEEP PURPLE/I've Been Carrying A Torch For You So Long .....(Atco 6273)		1.00	2.00	63
THEM (Featuring Van Morrison)				
GLORIA/If You And I Could Be As Two .... (Parrot 365)		5.00	10.00	65
HERE COMES THE NIGHT/All For Myself................. (Parrot 9749)		1.25	2.50	65
THOMAS, B.J.				
BILLY & SUE/Never Tell .... (Bragg 103)		5.00	10.00	64
HOOKED ON A FEELING/				
I've Been Down This Road Before .... (Scepter 12230)		1.00	2.00	68
THREE CHUCKLES (Features Teddy Randazzo)				
MIDNIGHT TIL DAWN/Fallen out of Love ....(Vik 0232)		2.00	4.00	57
RUNAROUND/At ast You Understand .... (Boulevard 100)		12.50	25.00	53
THREE DOG NIGHT				
JOY TO THE WORLD/I Can Hear You Calling .... (Dunhill 4272)		1.00	2.00	71
TILLOTSON, Johnny				
DREAMY EYES/Well, I'm Your Man .... (Cadence 1353)		2.50	5.00	58
POETRY IN MOTION/Princess, Princess.................. (Cadence 1384)		1.50	3.00	60
TOM & JERRY (Simon & Garfunkle)				
BABY TALK/Two Teenagers .... (Big 621)		15.00	30.00	58
HEY, SCHOOLGIRL/Dancin' Wild .... (Big 613)		3.50	7.00	57
TRASHMEN				
SURFIN' BIRD/King Of The Surf ....(Garrett 4002)		1.50	3.00	63
TREMELOES				
SILENCE IS GOLDEN/				
Let Your Hair Hang Down...........................(Epic 10184)		1.00	2.00	67
TROGGS				
WILD THING/With a Girl Like You ....(Atco 6415)		3.00	6.00	66
WILD THING/From Home...............................(Fontana 1548)		1.00	2.00	66
TURTLES (Formerly the Crossfires)				
HAPPY TOGETHER/Like the Seasons .... (White Whale 244)		1.00	2.00	67
UNIQUES (Featuring Joe Stampley)				
NOT TOO LONG AGO/Fast Way Of Living ....(Paula 219)		1.00	2.00	65
UNIT FOUR PLUS TWO				
CONCRETE AND CLAY/When I Fall in Love................ (London 9751)		1.00	2.00	65
VALLEY, Frankie (Frankie Valli)				
MY MOTHERS EYES/The Laugh's On Me....... ....(Corona 1234)		55.00	110.00	53

TITLE/Flip	LABEL & No.	GOOD	NEAR MINT	YR.
VAUGHAN, Sarah				
BROKEN-HEARTED MELODY/Misty .... (Mercury 71477)		1.25	2.50	59
VEE, Bobby				
SUZIE BABY/Flyin' High (Instrumental) .... (Soma 1110)		3.00	6.00	
(With the Shadows)				
TAKE GOOD CARE OF MY BABY/Bashful Bob .... (Liberty 55354)		1.25	2.50	61
VENTURES (A.K.A. The Marksmen)				
(Don Wilson & Bob Bogle)				
PERFIDIA/No Trespassing .... (Dolton 28)		1.25	2.50	60
WALK, DON'T RUN/Home .... (Blue Horizon 101)		4.00	8.00	60
VERNE, Larry				
MR. CUSTER/Okeefenokee Two Step .... (Era 3024)		1.50	3.00	60
VILLAGE VOICES (Features Bobby Valli-Brother				
of Frankie Valli)				
RED LIPS/Too Young To Start .... (Topix 6000)		15.00	30.00	61
(Yellow & Black Pressing)				
VITO & THE SALUTATIONS				
UNCHAINED MELODY/Hey, Hey, Baby .... (Herald 583)		2.50	5.00	63
YOUR WAY/Hey, Hey, Hey .... (Kram 1202)		10.00	20.00	62
VOGUES				
FIVE O'CLOCK WORLD/				
Nothing to Offer You .... (Co & Ce 232)		1.50	3.00	65
YOU'RE THE ONE/Some Words .... (Blue Star 229)		4.00	8.00	65
WASHER WINDSHIELD				
KATHY YOUNG FINDS THE INNOCENTS GUILTY/ .... (Indigo (no. #)		20.00	40.00	61
(Novelty/Break-In)				
WELK, Lawrence				
CALCUTTA/My Grandfathers Clock .... (Dot 16161)		1.00	2.00	60
WILLIAMS, Andy				
BUTTERFLY/It Doesn't Take Very Long .... (Cadence 1308)		1.25	2.50	57
WILSON, J. Frank & The Cavaliers				
LAST KISS/Carla .... (Le Cam 722)		4.00	8.00	64
(Different version-earlier than Tamara & Josie)				
(Shown only as J.Frank Wilson)				
WRAY, Link & His Wray Men				
RUMBLE/The Swag .... (Cadence 1347)		2.50	5.00	58
SLINKY/Rendezvous .... (Epic 9343)		7.50	15.00	59
(With Picture Sleeve)				
YARBROUGH, Glenn (Of the Limeliters)				
BABY THE RAIN MUST FALL/I've Been to Town .... (RCA 8498)		1.00	2.00	65
YOUNG, Kathy (With the Innocents)				
A THOUSAND STARS/Eddie My Darling.................... (Indigo 108)		1.25	2.50	60
YURO, Timi				
HURT/I Apologize................................. (Liberty 55343)		1.00	2.00	61
ZAGER & EVANS				
IN THE YEAR 2525/Little Kid's .... (Truth 8082)		3.50	7.00	69

Samples chosen for each artist represent the range of high and low values that artist's records usually bring.

Most artists in this section from the singles pop & rock book are also in *Record Albums 1948-1978*.

OUR MOST ANTICIPATED BOOK

Blacks and Blues is a sweeping endeavor that's been in the works by Jelly-roll Productions since 1975. Its two-fold purpose is to chronicle the history—the roots—of black American music and to be a price guide to that same music from World War II to present.

The base will be oriented in the blues, and will closely align with related folk music, the two being very similar in type and origin. For the first edition of this book, however, no attempt will be made to more than lightly touch gospel, which is a field in itself, nor to delve into black jazz or Dixieland, since those areas will be covered in still another price guide now in the works!

Though blues records have continued to be produced up to the present, an offshoot, which began in the late 1940s, heavily dominated black music in the 1950s—rhythm and blues—a sound by black groups that, essentially, added rhythm to the blues. This area has developed a heavy cult of collectors, and the inevitable high-priced records that follow such a demand will provide the main body of the work.

Soul music from the '60s, the Motown sound, and other interim music of blacks will round out a dramatic, important book worth waiting and watching for!

All artists shown in photos appear with listings in the guide these samples were taken from.

BLACK ROOTS OF POPULAR MUSIC
by Victoria Erickson

In the past few years, many people have been fascinated by the black history brought forward in Alex Haley's book, **Roots**. In light of this interest, it seems appropriate to bring to everyone's attention the equally fascinating question of the black roots of current popular music.

Perhaps surprising to some, the single most influential force in today's music traces back to those very same slave ships which delivered their human cargo onto American soil two centuries ago.

While blacks have always made music, the earliest recognized genre is the blues. During slavery, black people had no real sense of individuality because of the conditions maintained on plantations. Once the black people were freed, they became individuals who suddenly had to provide their own food, clothing, shelter and work; they found themselves in many new and terrifying situations. This was where the blues began.

The singing of the blues helped destitute, rootless, unhappy people to face their frustrating lot in life.

The original form of the blues, often called country blues, was very personal, and not primarily done for the entertainment of others. The point of the music was singing what was felt, and was basically introspective. The country blues were almost exclusively sung by male artists who had lived the hard lives of share-croppers. The blues tell the story of the facing of their lives with humor and strength, while at the same time describing their sorrows and pain.

A second form of early black music was the classic blues. This form, performed almost always by female vocalists, represents a more sophisticated blues than its relative from the country. The classic blues began after World War I, when a large part of the black population moved to northern industrial cities. The classic blues were the country blues reworked by professional black entertainers, who found growing demand for their music from blacks and whites during the twenties.

With the onset of the depression, the blues lost some of its popularity because white people found it too depressing in the face of their own misfortune. It was around this time that another significant area of black music found national acceptance: jazz. Jazz is an art form where improvisation is the key concept. Black artists are among the finest musicians and vocalists who have mastered this highly creative art.

After World War II, black music took on a new shape called rhythm and blues. R & B is usually composed of loud, electrically amplified music and almost unintelligible lyrics. The lyrics appear incomprehensible because the artists manipulate the words for their rhythmic value, rather than emphasizing their content. R & B was music used for escape from the new frustrations blacks faced on returning from the service. Made to go along with dancing, drinking, and whooping-it-up in general, it was a way of escaping from the anger, alienation and resentment that boiled inside a people who were still getting the "short end of the stick."

Whites didn't really accept black R & B, but they did like the R & B songs that white artists re-recorded, or "covered." A trend began with white "covers" of black R & B songs becoming big popular hits for the white artists. These were the first signs of the beginnings of rock and roll. In the late forties and early fifties, black artists found they could have big pop hits, too, if they sang white music. Black entertainers who were willing to compromise their black musical heritage to sing "white" were well accepted by white audiences, but received only the disdain of the blacks. But these artists helped to open the door to the world of popular music. These pioneers paved the way for uncompromising black artists who received, by this time, the acceptance of blacks and whites alike, while *singing black music*. At this point, black entertainers had reached something of a pinnacle—they were accepted and liked by the world of white listeners, just the way they were.

In the mid-fifties, the bi-racial, civil rights movement collapsed. The black nation was once again angry. This anger unleashed a new musical form which was fed with black pride, black power, black nationalism, and the conviction that black *alone* was all they needed. This new form was soul.

The time that has passed since the birth and flourishing of soul seems to have softened the attitudes which spawned it. Today, the various threads that make up the fabric of black musical history still exist . There are still blues artists, jazz artists, R & B-influenced artists and soul-influenced artists, but they are now both black and white, and the threads which were once only black are now mixed in all of the music we hear. Blacks have contributed 200 years of joy and anguish to our music, making it uniquely American and ultimately more human.

BLACKS AND BLUES NOTES

The percentage of selections chosen to represent **Blacks and Blues** is roughly in ratio to the price guide, except in the case of early blues, which we have not yet fully documented.

The albums are all taken from the second edition of **Record Albums 1948-1978**. It was decided to represent them here, rather than in the section on pages 19-37, because it accurately reflects one of the portions of our upcoming **Blacks and Blues** price guide, and also because these albums will *not* be in the third edition of the album book.

(A side note: we prematurely went ahead and deleted the blacks' singles from the second edition of the **Popular and Rock Records** price guide, because at that time we were anticipating an earlier press date for the blacks guide. We learned a lesson from this, having received a barbed criticism in print from **People** magazine, who reviewed the guide and accused us of "inexplicable gaps" in our listings, proceeding to "prove" their critique by pointing to the absence of several notable black artists. Apparently even reviewers don't always read the explanatory introductory material in the books they review.)

The price spread for condition is set at double on 45s, triple on 78s, and ranges from double to quadruple on albums, according to vintage. Occasionally, we list both a 45 and a 78 pressing of the same song by a performer to illustrate the comparative values. If two records are listed under an artist's name, one for, say, $5.00 and the other for $35, that shows the extremes, meaning that any other records by that same person would fall somewhere in-between in value.

Within the next 27 pages you'll find a notation on the most valuable record in the world.

Pearl Bailey

Alphabetical Listing: Records of Blacks & Blues

This section represents approximately 3½% of the listings to appear in the price guide. *Blacks and Blues.*

TITLE/Flip	LABEL & No.	GOOD	NEAR MINT
ACE, Johnny			
JOHNNY ACE MEMORIAL ALBUM (LP) .... *Duke (M) DLP 71*		8.00	32.00
ADAMS, Woodrow [Blues]			
PRETTY BABY BLUES/She's Done Come and Gone (45) .. *Checker 757*		43.00	86.00
PRETTY BABY BLUES/She's Done Come and Gone (78) .. *Checker 757*		20.00	60.00
WINE HEAD WOMAN/Baby You Just Don't Know (45) .... *Meteor 5018*		18.00	36.00
WINE HEAD WOMAN/Baby You Just Don't Know (78) .... *Meteor 5018*		5.00	15.00
ALLEN, Lee			
WALKIN' WITH MR. LEE (LP)			
(1st pressing, red label) .... *Ember (M) ELP 200*		11.00	44.00
ALLEN, Tony & The Night Owls			
ROCK AND ROLL WITH TONY ALLEN AND			
THE NIGHT OWLS (LP) .... *Crown (M) CLP 5231*		8.00	32.00
AMBASSADORS			
DARLING I'M SORRY/Willa-Bea (45) .... *Timely 1001*		162.50	325.00

(M) Monaural, (S) Stereo, (EP) Extended Play, (LP) Long Play, (45) 45 rpm, (78) 78 rpm.

TITLE/Flip	LABEL & No.	GOOD	NEAR MINT

ANDREWS, Lee & The Hearts
LONG, LONELY NIGHTS/The Clock (45) .... Chess 1665		2.00	4.00
WHITE CLIFFS OF DOVER/Much Too Much (45) .... Rainbow 250		50.00	100.00

AVONS
AVONS, THE (LP)............................... Hull (M) HLP 1000		12.50	50.00

BAKER, Lavern
I CRIED A TEAR/Dix-A-Billy (45) .... Atlantic 2007		1.25	2.50
TWEEDLEE DEE/Tomorrow Night (45) .... Atlantic 1047		2.00	4.00

BALLARD, Hank & The Midnighters
GLAD SONGS, SAD SONGS (LP) .... King (M) 927		4.00	12.00
LET'S GO, LET'S GO, LET'S GO/If You'd Forgive Me (45) ..... King 5400		1.25	2.50
THEIR GREATEST JUKE BOX HITS (LP) .... King (M) 541		9.00	36.00

BANISTER, James & His Combo [Blues]
GOLD DIGGER/Blues And Trouble (45) .... States 141		22.00	44.00
GOLD DIGGER/Blues And Trouble (78) .... States 141		10.00	30.00

BARNER, Juke Boy [Blues]
WELL BABY/Rock With Me Baby (45) .... Irma 111		18.00	36.00
WELL BABY/Rock With Me Baby (78) .... Irma 111		6.00	12.00

BATTLE, Joseph Von [Blues]
LOOKING FOR MY WOMAN/(flip by Robert Richard) (78) ... JVB 75828		15.00	45.00

BAUM, Allen (Allen Bunn) [Blues]
IT'S TOO LATE/Don't Ever Leave Me (45) .... Fire 1000		2.00	4.00
(Artist listed as TARHEEL SLIM)			
MY KINDA WOMAN/Too Much Competition (45) .... Red Robin 124		23.00	46.00

BELVIN, Jessie
GOODNIGHT MY LOVE/			
I Want You With Me At Christmas (45) .... Modern 1005		3.00	6.00
HERE'S A HEART/It Could've Been Worse (45) .... RCA Victor 7543		1.00	2.00

BENTON, Brook
IT'S JUST A MATTER OF TIME/Hurtin' Inside (45)...... Mercury 71394		1.25	2.50
LOVE MADE ME YOUR FOOL/Give Me A Sign (45) .... Epic 9177		2.25	4.50

BERRY, Chuck
AFTER SCHOOL SESSION (LP) .... Chess (M) LP 1426		7.00	21.00
IN MEMPHIS (LP) .... Mercury (S) SR 61123		4.00	8.00
JOHNNY B. GOODE/Around And Around (45) .... Chess 1691		1.50	3.00
MAYBELLENE/Wee Wee Hours (45) .... Chess 1604		3.00	6.00

BIG ED & HIS COMBO—see Eddie Burns

BIG MAYBELLE
BLUES, CANDY AND BIG MAYBELLE (LP)........ Savoy (M) MG 14011		4.00	16.00

BINGHAMPTON BLUES BOYS [Blues]
CROSS CUT SAW/Slim's Twist (45)............................ XL 901		15.00	30.00

BLACK DIAMOND [Blues]
T.P. RAILER/Lonesome Blues (78) .... Jaxyson 50		15.00	45.00

BLAIR, Sunny [Blues]
PLEASE SEND MY BABY BACK/			
(flip by Baby Face Turner) (45)..................... Meteor 5006		23.00	46.00
PLEASE SEND MY BABY BACK/			
(flip by Baby Face Turner) (78)..................... Meteor 5006		7.00	21.00

BLAND, Bobby Blue
HERE'S THE MAN (LP)........................... Duke (S) DLP 75		5.00	15.00
I PITY THE FOOL/Close To You (45) .... Duke 332		1.00	2.00

Samples chosen for each artist represent the range of high and low values that artist's records usually bring.

TITLE/Flip	LABEL & No.	GOOD	NEAR MINT

BLUE SMITTY & HIS STRING MEN [Blues]
CRYING/Sad Story (45) .... Chess 1522 — 20.00 — 40.00
CRYING/Sad Story (78) .... Chess 1522 — 9.00 — 27.00

BOINES, Houston [Blues]
GOING HOME/Relation Blues (78) ....Blues & Rhythm 7001 — 9.00 — 27.00

BOOKER T & THE M.G.'s
GREEN ONIONS (LP) .... Stax (M) 701 — 4.00 — 8.00
GREEN ONIONS/Behave Yourself (45) .... Stax 127 — 1.00 — 2.00

BOSTIC, Earl
BOSTIC FOR YOU (LP) .... King (M) 503 — 6.00 — 24.00
EARL BOSTIC AND HIS ALTO SAX (LP) .... King (EP) KEP 284 — 2.00 — 8.00
NEW SOUND (LP) .... King (M) 900 — 3.00 — 9.00

BOYD, Eddie [Blues]
I LOVE YOU/Save Her Doctor (45) .... J.O.B. 1114 — 10.00 — 20.00
YOU GOT TO LOVE THAT GAL/
   Unfair Lovers (78) .... RCA Victor 22-2555 — 1.50 — 4.50

BRADIX, Big Charlie [Blues]
BOOGIE LIKE YOU WANNA/Dollar Diggin' Woman (78) ....Colonial 108 — 3.00 — 9.00
NUMBERED DAYS/Wee Wee Hours (45) .... Aristocrat 418 — 18.00 — 36.00

BRADSHAW, Tiny
SELECTIONS (LP) .... King (M) LP 501 — 10.00 — 40.00
24 GREAT SONGS (LP) .... King (M) 953 — 3.00 — 12.00

BRIM, John [Blues]
DARK CLOUDS/Lonesome Man Blues (78) .... Random 201 — 10.00 — 30.00
TOUGH TIMES/Gary Stomp (45) ....Parrot 799 — 18.00 — 36.00

BROONZY, Big Bill [Blues]
HEY HEY/Walkin' That Lonesome Road (45) .... Mercury 8271 — 4.00 — 8.00
LITTLE CITY WOMAN/Lonesome (45) .... Chess 1546 — 6.00 — 12.00
PLEASE BELIEVE ME/Why Did You Do That (78) .... Hub 3003 — 1.00 — 3.00

BROWN, Buster
GET DOWN WITH BUSTER BROWN (LP) .... Souffle (M) 2014 — 2.00 — 4.00
NEW KING OF THE BLUES, THE (LP) ....Fire (M) FLP 102 — 12.00 — 48.00

The left hand price column represents the true value of the average, used record.

Chuck Berry

The Blossoms

TITLE/Flip	LABEL & No.	GOOD	NEAR MINT

BROWN, Charles
BALLADS MY WAY (LP) .... Mainstream (M) 6035 — 4.00 / 12.00
MOOD MUSIC (10" LP) (Red Vinyl) .... Aladdin (M) 702 — 40.00 / 160.00
MOOD MUSIC (10" LP) (Black Vinyl) .... Aladdin (M) 702 — 30.00 / 120.00

BROWN, Clarence "Gatemouth" [Blues]
MY TIME'S EXPENSIVE/Mary Is Fine (78) .... Peacock 1504 — 2.00 / 6.00

BROWN, James & The Famous Flames
PAPA'S GOT A BRAND NEW BAG/
   Papa's Got a Brand New Bag (Pt. 2) (45) .... King 5999 — 1.00 / 2.00
TRY ME/Tell Me What I Did Wrong (45) .... Federal 12337 — 3.00 / 6.00

BROWN, Nappy
NAPPY BROWN SINGS (LP) .... Savoy (M) MG 14002 — 6.00 / 24.00

BROWN, Ruth
LUCKY LIPS/My Heart Is Breaking Over You (45) .... Atlantic 1125 — 3.00 / 6.00
REAL RUTH BROWN (LP) .... Cobblestone (M) 9007 — 3.00 / 6.00
RUTH BROWN SINGS (10" LP) .... Atlantic (M) 115 — 25.00 / 100.00
SHAKE A HAND/Say It Again (45) .... Philips 40028 — 1.00 / 2.00

㉜ BUCCANEERS
STARS WILL REMEMBER, THE/Come Back My Love (45) ..... Rama 21 — 175.00 / 350.00

BULLARD, John [Blues]
DON'T TALK DEM TRASH/Callin' The Blues (78) .... Index 300 — 6.00 / 18.00
WESTERN UNION BLUES/Spoiled Hambone Blues (45) ...Deluxe 6019 — 11.00 / 22.00

BURKE, Solomon
I WISH I KNEW (LP) .... Atlantic (S) SD 8185 — 3.00 / 9.00
GOT TO GET YOU OFF MY MIND/Peepin' (45) .... Atlantic 2276 — 1.00 / 2.00
SOLOMON BURKE (LP) .... Apollo (M) ALP 498 — 9.00 / 36.00

BURNS, Eddie [Blues]
ORANGE DRIVER/Hard Hearted Woman (45) .... Harvey 111 — 2.50 / 5.00
PAPA'S BOOGIE/Bad Woman Blues (78)....................... Palda — 9.00 / 27.00
   (Artist listed as Slim Pickens)
SUPERSTITION/Biscuit Baking Mama (45) .... Checker 790 — 13.00 / 26.00
   (Artist listed as Big Ed & His Combo)

BUTLER, Jerry
AWARE OF LOVE (LP)................................ Vee Jay (S) 1038 — 5.00 / 15.00
FOR YOUR PRECIOUS LOVE/Sweet Was The Wine (45) .... Vee Jay 280 — 6.00 / 12.00
HE WILL BREAK YOUR HEART/Thanks To You (45) .... Vee Jay 354 — 1.25 / 2.50

BYRD, Roy & His Blues Jumpers [Blues]
BALD HEAD/Hey Now Baby (78) .... Mercury 8175 — 2.00 / 6.00
CUTTIN' OUT/If I Only Knew (45) .... Ron 326 — 3.00 / 6.00
   (Artist listed as Professor Longhair)
SHE AIN'T GOT NO HAIR/Bye Bye Baby (45) .... Talen 808 — 20.00 / 40.00
   (Artist listed as Professor Longhair & His Shuffling Hungarians)
SHE AIN'T GOT NO HAIR/Bye Bye Baby (78) .... Talen 808 — 9.00 / 27.00

CADILLACS
FABULOUS CADILLACS, THE (Blue label LP) .... Jubilee (M) JGM 1045 — 15.00 / 60.00
FABULOUS CADILLACS, THE (Black label LP) ... Jubilee (M) JGM 1045 — 10.00 / 40.00
FABULOUS CADILLACS, THE
   (Multi-color label LP) .... Jubilee (M) JGM 1045 — 5.00 / 20.00
SPEEDOO/Let Me Explain (45) .... Josie 785 — 2.50 / 5.00

CAROLINA SLIM [Blues]
GEORGIA WOMAN/Money Blues (45)...................... Savoy 854 — 8.00 / 16.00
   (Artist listed as Lazy Slim Jim)
MAMA'S BOOGIE/Black Chariot Blues (78) .... Acorn 3015 — 3.00 / 9.00
MOTHER DEAR MOTHER/Side Walk Boogie (45) .... King 4573 — 13.00 / 26.00
   (Artist listed as Country Paul)

Many albums in this forthcoming book are included in the current *Record Albums 1948-1978* price guide.

TITLE/Flip	LABEL & No.	GOOD	NEAR MINT

CARTER, Goree [Blues]
DRUNK OR SOBER/(flip by Clarence Samuels) (45) .... *Bayou 010* — 10.00 / 20.00
SERENADE/Come On Let's Boogie (78) .... *Freedom 1536* — 4.00 / 12.00

CHANDLER, Gene
DUKE OF EARL, THE (LP) .... *Up Front (M) UPF 105* — 2.00 / 4.00
DUKE OF EARL, THE (LP) .... *Vee Jay (S) SR 1040* — 4.00 / 16.00
DUKE OF EARL/Kissin' In The Kitchen (45) .... *Vee Jay 416* — 1.00 / 2.00

CHANTELS
HE'S GONE/The Plea (45) .... *End 1001* — 4.00 / 8.00
LOOK IN MY EYES/Glad To Be Back (45) .... *Carlton 55* — 1.50 / 3.00

CHARLES, Ray
BABY LET ME HOLD YOUR HAND/Lonely Boy (45) ..... *Swingtime 250* — 5.00 / 10.00
TAKE THESE CHAINS FROM MY HEART/
No Letter Today (45) .... *ABC Paramount 10435* — 1.00 / 2.00

(36) CHARMERS
CHURCH ON THE HILL/Battle Axe (45).................... *Timely 1011* — 160.00 / 320.00

CHARMS (Featuring Otis Williams)
CHARMS VOL. 2, THE (LP) .... *King (EP) EP 364* — 3.00 / 12.00
LING, TING, TONG/Razoom (45) .... *Deluxe 6076* — 3.50 / 7.00
OTIS WILLIAMS & THE CHARMS (LP) .... *King (M) LP 570* — 17.00 / 51.00
(A bootleg copy of this album is known to exist which has a dark red cover.)

CHECKER, Chubby
DANCING DINOSAUR/Those Private Eyes (45) .... *Parkway 810* — 3.00 / 6.00
FOR TEEN TWISTERS ONLY (LP) .... *Parkway (M) P 7009* — 3.00 / 9.00
LET'S TWIST AGAIN/
Everything's Gonna Be All Right (45).................. *Parkway 824* — 1.00 / 2.00

The Channels

The Charms

TITLE/Flip	LABEL & No.	GOOD	NEAR MINT

CHENIER, Clifton [Blues]
COUNTRY BRED/Rockin' The Bop (45)	Post 2010	9.00	18.00
IT HAPPENED SO FAST/Goodbye Baby (45)	Zynn 506	1.50	3.00
LOUISIANA STOMP/Louisiana Stomp (78)	Elko 920	7.00	21.00

CHICAGO SUNNY BOY [Blues]
RE JACK POT/Western Union Man (45)	Meteor 5008	33.00	66.00
RE JACK POT/Western Union Man (78)	Meteor 5008	5.00	15.00

CHIFFONS
HE'S SO FINE (LP)	Laurie (M) LLP 2018	5.00	15.00

CHIPS
BYE BYE MY LOVE/What A Lie (45)	Ember 1077	1.50	3.00
RUBBER BISCUIT/Oh My Darlin' (45)	Josie 803	5.00	10.00

CHORDCATS (Chords)
GIRL TO LOVE, A/Hold Me Baby (45)	Cat 112	4.50	9.00

CHORDS
SH-BOOM/Cross Over The Bridge (45)	Cat 104	6.00	12.00
ZIPPITY ZUM/Bless You (45)	Cat 109	2.50	5.00

CLARK, Dee
HOLD ON, IT'S DEE CLARK (LP)	Vee Jay (M) 1037	5.00	20.00
JUST KEEP IT UP/Whispering Grass (45)	Abner 1026	1.50	3.00
24 BOY FRIENDS/Seven Nights (45)	Falcon 1005	3.00	6.00

CLEFTONES
HEART AND SOUL/How Do You Feel (45)	Gee 1064	1.50	3.00
YOU BABY YOU/I Was Dreaming (45)	Gee 1000	2.50	5.00

Chubby Checker

The Coasters

The Contours   **Sam Cooke**

TITLE/Flip	LABEL & No.	GOOD	NEAR MINT
CLIQUES (With Jessie Belvin)			
GIRL IN MY DREAMS, THE/I Wanna Know Why (45)	Modern 987	3.00	6.00
MY DESIRE/I'm In Love With A Girl (45)	Modern 995	1.50	3.00
CLOVERS			
CLOVERS, THE (LP)	Atlantic (M) 1248	12.00	48.00
LOVE, LOVE, LOVE/Your Tender Lips (45)	Atlantic 1094	2.00	4.00
THEIR GREATEST RECORDINGS (LP)	Atco (S) SD 33374	3.00	6.00
COASTERS			
ALONG CAME JONES/That Is Rock And Roll (45)	Atco 6141	1.50	3.00
COASTERS (LP)	Atco (M) 101	5.00	20.00
ONE KISS LED TO ANOTHER/Brazil (45)	Atco 6073	3.00	6.00
THAT'S ROCK AND ROLL (LP)	Clarion (M) 605	4.00	8.00
CONFINERS [Blues]			
HARMONICA BOOGIE/The Toss Bounce (45)	Electro 261	43.00	86.00
COOKE, Sam			
CUPID/Farewell My Love (45)	RCA Victor 7883	1.00	2.00
LOVEABLE/Forever (45)	Specialty 596	2.50	5.00
MR. SOUL (LP)	RCA Victor (M) 2673	4.00	8.00
COTTON, James [Blues]			
COTTON CROP BLUES/Hold Me In Your Arms (45)	Sun 206	43.00	86.00
MY BABY/Straighten Up Baby (45)	Sun 199	33.00	66.00
COUNTRY JIM [Blues]			
HOT ROD BOOGIE/Worried Blues (45) (Artist listed as Hot Rod Happy)	Pacemaker 1014	20.00	40.00
OLD RIVER BLUES/I'll Take You Back Baby (78)	Imperial 5073	7.00	21.00
COUNTRY PAUL—see Carolina Slim			
CRAYTON, Pee Wee [Blues]			
AFTER HOURS BOOGIE/Why Did You Go (78)	Four Star 1304	4.00	12.00
FROSTY NIGHT, A/The Telephone Is Ringing (45)	Vee Jay 214	2.00	4.00
PAPPY'S BLUES/Crying And Walking (45)	RIH 408	9.00	18.00
POPPA STOPPA/Thinking Of You (45)	Modern 20-816	2.00	4.00

Halfway between good and mint is the true value and the best condition usually available in old records. Mint is rare.

The Crowns   The Crickets

TITLE/Flip	LABEL & No.	GOOD	NEAR MINT
CRUDUP, Big Boy [Blues]			
COOL DISPOSITION/			
Keep Your Arms Around Me (78)	Bluebird 34-0738	2.50	5.00
CRUDUP'S VICKSBURG BLUES/			
Shout Sister Shout (45)	RCA Victor 50-0013	7.00	14.00
I WONDER/My Baby Boogies All The Time (78)	Champion	20.00	40.00
CHRYSTALS			
DA DOO RON RON/Git It (45)	Philles 112	1.50	3.00
HE'S A REBEL (LP)	Philles (M) PHLP 4001	9.00	36.00
SCREW, THE (DO) (Pt. 1)/(Do) The Screw, (Pt. 2) (45)	Philles 111	50.00	100.00
(Only known to exist on promotional copy)			
DANLEERS			
ONE SUMMER NIGHT/Wheelin' And A-Dealin' (45)	AMP 3 Inc. 2115	5.50	11.00
ONE SUMMER NIGHT/Wheelin' And A-Dealin' (45)	Mercury 71322	1.75	3.50
DAVIS, Sonny Boy [Blues]			
RHYTHM BLUES/I Don't Live Here No More (78)	Talent 802	9.00	27.00
DAY, Bobby			
ROCKIN' WITH ROBIN (LP)	Class (M) LP 5002	8.00	32.00
THAT'S ALL I WANT/Say Yes (45)	Class 245	1.25	2.50
DE BERRY, Jimmy [Blues]			
TAKE A LITTLE CHANCE/Time Has Made A Change (45)	Sun 185	43.00	86.00
DEL VIKINGS			
COME GO WITH THE DEL VIKINGS (LP)	Luniverse (M) LP 1000	20.00	80.00
COME GO WITH ME/How Can I Find True Love (45)	FeeBee 205	15.00	30.00
THEY SING-THEY SWING (LP)	Mercury (M) MG 20314	9.00	36.00
WHISPERING BELLS/Don't Be A Fool (45)	Dot 15592	1.50	3.00
DELLS			
LIKE HIS (LP)	Cadet (S) 837	3.00	6.00
OH WHAT A NIGHT (LP)	Vee Jay (M) 1010	8.00	24.00
DELTA RHYTHM BOYS			
DRY BONES (10" LP)	RCA Victor (M) LPM 3085	9.00	36.00

TITLE/Flip	LABEL & No.	GOOD	NEAR MINT
DETROIT COUNT [Blues]			
HASTINGS STREET OPERA Pt. 1/			
Hastings Street Opera Pt. 2 (78)	JVB 75830	9.00	27.00
LITTLE TILLIE WILLIE/My Last Call (78)	King 4279	4.00	12.00
DIDDLEY, Bo [Blues]			
BO DIDDLEY (LP)	Checker (M) 1431	10.00	20.00
CLOCK STRIKES TWELVE, THE/Say Man (45)	Checker 931	1.50	3.00
DIDDLEY DADDY/She's Fine, She's Mine (45)	Checker 819	3.50	7.00
ORIGINATOR, THE (LP)	Checker (M) LP 3001	4.00	8.00
DIXIE BLUES BOYS [Blues]			
MONTE CARLO/My Baby Left Town (45)	Flair 1072	15.00	30.00
DIXIE CUPS			
CHAPEL OF LOVE (LP)	Red Bird (S) RBS 20-100	5.00	15.00
DIXON, Floyd [Blues]			
DALLAS BLUES/Helen (78)	Modern 20-653	1.00	3.00
MARRIED WOMAN/Lovin' (45)	Aladdin 3196	10.00	20.00
DOGGETT, Bill			
HONKY TONK, Pt. 2/Honky Tonk, Pt. 1 (45)	King 4950	1.50	3.00
DOMINO, Fats			
COOKING WITH FATS (LP)	United Artists (M) 122	3.00	6.00
EVERY NIGHT ABOUT THIS TIME/Korea Blues (45)	Imperial 5099	18.00	36.00
FATS (LP)	Reprise (M) 6439	8.00	32.00
I'M WALKIN'/I'm In The Mood For Love (45)	Imperial 5428	1.50	3.00
DOMINOES			
SIXTY MINUTE MAN/I Can't Escape From You (45)	Federal 12022	25.00	50.00
DOUGLAS, K.C. [Blues]			
LONELY BLUES/K.C. Boogie (78)	Rhythm 1780	7.00	21.00
DREAMLOVERS			
WHEN WE GET MARRIED/Just Because (45)	Heritage 102	1.50	3.00
DRIFTERS			
CLYDE McPHATTER AND THE DRIFTERS (LP)	Atlantic (M) 8003	9.00	36.00
NOW (LP)	Bell (M) 219	4.00	8.00
STEAMBOAT/Adorable (45)	Atlantic 1078	3.00	6.00
UNDER THE BOARDWALK/			
I Don't Want To Go On Without You (45)	Atlantic 2237	1.00	2.00
DUBS			
BE SURE MY LOVE/Song In My Heart (45)	Mark X 8008	1.00	2.00
DON'T ASK ME/Darling (45)	Gone 5002	4.00	8.00
DUPREE, Champion Jack [Blues]			
AIN'T NOE MEAT ON DE BONE/			
Please Tell Me Baby (45)	King 4651	2.00	4.00
BLUES FROM THE GUTTER (LP)	Atlantic (S) SD 8019	5.00	20.00
CHAMPION JACK DUPREE (LP)	Folkways (M) 3825	2.50	5.00
HIGHWAY BLUES/Shake Baby Shake (45)	Red Robin 112	20.00	40.00
ONCE I HAD A GIRL/Black Woman Blues (78)	Solo 10-014	2.00	6.00
EDWARDS, Honeyboy [Blues]			
BUILD A CAVE/			
Who May Your Regular Be (78)	Artist Record Co. 102	15.00	45.00
ELBERT, Donnie			
MY CONFESSION OF LOVE/Peek-A-Boo (45)	Deluxe 6161	4.00	8.00
WHAT CAN I DO/Hear My Plea (45)	Deluxe 6125	2.00	4.00
ELDORADOS			
CRAZY LITTLE MAMA (LP)	Vee Jay (M) VJLP 1001	15.00	60.00

(M) Monaural, (S) Stereo, (EP) Extended Play, (LP) Long Play, (45) 45 rpm, (78) 78 rpm.

The Drifters

TITLE/Flip	LABEL & No.	GOOD	NEAR MINT
ENCORES			
WHEN I LOOK AT YOU/Young Girls, Young Girls (45)	Checker 760	240.00	480.00
ESQUERITA			
ESQUERITA (LP)	Capitol (M) T 1186	18.00	72.00
FIVE KEYS			
BEST OF THE FIVE KEYS (LP)	Group Classics (M) 304	3.00	6.00
BEST OF THE FIVE KEYS, Vol. 3 (LP)	Aladdin (M) 810	25.00	100.00
LING, TING, TONG/I'm Alone (45)	Capitol 2945	4.25	8.50
5 ROYALES			
ALL TIME HITS (LP)	King (M) 955	9.00	36.00
DEDICATED TO THE ONE I LOVE/Miracle Of Love (45)	King 5453	2.50	5.00
ROCKIN' 5 ROYALES (LP)	Apollo (M) LP 488	15.00	60.00
FIVE SATINS			
FIVE SATINS SING (LP)	Ember (M) ELP 100	12.00	48.00
I REMEMBER (IN THE STILL OF THE NIGHT)/ The Jones Girl (45)	Standard 200	50.00	100.00
TO THE AISLE/Wish I Had My Baby (45)	Ember 1019	2.50	5.00
FIVE SHARPS			
STORMY WEATHER/Sleepy Cowboy (78)	Jubilee 5104	1,500.00	4,500.00
FLAMINGOS			
I ONLY HAVE EYES FOR YOU/At The Prom (45)	End 1046	1.50	3.00
LOVERS NEVER SAY GOODBYE/That Love Is You (45)	End 1035	3.00	6.00
FOREST CITY JOE [Blues]			
MEMORY OF SONNY BOY/ A Woman On Every Street (78)	Aristocrat 3101	15.00	45.00
FOSTER, Leroy [Blues]			
ROLLIN' AND TUMBLIN' Pt. 1/ Rollin' And Tumblin', Pt. 2 (78)	Parkway 501	22.00	66.00

The left hand price column represents the true value of the average. used record.

The Five Keys

TITLE/Flip	LABEL & No.	GOOD	NEAR MINT
FOSTER, Little Willie [Blues]			
FALLING RAIN BLUES/Four Day Jump (45) ....Parrot 813		21.00	42.00
FOUR TOPS			
FOUR TOPS (LP) .... Motown (M) 622		5.00	10.00
I CAN'T HELP MYSELF/Sad Souvenirs (45) ....Motown 1076		1.00	2.00
JAZZ IMPRESSIONS (LP) .... Workshop (M) 217		15.00	60.00
MAIN STREET PEOPLE (LP) ....Dunhill (S) X 50144		2.00	4.00
FOX, Norman & The Rob-Roys			
DANCE GIRL DANCE/My Dearest One (45)............ Back Beat 508		3.00	6.00
DREAM GIRL/Pizza Pie (45)............................ Capitol 4128		1.50	3.00
FRANKLIN, Aretha			
ROCK-A-BYE YOUR BABY WITH A DIXIE MELODY/			
Operation Heartbreak (45) ....Columbia 42157		1.25	2.50
SONGS OF FAITH (LP) ....Checker (M) 10009		5.00	10.00
YOUNG, GIFTED & BLACK (LP) .... Atlantic (S) 7213		2.50	5.00
FREEMAN, Bobby			
BABY WHAT WOULD YOU DO/Miss You So (45) .... Josie 886		1.25	2.50
MY GUARDIAN ANGEL/Where Did My Baby Go (45)......... Josie 867		2.00	4.00
FULLER, Playboy [Blues]			
SUGAR CANE HIGHWAY/Gonna Play My Guitar (45).........Fuller 171		137.50	275.00
SUGAR CANE HIGHWAY/Gonna Play My Guitar (78)......Fuller OP 171		45.00	135.00
FULSON, Lowell [Blues]			
CRYING BLUES/			
You're Going To Miss Me When I'm Gone (78) .... Swing Time 110		1.50	4.50
RAGGEDY DADDY BLUES/Goodbye (45) .... Swing Time 315		6.00	12.00
GAYE, Marvin			
I HEARD IT THROUGH THE GRAPEVINE (LP)............ Tamla (S) 285		3.00	6.00
LET YOUR CONSCIENCE BE YOUR GUIDE/			
Never Let You Go (45) .... Tamla 54041		4.00	8.00
STUBBORN KIND OF FELLOW/It Hurt Me Too (45) .... Tamla 54068		1.25	2.50
GENE & EUNICE			
POCO-LOCO/Go On Ko Ko Mo .... Case 1001		1.25	2.50
THIS IS MY STORY/Move It Over Baby...................Aladdin 3282		4.00	8.00
GLADIOLAS			
LITTLE DARLIN'/Sweetheart Please Don't Go (45) .... Excello 2101		3.50	7.00

TITLE/Flip	LABEL & No.	GOOD	NEAR MINT

GLENN, Lloyd
LLOYD GLENN (10" LP) . . . . Swingtime (M) 1901 | 17.00 | 68.00

GREEN, Boy [Blues]
A AND B BLUES/Play My Juke Box (78) . . . . Regis 120 | 12.00 | 36.00

GREEN, L.C. [Blues]
GOING DOWN TO THE RIVER BLUES/
Ramblin' Around Blues (78) . . . . Von 42 | 15.00 | 45.00

GREEN, R. & Turner (Slim Green) [Blues]
ALLA BLUES/
Central Ave. Blues (78) . . . . J&M Fullbright 123 | 10.00 | 30.00
MY WOMAN DONE QUIT ME/(flip by Al Simmons) (45) . . . . Dig 142 | 6.00 | 12.00
(Artist shown as Slim Green)

GUITAR SLIM (Eddie Jones) [Blues]
BAD LUCK IS ON ME (WOMAN TROUBLES)/
Cryin' In The Mornin' (45) . . . . Imperial 5278 | 11.00 | 22.00
THINGS THAT I USED TO DO, THE/
Well I Done Got Over It (45) . . . . Specialty 482 | 2.00 | 4.00

HAMILTON, Roy
UNCHAINED MELODY/From Here To Eternity (45) . . . . Epic 9102 | 1.25 | 2.50

HARMONICA FRANK (Frank Floyd) [Blues]
GREAT MEDICAL MENAGERIST, THE/
Rockin' Chair Daddy (45) . . . . Sun 205 | 65.00 | 130.00
GREAT MEDICAL MENAGERIST, THE/
Rockin' Chair Daddy (78) . . . . Sun 205 | 25.00 | 75.00
ROCK A LITTLE BABY/Monkey Love (45) . . . . F & L 100 | 50.00 | 100.00

HARPTONES
WHAT WILL I TELL MY HEART/Foolish Me (45) . . . . Companion 103 | 2.50 | 5.00

HARRIS, Thurston
LITTLE BITTY PRETTY ONE/
I Hope You Won't Hold It Against Me (45) . . . . Aladdin 3398 | 1.50 | 3.00

HARRISON, Wilbert
KANSAS CITY/Listen My Darling (45) . . . . Fury 1023 | 1.75 | 3.50

HAWKINS, Screamin' Jay
AT HOME WITH SCREAMIN' JAY HAWKINS (LP) . . . . . . Epic (M) LN 3448 | 8.00 | 32.00
WHAT THAT IS (LP) . . . . Philips (S) PHS 600-319 | 4.00 | 12.00

HAYES, Isaac
ISAAC HAYES MOVEMENT, THE (LP) . . . . Enterprise (S) ENS 1010 | 3.00 | 6.00

HEARTBEATS
THOUSAND MILES AWAY, A/Oh Baby Don't (45) . . . . Rama 216 | 2.50 | 5.00
TORMENTED/ (45) . . . . Network | 15.00 | 30.00

HENDRICKS, Bobby
BUSY FLIRTIN'/I Want That (45) . . . . Sue 729 | 1.25 | 2.50
ITCHY TWITCHY FEELING/A Thousand Dreams (45) . . . . Sue 706 | 3.00 | 6.00

HIBBLER, Al
HE/Breeze (45) . . . . Decca 29660 | 1.00 | 2.00

⑤ HIDEAWAYS
CAN'T HELP LOVING THAT GIRL OF MINE/
I'm Coming Home (45) . . . . Ronnie 1000 | 650.00 | 1300.00

HI-FIVES
FELICIA/Windy City Special (45) . . . . Bingo 1006 | 1.25 | 2.50
MY FRIEND/How Can I Win (45) . . . . Decca 30576 | 6.00 | 12.00

Many albums in this forthcoming book are included in the current *Record Albums 1948-1978* price guide.

TITLE/Flip	LABEL & No.	GOOD	NEAR MINT
HOGG, Andrew [Blues]			
HE KNOWS HOW MUCH WE CAN BEAR/I Don't Want Nobody's Bloodstains On My Hands (78) ....*Exclusive 89*		4.00	12.00
HOOKER, John Lee [Blues]			
BORN IN MISSISSIPPI (LP)................................ *ABC (M) 768*		2.00	4.00
CANAL STREET BLUES/Huckle Up Baby (78) .... *Sensation 26*		2.00	6.00
DON'T TURN ME FROM YOUR DOOR (LP)............ *Atco (M) 151*		4.00	16.00
MAD MAN BLUES/Boogie Now (78) ....*Gone 60*		5.00	15.00
(Artist shown as John Lee Booker)			
HOPKINS, Lightnin' [Blues]			
CAN'T YOU DO LIKE YOU USED TO DO/ West Coast Blues (78) .... *Aladdin 165*		2.00	6.00
COUNTRY BLUES (LP) .... *Tradition (M) TLP 1035*		2.00	4.00
LIGHTNIN' HOPKINS STRUMS THE BLUES (LP) ....*Score (M) 4022*		7.00	28.00
ROLLIN' BLUES (ROLLIN' AND ROLLIN')/ Shotgun Blues (45) .... *Aladdin 3063*		13.00	26.00
HOT ROD HAPPY—see Country Jim			
HOWLIN' WOLF [Blues]			
ALL NIGHT BOOGIE/I Love My Baby (45) .... *Chess 1557*		5.00	10.00
RIDING IN THE MOONLIGHT/Morning At Midnight (78) ...... *RPM 333*		3.00	9.00
SADDLE MY PONY/Worried All The Time (45) .... *Chess 1515*		8.00	16.00
SADDLE MY PONY/Worried All The Time (78) .... *Chess 1515*		2.50	5.00
㊻ HUNT, D.A.			
LONESOME OL' JAIL/Greyhound Blues (45) ....*Sun 183*		140.00	280.00
HUNTER, Ivory Joe			
I ALMOST LOST MY MIND/I Give You My Love (45) .... *MGM 10578*		2.50	5.00
SINCE I MET YOU BABY/ I Can't Stop This Rocking And Rolling (45) .... *Atlantic 1111*		1.25	2.50
HUTTO, J.B. [Blues]			
PET CREAM MAN/Lovin' You (45) .... *Chance 1160*		33.00	66.00
PET CREAM MAN/Lovin' You (78) .... *Chance 1160*		7.00	21.00
INK SPOTS			
INK SPOTS, Vol. 1 (10" LP)............................ *Decca (M) 5056*		5.00	20.00
SOMETIME/I Was Dancing With Someone (45) .... *Decca 27102*		1.50	3.00
ISLEY BROTHERS			
ANGELS CRIED/The Cow Jumped Over The Moon (45) .. *Teenage 1004*		15.00	30.00
SHOUT Pt. 1/Shout Pt. 2 (45) .... *RCA Victor 7588*		1.25	2.50
JACKS			
WHY DON'T YOU WRITE ME/My Darling (45) .... *RPM 428*		5.00	10.00
JACKSON, Chuck			
ANY DAY NOW/The Prophet (45)........................... *Wand 122*		1.25	2.50
JACKSON, Lil' Son [Blues]			
LONELY BLUES/Freight Train Blues (No Money) (45).... *Imperial 5229*		10.00	20.00
ROBERTA BLUES/Freedom Train Blues (78) .... *Gold Star 638*		2.00	6.00
JAMES, Elmore [Blues]			
I BELIEVE/I Held My Baby Last Night (45) .... *Meteor 5000*		10.00	20.00
(Yellow label)			
I BELIEVE/I Held My Baby Last Night (78) .... *Meteor 5000*		3.00	9.00
JAMES, Etta			
DANCE WITH ME HENRY/Hold Me, Squeeze Me (45)...... *Modern 947*		3.00	6.00
ETTA JAMES (LP) .... *Chess (M) CH 50042*		4.00	8.00
IT'S TOO SOON TO KNOW/Seven Day Fool (45) .... *Argo 5402*		1.00	2.00
JEFFERSON, Blind Lemon [Blues]			
FOLK BLUES (LP) .... *Riverside (M) RLP 1014*		6.00	18.00

The left hand price column represents the true value of the average, used record.

The Ink Spots

The Isley Brothers

TITLE/Flip	LABEL & No.	GOOD	NEAR MINT
JENKINS, Robert [Blues]			
STEELIN' BOOGIE Pt. 1/Steelin' Boogie Pt. 2 (78) .... *Parkway 103*		20.00	60.00
JESTERS			
SO STRANGE/Love No One But You (45) .... *Winley 218*		3.00	6.00
TIGER TAIL/Panther Pounce (45) .... *Feature 101*		1.25	2.50
JIVE FIVE			
HULLY GULLY CALLING TIME/No Not Again (45) .... *Beltone 2019*		3.00	6.00
MY TRUE STORY/When I Was Single (45)............... *Beltone 1006*		1.50	3.00
JOHNNIE & JOE			
OVER THE MOUNTAIN, ACROSS THE SEA/ My Baby's Gone, On, On (45)............................ *J & S 1654*		15.00	30.00
OVER THE MOUNTAIN, ACROSS THE SEA/ My Baby's Gone, On, On (45)............................ *Chess 1654*		2.00	4.00

(M) Monaural, (S) Stereo, (EP) Extended Play, (LP) Long Play, (45) 45 rpm, (78) 78 rpm.

TITLE/Flip	LABEL & No.	GOOD	NEAR MINT

JOHNSON, Sonny Boy & His Blue Blazers [Blues]
SWIMMING POOL BLUES/
   I'm Drinking My Last Drink (78) ....Murray 507 — 10.00 — 30.00

JONES, Floyd [Blues]
BIG WORLD/Dark Road (78) .... JOB 1001 — 6.00 — 18.00
STOCKYARD BLUES/Keep What You Got (78) .... Marvel — 15.00 — 45.00

JORDAN, Louis
COME BLOW YOUR HORN (LP)........................Score (M) 4007 — 14.00 — 56.00
MAN WE'RE WAILIN' (LP) .... Mercury (M) MG 20331 — 3.00 — 12.00

K-DOE, Ernie
MOTHER-IN-LAW/Wanted $10,000 Reward (45) .... Minit 623 — 1.25 — 2.50
MY LOVE FOR YOU/Shirley Tuff (45) ....Ember 1075 — 3.00 — 6.00

KING, B.B. [Blues]
ELECTIVE, THE (LP) .... Bluesway (M) 6022 — 2.50 — 5.00
I LOVE YOU BABY/The Woman I Love (45) ....RPM 408 — 1.50 — 3.00
MISS MARTHA KING/
   When Your Baby Packs Up And Goes (78) ....Bullet 309 — 5.00 — 15.00
3 O'CLOCK BLUES/That Ain't The Way To Do It (45)..........RPM 339 — 9.00 — 18.00

KING, Ben E.
DON'T PLAY THAT SONG (LP)........................... Atco (M) 142 — 5.00 — 15.00
STAND BY ME/On The Horizon (45)......................Atco 6194 — 1.00 — 2.00

KING, Freddie
BURGLAR (LP) ....RSO (S) 4803 — 2.50 — 5.00
FREDDY KING SINGS (LP) .... King (M) 762 — 10.00 — 40.00
SAN-HO-ZAY/See See Baby (45) ....Federal 12428 — 1.00 — 2.00

KNIGHT, Gladys & The Pips
ALL IN A NIGHT'S WORK (LP)......................Soul (S) SS 730 — 4.00 — 8.00
EVERY BEAT OF MY HEART/Room In Your Heart (45) ... Huntom 2510 — 10.00 — 20.00
LETTER FULL OF TEARS (LP).........................Fury (M) F 1003 — 8.00 — 32.00
LETTER FULL OF TEARS/You Broke Your Promise (45) ...... Fury 1054 — 1.50 — 3.00

KNIGHT, Sonny
CONFIDENTIAL/Jail Bird (45) ....Dot 15507 — 1.50 — 3.00
DEDICATED TO YOU/Short Walk (45)........................ Starla 1 — 5.00 — 10.00

LAZY BILL & HIS BLUE RHYTHMS [Blues]
SHE GOT ME WALKIN'/I Had A Dream (45).............Chance 1148 — 30.00 — 60.00
SHE GOT ME WALKIN'/I Had A Dream (78).............Chance 1148 — 7.00 — 21.00

LAZY SLIM JIM—see Carolina Slim

LEADBELLY [Blues]
HUDDIE LEDBETTER MEMORIAL ALBUM, Vol. 1
   (10" LP) ....Folkways (M) 2013 — 7.50 — 15.00
ON A MONDAY/John Henry (45) ....Asch 343-3 — 2.00 — 4.00

LEE, Curtis
NEVER KNEW WHAT LOVE COULD DO/Gotta Have You (45) ..... Hot 7 — 2.50 — 5.00
PICKIN' UP THE PIECES OF MY HEART/
   Mr. Mistaker (45).................................... Dunes 2021 — 1.00 — 2.00

LEE, John [Blues]
RHYTHM ROCKIN' BOOGIE/
   Knockin' On Lula Mae's Door (45) .... JOB 114 — 35.00 — 70.00
RHYTHM ROCKIN' BOOGIE/
   Knockin' On Lula Mae's Door (78) .... JOB 114 — 15.00 — 45.00

LEGENDS
LEGENDS LET LOOSE (LP) ....Capitol (M) T 1925 — 7.00 — 28.00

LENOIR, J.B. [Blues]
EISENHOWER BLUES/I'm In Korea (45) ....Parrot 802 — 15.00 — 30.00
PEOPLE ARE MEDDLIN' IN OUR AFFAIRS/Let's Roll (78) ...... JOB 112 — 5.00 — 15.00

TITLE/Flip	LABEL & No.	GOOD	NEAR MINT

LIGHTNIN' SLIM [Blues]
BAD LUCK/Rock Me Mama (45) .... Feature 3006		38.00	76.00
BAD LUCK/Rock Me Mama (78) .... Feature 3006		7.00	14.00

LITTLE ANTHONY & THE IMPERIALS
HURT SO BAD/Reputation (45) .... DCP 1128		1.00	2.00
ON A NEW STREET (LP) .... Avco (S) 11012		3.00	6.00
TEARS ON MY PILLOW/Two People In The World (45) .... End 1027		2.00	4.00

LITTLE CAESAR & THE ROMANS
MEMORIES OF THOSE OLDIES BUT GOODIES/ Fever (45) .... Del-Fi 4166		6.00	12.00
TEN COMMANDMENTS OF LOVE/C C Rider (45) .... Del-Fi 4170		1.50	3.00

LITTLE COOPER & THE DRIFTERS
EVENING TRAIN/Moving Slow (45) .... Stevens 105		33.00	66.00

LITTLE EVA
LOCO-MOTION, THE/He Is The Boy .... Dimension 1000		1.25	2.50

LITTLE MILTON
WE'RE GONNA MAKE IT/ Can't Hold Back The Tears (45) .... Checker 1105		1.00	2.00

LITTLE RICHARD
EVERY HOUR/Taxi Blues (45) .... RCA Victor 4392		25.00	50.00
FABULOUS LITTLE RICHARD, THE (LP) .... Specialty (M) SP 2104		4.00	8.00
RIP IT UP/Ready Teddy (45) .... Specialty 579		1.00	2.00

LITTLE WALTER [Blues]
JUKE/Can't Hold Out Much Longer (45) .... Checker 758		4.00	8.00
MUSKADINE BLUES/Bad Acting Woman (78) .... Regal 3296		15.00	45.00

LITTLE WILLIE JOHN
ALL AROUND THE WORLD/Don't Leave Me Dear (45) .... King 4818		2.00	4.00
FEVER (LP with Brown Cover) .... King (M) 564		7.00	28.00
TALK TO ME/Let Them Talk (45) .... King 5799		1.00	2.00

LOUIS, Joe Hill [Blues]
DOROTHY MAY/When I'm Gone (45) .... Checker 763		20.00	40.00
DOROTHY MAY/When I'm Gone (78) .... Checker 763		3.00	9.00

LYMON, Frankie & The Teenagers
I WANT YOU TO BE MY GIRL/I'm Not A Know It All (45) ..... Gee 1012		2.50	5.00

MABON, Willie [Blues]
LIGHT UP YOUR LAMP/Rosetta, Rosetta (45) .... Federal 12306		1.50	3.00
WORRY BLUES/I Don't Know (45) .... Chess 1531		3.50	7.00

MARCELS
BLUE MOON/Goodbye To Love (45) .... Colpix 186		1.50	3.00
ONE LAST KISS/Teeter Totter Love (45) .... Colpix 694		7.00	14.00

MARTHA & THE VANDELLAS
COME AND GET THESE MEMORIES (LP) .... Gordy (M) 902		5.00	15.00
QUICKSAND/Darling I Hum Our Song (45) .... Gordy 7025		1.00	2.00

MARVELETTES
AS LONG AS I KNOW HE'S MINE/Little Girl Blue (45) .... Tamla 54088		1.50	3.00

MAYFIELD, Curtis
HIS EARLY YEARS WITH THE IMPRESSIONS (LP) .... ABC (S) X 780		3.00	6.00

McDANIELS, Gene
TOWER OF STRENGTH/Secret (45) .... Liberty 55371		1.50	3.00

McGHEE, Brownie [Blues]
DON'T DOG YOUR WOMAN/Daisy (45) .... Red Robin 111		15.00	30.00
THAT'S THE STUFF (WATCH OUT)/ Knockabout Blues (Carolina Blues) (78) .... Savoy 5533		1.00	3.00

TITLE/Flip	LABEL & No.	GOOD	NEAR MINT

McNEELY, Big Jay
BIG JAY McNEELY (10" LP) .... Federal (M) 29596 — 13.00 — 52.00
JUST CRAZY, Vol. 1 (LP) .... King (EP) 245 — 2.00 — 6.00

McPHATTER, Clyde
I'M LONELY TONIGHT/Thirty Days (45)................. Atlantic 1106 — 2.00 — 4.00
LIVE AT THE APOLLO (LP) .... Mercury (M) MG 20915 — 5.00 — 15.00

McTELL, Blind Willie [Blues]
BROKE DOWN ENGINE BLUES/Kill It Kid (78) .... Atlantic 891 — 9.00 — 27.00

(38) MELLO MOODS
I COULDN'T SLEEP A WINK LAST NIGHT/
And You Just Can't Go Through Life Alone .... Red Robin 104 — 150.00 — 300.00 Tie

MEMPHIS SLIM [Blues]
BORN WITH THE BLUES (LP) .... Jewell (M) 5004 — 2.00 — 4.00
HARLEM BOUND/Life Is Like That (78)................. Miracle M 111 — 1.00 — 3.00
JUST BLUES (LP) .... Prestige (M) BV 1018 — 5.00 — 15.00

MICKEY & SYLVIA
LOVE IS STRANGE/I'm Going Home (45) .... Groove 0175 — 1.50 — 3.00

MIDNIGHTERS
MIDNIGHTERS (LP; label is yellow and gray) .... Federal (M) 541 — 15.00 — 60.00
MIDNIGHTERS: THEIR GREATEST HITS, THE
(10" LP) .... Federal (M) 295 90 — 40.00 — 160.00

MILBURN, Amos [Blues]
BLUES BOSS (LP) .... Motown (M) 608 — 4.00 — 12.00
ROCKIN' THE BOOGIE (10" LP, red vinyl) .... Aladdin (M) 704 — 40.00 — 160.00
ROCKIN' THE BOOGIE (10" LP, black vinyl) .... Aladdin (M) 704 — 30.00 — 120.00

The Moonglows

TITLE/Flip	LABEL & No.	GOOD	NEAR MINT
MIRACLES			
BAD GIRL/I Need Your Baby (45) .... Motown 1		5.00	10.00
GOING TO A-GO-GO (LP) .... Tamla (S) 267		4.00	8.00
SHOP AROUND/Who's Lovin' You (45) .... Tamla 54034		1.25	2.50
MUDDY WATERS [Blues]			
I'M READY/I Don't Know Why (45) .... Chess 1579		3.50	7.00
SCREAMIN' AND CRYIN'/			
Where's My Woman Been (78) .... Aristocrat 406		7.00	21.00
YOU'RE GONNA NEED MY HELP I SAID/			
Sad Letter Blues (78) .... Chess 1434		3.00	6.00
NASH, Johnny			
AS TIME GOES BY/The Voice Of Love (45) .... ABC Paramount 9996		1.00	2.00
THOUSAND MILES AWAY/			
I Need Someone To Stand By Me (45) .... ABC Paramount 10212		3.00	6.00
NUTONES			
(38) BELIEVE/Annie Kicked The Bucket (45) .... Hollywood Star 798		150.00	300.00 Tie
OLYMPICS			
BIG BOY PETE/Stay Away From Joe (45) .... Arvee 595		1.00	2.00
DOOLEY/Stay Where You Are (45) .... Arvee 5031		3.00	6.00
ORIOLES			
CRYING IN THE CHAPEL/			
Don't You Think I Ought To Know (45) .... Jubilee 5122		4.50	9.00
ORLONS			
MR. 21/Please Let It Be Me (45) .... Cameo 211		4.00	8.00
SOUTH STREET/Them Terrible Boots (45) .... Cameo 243		1.00	2.00
OTIS, Johnny			
COLD SHOT (LP) .... Kent (M) KST 534		3.00	6.00
ROCK AND ROLL HIT PARADE (LP) .... Dig (M) LP 104		9.00	36.00
STAR OF LOVE/It's Too Soon To Know (45) .... Capitol 3802		2.00	4.00
PELICANS			
(34) AURELIA/White Cliffs Of Dover (45) .... Parrot 793		165.00	330.00
PENGUINS			
BELIEVE ME/Pony Rock (45) .... Sun State 001		3.00	6.00
COOL COOL PENGUINS (LP) .... Dooto (M) DTL 242		8.00	16.00
EARTH ANGEL/Hey Senorita (45) .... Dootone 348		5.00	10.00
PHILLIPS, Little Esther			
RELEASE ME/Don't Feel Rained In (45) .... Lenox 5555		1.00	2.00
PLATTERS			
MOONLIGHT MEMORIES (LP) .... Mercury (M) MG 20759		3.00	6.00
MY PRAYER/Heaven On Earth (45) .... Mercury 70893		1.75	3.50
ONLY YOU/You Made Me Cry (45) .... Federal 12244		15.00	30.00
PLATTERS (LP) .... Federal (M) 549		8.00	32.00
POINTER SISTERS			
LIVE AT THE OPERA HOUSE (LP) .... Blue Thumb (S) 8002		4.00	8.00
PRISONAIRES			
(17) THERE IS LOVE IN YOU/What'll You Do Next (45) .... Sun 207		237.50	475.00
PROFESSOR LONGHAIR—see Roy Byrd			
PROFESSOR LONGHAIR & HIS SHUFFLING HUNGARIANS—see Roy Byrd			
PRYOR, Snooky [Blues]			
BOOGIE/Telephone Blues (78) .... Planet 101		20.00	60.00
CRYIN' SHAME/Eighty Nine Ten (45) .... JOB 1014		25.00	50.00
CRYIN' SHAME/Eighty Nine Ten (78) .... JOB 1014		6.00	18.00

This section represents approximately 3½% of the listings to appear in the price guide. *Blacks and Blues.*

The Pointer
Sisters

The Platters

TITLE/Flip	LABEL & No.	GOOD	NEAR MINT
RAINEY, _Big Memphis Ma_ [Blues]			
CALL ME ANYTHING, BUT CALL ME/Baby, No, No (45)	Sun 184	38.00	76.00
CALL ME ANYTHING, BUT CALL ME/Baby, No, No (78)	Sun 184	20.00	60.00
RATTLESNAKE COOPER [Blues]			
RATTLESNAKE BLUES/Lost Woman (78)	Talent 804	10.00	30.00
REESE, _Della_			
DON'T YOU KNOW/Soldier, Won't You Marry Me (45)	RCA Victor 7591	1.00	2.00
RAVENS			
COUNT EVERY STAR/ I'm Gonna Paper All My Walls With Your Love Letters (45)	National 9111	190.00	380.00
RIPLEY COTTON CHOPPERS			
BLUES WALTZ/Silver Bells (78)	Sun 190	210.00	420.00
RIVINGTONS			
PAPA-OOOM-MOW-MOW/Deep Water (45)	Liberty 55427	1.25	2.50
ROSS, _Diana_			
TOUCH ME IN THE MORNING (LP)	Motown (S) 772	2.50	5.00
RUFUS (Featuring Chaka Khan)			
STREET PLAYER (LP) (picture record)	Abe (S) AA 1049	12.00	24.00
SCHOOLBOYS			
SHIRLEY/Please Say You Want Me (45)	Okeh 7076	4.50	9.00

The Rivingtons

TITLE/Flip	LABEL & No.	GOOD	NEAR MINT
SHARP, Dee Dee			
MASHED POTATO TIME/Set My Heart At Ease (45)........*Cameo 212*		1.00	2.00
WHERE DID I GO WRONG/Willyam, Willyam (45)..........*Cameo 296*		2.00	4.00
SHEP & THE LIMELITES			
DADDY'S HOME/This I Know (45) ....*Hull 740*		1.25	2.50
WHAT DID DADDY DO/Teach Me How To Twist (45) .... *Hull 751*		3.00	6.00
SHIRELLES			
DEDICATED TO THE ONE I LOVE/Look A Here Baby (45) .*Scepter 1203*		1.50	3.00
FOOLISH LITTLE GIRL (LP).......................*Scepter (M) S 511*		4.00	12.00
MY LOVE IS A CHARM/Slop Time (45)..................*Decca 30669*		5.00	10.00
SHIRLEY & LEE			
I FEEL GOOD/Now That It's Over (45) ....*Aladdin 3338*		2.00	4.00
LEGENDARY MASTERS-SHIRLEY AND LEE			
(LP) .... *United Artists (S) UALA 026 G2*		5.00	10.00
LET THE GOOD TIMES ROLL (LP).....................*Aladdin (M) 807*		14.00	56.00
LET THE GOOD TIMES ROLL/			
Do You Mean To Hurt Me (45) ....*Aladdin 3325*		5.00	10.00
SLIM PICKENS—see Eddie Burns			
SLY & THE FAMILY STONE			
WHOLE NEW THING, A(LP) .... *Epic (M) LN 24324*		4.00	8.00
SMITH, Bessie			
BESSIE SMITH STORY (LP) .... *Columbia (M) ML 4807*		4.00	8.00
SMITH, Thunder [Blues]			
TRAIN IS LEAVING, THE/			
Thunder's Unfinished Boogie (78) ....*Down Town 2011*		4.00	12.00

Samples chosen for each artist represent the range of high and low values that artist's records usually bring.

TITLE/Flip	LABEL & No.	GOOD	NEAR MINT

SONNY TERRY [Blues]
BABY LET'S HAVE SOME FUN/Four O'Clock Blues (45)......Gotha 517		5.00	10.00
SWEET WOMAN/Fox Chase (78) ....Solo 10-004		2.00	6.00
THAT WOMAN IS KILLING ME/Harmonica Train (45)....Jackson 2302		13.00	26.00

SPANIELS
30
BABY IT'S YOU/Bounce (45) ....VeeJay 101		187.50	375.00
(Pressed in red vinyl)			

SPINNERS
I'LL ALWAYS LOVE YOU/			
Tomorrow May Never Come (45) ....Motown 1078		1.00	2.00
ORIGINAL SPINNERS, THE (LP) ....Motown (M) 639		4.00	8.00
THAT'S WHAT GIRLS ARE MADE FOR/			
Heebie Jeebies (45) ....Tri-Phi 1001		3.00	6.00

SUNNYLAND SLIM [Blues]
HARD TIMES/School Days (78) ....Tempo Tone 1001		20.00	60.00
IT'S YOU BABY/Highway 51 (45)......................Cobra 5006		7.00	14.00
ORPHAN BOY BLUES/When I Was Young (78) ....Regal 3327		2.00	6.00

SUPREMES
BACK IN MY ARMS AGAIN/			
Whisper You Love Me Boy (45) ....Motown 1075		1.00	2.00
I WANT A GUY/Never Again (45)......................Tamla 54038		7.50	15.00
MEET THE SUPREMES (LP) ....,...Motown (M) MLP 606		9.00	36.00
(Original LP with girls sitting on stools)			
MEET THE SUPREMES (LP) ....Motown (M) MLP 606		3.00	9.00
(Later pressing with girls' faces on cover)			

SWALLOWS
33
SINCE YOU BEEN AWAY/Wishing For You (45).............King 4466		170.00	340.00

SYKES, Roosevelt [Blues]
HONEYSUCKLE ROSE/Jivin' The Jive (78) ....Bluebird 34-0729		1.50	4.50
RAINING IN MY HEART/Heavy Heart (45) ....United 120		6.00	12.00

TAMPA RED [Blues]
DETROIT BLUES/Sure Enough I Do (78) ....Bluebird 34-0731		2.00	6.00
SO CRAZY ABOUT YOU BABY/			
So Much Trouble (45) ....RCA Victor 20-5523		6.00	12.00

TARHEEL SLIM—see Allen Baum

TEENAGERS (Featuring Frankie Lymon)
TEENAGERS FEATURING FRANKIE LYMON, THE			
(Red label LP)....................................Gee (M) GLP 701		10.00	40.00
TEENAGERS FEATURING FRANKIE LYMON, THE			
(Gray label LP) ....Gee (S) GLP 701		4.00	16.00

TEMPTATIONS
DREAM COME TRUE/Isn't She Pretty (45) ....Gordy 7001		5.00	10.00
GETTIN' READY (LP).................................Gordy (S) 918		4.00	8.00
MY GIRL/Nobody But My Baby (45) ....Gordy 7038		1.00	2.00

THOMAS, Jessie [Blues]
GUESS I'LL WALK ALONE/Let's Have Some Fun (78) ....Freedom 1513		3.00	9.00
MELODY IN C/You Are My Dreams (78) ....Club		10.00	30.00

THORNTON, Willie Mae "Big Mama" [Blues]
PARTNERSHIP BLUES/All Fed Up (45) ....Peacock 1567		5.00	10.00
PARTNERSHIP BLUES/All Fed Up (78) ....Peacock 1567		1.25	2.50

TUNE WEAVERS
HAPPY HAPPY BIRTHDAY BABY/			
Ol Man River (45) ....Casa Grande 4037		4.50	9.00
I REMEMBER DEAR/Pamela Jean (45).............Casa Grande 4038		2.50	5.00

All artists shown in photos appear with listings in the guide these samples were taken from.

The Spaniels

TITLE/Flip	LABEL & No.	GOOD	NEAR MINT
TURNER, Baby Face [Blues]			
BLUE SERENADE/Gonna Let You Go (45) .... Modern 882		18.00	36.00
BLUE SERENADE/Gonna Let You Go (78) .... Modern 882		6.00	18.00
TURNER, Ike & Tina			
COME TOGETHER (LP) .... Liberty (S) LST 7637		2.50	5.00
FINGER POPPIN'/It's All Over (45) .... Warner Bros. 5481		1.00	2.00
FOOL IN LOVE, A/The Way You Love Me (45) .... Sue 730		2.00	4.00
RIVER DEEP, MOUNTAIN HIGH (LP) .... Philles (M) LP 4011		20.00	40.00

This section represents approximately 3½% of the listings to appear in the price guide, *Blacks and Blues*.

TITLE/Flip	LABEL & No.	GOOD	NEAR MINT
TURNER, Joe			
BIG JOE RIDES AGAIN (LP) .... Atlantic (S) SD 1332		6.00	24.00
JUMPIN' THE BLUES (LP) .... Arhoolie (M) R 2004		4.00	8.00
㉗ VELVETEERS			
TELL ME YOU'RE MINE/Boo Wacka Boo (45) .... Spitfire 15		212.50	425.00
WALKER, T-Bone [Blues]			
I GOT A BREAK BABY/Mean Old World (78) .... Capitol 10033		1.50	4.50
NO REASON/Look Me In The Eye (45) .... Imperial 5117		8.00	16.00
WARD, Billy & The Dominoes			
BILLY WARD AND HIS DOMINOES (LP) .... Federal (M) 548		30.00	120.00
㉛ BILLY WARD AND HIS DOMINOES (10" LP) .... Federal (M) 295 94		90.00	360.00
(One of the rarest and most sought after 10" LP's. Price may vary widely.)			
BILLY WARD AND HIS DOMINOES (LP) .... Decca (M) DL 8621		10.00	60.00
(Features Jackie Wilson singing the lead on some songs)			
DEEP PURPLE/Do It Again (45) .... Liberty 55099		1.50	3.00
SEA OF GLASS (LP) .... Liberty (M) LRP 3056		3.00	9.00

(M) Monaural, (S) Stereo. (EP) Extended Play, (LP) Long Play, (45) 45 rpm, (78) 78 rpm.

Joe Turner

The Tune Weavers

Billy Ward and His Dominoes

TITLE/Flip	LABEL & No.	GOOD	NEAR MINT
WARREN, Baby Boy [Blues]			
LONESOME CABIN BLUES/			
Don't Want No Skinny Woman (78)	Staff 707	12.00	36.00
WELLS, Junior [Blues]			
JUNIOR'S WAIL/Hodo Man (45)	States 134	15.00	30.00
JUNIOR'S WAIL/Hodo Man (78)	States 134	2.50	7.50
WHITE, Barry			
I'VE GOT SO MUCH TO GIVE (LP)	20th Century Fox (S) 407	2.00	4.00
WILLIAMS, Otis & His Charms			
IVORY TOWER/In Paradise (45)	Deluxe 6093	5.00	10.00
OTIS WILLIAMS AND HIS CHARMS SING			
THEIR ALL TIME HITS (LP)	Deluxe (M) 570	15.00	60.00
THAT'S YOUR MISTAKE/Too Late I Learned (45)	Deluxe 6091	1.50	3.00
THIS IS OTIS WILLIAMS AND HIS CHARMS (LP)	King (M) 614	6.00	24.00
WILLIAMSON, Sonny Boy [Blues]			
EYESIGHT TO THE BLIND/Crazy About You Baby (78)	Trumpet 129	2.00	6.00
I CROSS MY HEART/West Memphis Blues (45)	Trumpet 144	6.00	12.00

Halfway between good and mint is the true value and the best condition usually available in old records. Mint is rare.

The following section contains excerpts from:

55 Years of Recorded Country/Western Music

This popular price guide has listed recordings dating back to 1921. It traces the history of country/western music from those early days into the revolutionary "Rockabilly" explosion of the early '50s and on up to now. The values of these many thousands of old 78s and newer 45s are documented between its covers.

The excerpts from our exclusive interview with Gene Autry — fully presented in *55 Years of Recorded Country/Western Music* — are but a taste of the views, memories and predictions of this famous singing Cowboy.

Each of our price guides includes a special *Dealers and Collectors Directory* listing hundreds of buyers and sellers of collectible records!

$6.95

buy from your local book or record store
or send check or money order to:

O'Sullivan Woodside & Company
2218 East Magnolia
Phoenix, Arizona 85034

please add 75¢ per book for postage and handling

HARD COVERS AVAILABLE

A SPECIAL, PERMANENT, LIMITED-EDITION OF HARD COVER COPIES ARE AVAILABLE WHILE THE VERY LIMITED SUPPLY LASTS!

If you wish to order direct, send $13.95 to:
Jellyroll Productions
Box 3017
Scottsdale, Arizona 85257

Country/Western
Price Guide of Current
Collectible Records (8½" x 11" 208 pages)

Gene Autry...Fifty Years Of Country/Western Music

The following are excerpts from a personal interview with Gene, conducted by Jerry Osborne and Bruce Hamilton.

Jerry: When did your career begin?

I was born in Tioga, Texas. I actually started in radio in 1927, on station KVOO back in Oklahoma. I made my first recording for a company called **Paramount Records**, up in Wisconsin.

Bruce: What was the name of the first song you recorded?

The very first I ever made was a number called, "No One To Call Me Darling."

Jerry: Who started the singing cowboy concept?

Ken Maynard did a couple of pictures with songs in them, but did not actually sing himself. The first picture I ever made was with Ken Maynard, *In Old Santa Fe.* I came out to California and did three songs in the picture and also appeared in a barn dance sequence.

Bruce: Could you tell us the difference, as you see it, between the western music of the cowboy era, as opposed to the country music of those same years?

Well, I don't think there was too much difference. Some of mine were known as cowboy songs, but they really weren't at all. "Silver Haired Daddy of Mine" was more Country/Western than cowboy. I did things like "Boots and Saddles" and "The Last Roundup," but I also did numbers like "You're The Only Star In My Blue Heaven." I really had a mixture of songs.

Jerry: How many pictures did you make?

I made fifty-six pictures for **Republic**, one picture for **Twentieth Century Fox** and a fifteen-chapter serial for **Mascot Pictures**. I spent three years as a pilot in World War II. After I came back, I went to **Columbia** with my own company, where I made thirty-two pictures. Then, when television came in, I made one hundred half-hour films for TV, not to mention countless radio programs.

Bruce: Do you think we might see a return of the singing cowboy star?

Yes, I think so. This kind of picture is beginning to be in vogue again, and I think the time is right for a young, good-looking, singing cowboy to make a comeback.

Jerry: I don't think anyone in history has been associated with doing Christmas and Easter songs as much as you have. Was it difficult for someone to talk you into singing a song about a red-nosed reindeeer, or was it something you willingly went into?

Well, "Rudolph, The Red-Nosed Reindeer" came along as an accident. The year before, I had a big record on **Columbia** called "Here Comes Santa Claus." I had been Grand Marshal of the Santa Claus Parade in Hollywood that year. While I was riding my horse, I kept hearing the kids saying, "Here comes Santa Claus! Here comes Santa Claus!" because the sleigh was right behind me. So I got the idea for the song, wrote it and recorded it. The first year we sold over a million copies. I was looking for another song as a follow-up for the next year, and a writer in New York, Johnny Marx, sent me an acetate of "Rudolph." When I first heard it, I didn't think too much of it, but my wife said she liked the song because Rudolph reminded her of the story of the "Ugly Duckling."

She said, "I like that line in there where they say they wouldn't let poor Rudolph join in any reindeer games." So, I said, all right. I didn't have anything better, so I recorded it and didn't think it was going to be that big a number. But we sold two million records the first year it was out, and, up to now, I think it's over seven million.

Bruce: I suppose you're aware that they really are getting high prices today from collectors for some old records?

Yes, they certainly are! We ran into a fellow a while back who was bootlegging some records of mine.

Bruce: It's unfortunate, because the artists don't get their just royalties from bootlegs.

They bootleg movies, too, but here recently the FBI has been running down those people because they have no right whatsoever to do that.

Jerry: When did you make your last record?

I did some recording about five years ago.

Bruce: Do you have any final comments?

I have been in country and western music from practically its infancy. I've seen the trends change. I've seen it go strictly country like Vernon Dalhart, to Gene Austin and his particular style; to the type of numbers I did; to Roy Acuff, Red Foley, Eddy Arnold and Tex Ritter, right on down to Elvis Presley and the present groups. I can truthfully say I have enjoyed hearing all their records, and I can understand why the American public today still loves a good song and a good artist.

*(Note: The full interview with Gene appears in the introduction to **55 Years of Country/Western Music.**)*

It's Called Rockabilly
By Ronny Weiser

Pure rockabilly (if there is such a thing), the musical hybrid which consists of about equal parts black blues and southern hillbilly jarred to a wild, orgasmic rock 'n' roll beat, didn't last too long; around 1958 most of it had disappeared, thought to be dead and buried forever.

While the seeds of rockabilly always existed in blues singers such as Arthur Crudup and in country singers like Hank Williams, the music actually started as a defined art form in 1954 with Elvis on Memphis' legendary *Sun* label. Other rockabilly greats included Carl Perkins, Mac Curtis, Jackie Lee Cochran, Ray Campi, Johnny Carroll and His Hot Rocks, Sid King, etc.

Lou Campi   The Best of CARL PERKINS   Elvis Presley

"Pure" rockabilly at its climactic raunchiest is a particular genre of rock 'n' roll with the characteristics of a hiccupy, breathy, neurotic voice usually with a southern accent and tape echo added to it; a galloping, standup, slappin' bass; an open chords, acoustic rhythm guitar; a clear, piercing, screeching, growling electric guitar, sometimes with echo and sometimes with reverberation; and hot, crashing drums, not much with cymbals, but, instead, a loud consistent downbeat to keep the music rocking.

Of course, there are many exceptions to the above conditions. Some rockabilly songs have a saxophone, many have a piano, and some have no drums. What is astounding is that this happened spontaneously with no real commercial effort.

Where is rockabilly headed in America? It seems that increasing numbers of teenagers are becoming tired of the "heavy metal" groups; they're becoming annoyed by the whole drug/bisex culture. They're searching for something new, something healthy, something positive, something with a happy dancing beat and a spontaneous down-to-earth feeling.

Fonzie is already Number One.

Rockabilly is next in line.

A Guide To America's "Country"

Country music is the music of the American people, of their down-to-earth struggles, accomplishments and attempts to get by as best they can. Country music—not unlike its cousin, folk music—deals with the cold, hard facts of life.

Cowboy, or western music, is specifically of the West or the move to the West, from the traditional railroad songs of the early days, to the saddle songs, the songs of the border, and to the prairies, tumbleweeds and cool, cool water.

Country/western over the years has become the label applied to either or both of the above, although today this, too, is almost universally shortened to just "country." The definition remains just as broad, though, when used in this context.

The most common country/western type of music with a handle all its own is bluegrass. The best of this earthy, driving, country rhythm-making, with emphasis on the banjo and fiddles, comes from notables such as Flatt and Scruggs, Bill Monroe and others. From the long lists of their recordings in *55 Years of Recorded Country/Western Music*, and we have sprinkled a fair sampling in this *Guide to Record Collecting*.

Cedric Rainwater   The Shoemates   Mac Wiseman   Earl Scruggs   Lester Fla

Elvis Presley cannot go without mention, being the only artist to appear in three sections of our compendium, and with records ranked and listed in color in each that placed in the *World's 50 Most Valuable Records*.

Please note the anomaly that most of the stars in the following pages also have albums documented in our price guide of *Record Albums 1948-1978*, though none appear in the album section of this book.

The mixture of 45s and 78s will explain the vaccilating condition-range for records in good or near mint grades, set at either double or triple as explained in detail earlier.

For one last word on investment potential, please note that in the country/western field we've listed a larger percentage of the obscure names and higher values of those artists who specialized in rockabilly, the genre begun by Elvis. It's an absolute can't-miss, if you buy wisely, avoiding the bootlegs!

Alphabetical Listing of Country/Western Records

This section represents approximately 5% of the artists and songs listed in *55 Years of Recorded Country/Western Music.*

All records are listed by rpm speed. (45) or (78).

TITLE	LABEL & No.	GOOD to VERY GOOD	NEAR MINT
ACUFF, Roy			
GONNA RAISE A RUCKUS TONIGHT (78) .... Perfect 7-01-60		2.50	7.50
GREAT SPECKLE BIRD (78) .... Conqueror 8740		3.00	9.00
PINS AND NEEDLES (IN MY HEART) (78) .... Columbia 36856		1.00	3.00
PLINEY JANE (45) .... Columbia 20804		1.50	3.00
STEAMBOAT WHISTLE BLUES (78) .... Vocalion-Okeh 03255		2.50	7.50
ADAMS, Nick			
TIRED AND LONELY REBEL (45) .... RCA Victor 8073		1.00	2.00
ALLEN, Harold			
I NEED SOME LOVIN (45) .... Marvel 1201		8.00	16.00
ALLEN, Milton			
DON'T BUG ME BABY (45) .... RCA Victor 7116		8.00	16.00
ALLEN, Rex			
CRYING IN THE CHAPEL (45) .... Decca 28758		1.00	2.00
KNOCK, KNOCK RATTLE (45) .... Decca 30651		5.00	10.00
ALMOND, Lucky Joe			
EVERY DAY OF THE WEEK (45)......................... Trumpet 233		3.00	6.00
GONNA ROLL & ROCK (45) .... Trumpet 221		7.50	15.00
ANDERSON, Bill			
MAMA SANG A SONG (45)............................. Decca 31404		1.00	2.00
MY LIFE (45) .... Decca 32445		1.00	2.00
ANDERSON, Liz			
MAMA SPANK (45) .... RCA Victor 9163		1.00	2.00
ANDERSON, Lynn			
ROSE GARDEN (45) .... Columbia 45252		1.00	2.00
ANERSON, Doug			
BOP MAN BOP (45) .... Intra State		10.00	20.00

Mrs. Acuff, Tubb and Snow with Roy Acuff

TITLE	LABEL & No.	GOOD	NEAR MINT

ARNOLD, Eddy
CATTLE CALL (78)	Bluebird 33-0527	7.50	22.50
DON'T ROB ANOTHER MAN'S CASTLE (45)	RCA Victor 0042	1.50	3.00
EASY ROCKING CHAIR (78)	RCA Victor 20-2481	2.50	7.50
I TALK TO MYSELF ABOUT YOU (78)	RCA Victor 20-1801	5.00	15.00
MOMMY PLEASE STAY HOME WITH ME (78)	Bluebird 33-0520	10.00	30.00
(Eddy Arnold's first record)			

ASHLEY, John
LET YOURSELF GO (45)	Intro 6097	3.00	6.00
LITTLE LOU (45)	Capehart	7.50	15.00

ASHLEY, Leon
LAURA (WHAT'S HE GOT THAT I AIN'T GOT) (45)	Ashley 2003	1.00	2.00

ASHWORTH, Ernest
TALK BACK TREMBLING LIPS (45)	Hickory 1214	1.00	2.00

ASLEEP AT THE WHEEL
TAKE ME BACK TO TULSA (45)	United Artists 245	1.00	2.00

ATKINS, Chet
I'VE BEEN WORKING ON THE GUITAR (78)	Bluebird 58-0072	1.00	3.00
(With his Colorado Mountain Boys)			
YAKETY AXE (45)	RCA Victor 8590	1.00	2.00

AUTRY, Gene
BLUEBERRY HILL (78)	Okeh 05779	1.50	4.50
BLUE DAYS (78)	Conqueror 7831	12.50	37.50
BLUE YODEL # 4 (78)	Velvet Tone 7058-V	10.00	30.00
BLUE YODEL # 5 (78)	Harmony 1046-H	10.00	30.00
CRIME I DIDN'T DO, THE (78)	Conqueror 8000	10.00	30.00
DEATH OF JIMMIE RODGERS, THE (78)	Conqueror 8168	20.00	60.00
DEATH OF MOTHER JONES, THE (78)	Conqueror 7702	15.00	45.00
FRANKIE AND JOHNNY (78)	Clarion 5026	12.50	37.50
GANGSTER'S WARNING, A (78)	Perfect 12695	10.00	30.00
HOBO YODEL (78)	Champion (Gennett) 16096	15.00	45.00
I'M THINKING TONIGHT OF MY BLUE EYES (78)	Columbia 37023	1.00	3.00
IN THE VALLEY OF THE MOON (78)	Columbia C 558	10.00	30.00
LIFE OF JIMMIE RODGERS, THE (78)	Vocalion 5504	20.00	60.00
MISSOURI I'M CALLING (78)	Conqueror 7914	5.00	15.00
MONEY AIN'T NO USE ANYHOW (78)	Decca 5426	12.50	37.50
OLE FAITHFUL (78)	Conqueror 8468	4.00	12.00
PETER COTTONTAIL (45)	Columbia 38750	1.50	3.00
SILVER SPURS (ON THE GOLDEN STAIRS) (78)	Columbia 36904	1.50	4.50
STAY AWAY FROM MY CHICKEN HOUSE (78)	Okeh 45462	2.50	7.50
THAT SILVER HAIRED DADDY OF MINE (78)	Vocalion 5489	7.50	22.50
THERE'S A GOOD GIRL IN THE MOUNTAINS (78)	Perfect 12837	7.50	22.50
TUMBLING TUMBLEWEEDS (78)	Vocalion 03007	5.00	15.00
WAITING FOR A TRAIN (78)	Diva 6031	12.50	37.50
WHEN IT'S SPRINGTIME IN THE ROCKIES (78)	Perfect 8-03-51	5.00	15.00

AXTON, Hoyt
BONEY FINGERS (45)	A&M 1607	1.00	2.00

BAILEY, De Ford
DAVIDSON COUNTY BLUES (78)	Bluebird 5147	12.50	37.50
MUSCLE SHOAL BLUES (78)	Brunswick 147	12.50	37.50

BARE, Bobby
EDUCATED ROCK AND ROLL (45)	Fraternity 838	2.00	4.00
MARIE LAVEAU (45)	RCA Victor 0261	1.00	2.00

BEARD, Dean & Crewcats
RAKIN AND SCRAPIN (45)	Atlantic 1137	8.00	16.00
RAKIN AND SCRAPIN (45)	(Original label unknown)	12.50	25.00

BEE, Molly
DOGGIE ON THE HIWAY (45)	Capitol 2494	1.00	2.00
KIDS WHO PAY (45)	Capitol 2258	1.50	3.00

Gene Autry

Eddy Arnold

TITLE	LABEL & No.	GOOD	NEAR MINT
BELEW, Carl			
COOL GATOR SHOES (45)	Decca 30947	1.50	3.00
BENNET, Boyd			
TENNESSEE ROCK & ROLL (45)	King 1475	2.00	4.00
WATERLOO (45)	King 1413	1.50	3.00
BLAKE, Tommy			
FLAT FOOT (45)	Sun 278	4.00	8.00
I DIG YOU BABY (45)	Sun 300	25.00	50.00
BLUE SKY BOYS			
SUNNY SIDE OF LIFE (78)	Bluebird 6457	5.00	15.00
BOB & LUCILLE			
EENY MENY MINEY MO (45)	Ditto 121	12.50	25.00
EENY MENY MINEY MO (45)	King 5631	7.50	15.00
BOND, Eddie			
BOPPIN BONNIE (45)	Mercury 70941	13.00	26.00
JUKE JOINT JOHNNIE (45)	Tab 669	2.50	5.00
SLIP, SLIP, SLIPPIN IN (45)	Mercury 70882	15.00	30.00
BOND, Johnny			
LOUISIANA SWING (45)	Columbia 21783	2.00	4.00
TEN LITTLE BOTTLES (45)	Columbia 21222	1.50	3.00
BOWSER, Donnie			
GOT THE BEST OF ME (45)	Sage 276	8.00	16.00
I LOVE YOU BABY (45)	Sage 265	1.50	3.00
BOYD, Bill & His Cowboy Ramblers			
MAMA'S GETTING HOT AND PAPA'S GETTING COLD (78)	Bluebird 6323	2.50	7.50
UNDER THE DOUBLE EAGLE (78)	Bluebird 5945	1.50	4.50

All records are listed by rpm speed. (45) or (78).

TITLE	LABEL & No.	GOOD	NEAR MINT
BRITT, Elton			
CANDY KISSES (45) .... RCA Victor 0006		1.50	3.00
GOODBYE, LITTLE DARLIN', GOODBYE (78) .... Bluebird 8511		1.50	4.50
WAVE TO ME, MY LADY (78) .... RCA Victor 20-1789		1.00	3.00
BROWNS			
THREE BELLS, THE (45) .... RCA Victor 7555		1.00	2.00
BROWN, Jim Ed			
POP A TOP (45) .... RCA Victor 9192		1.00	2.00
BROWN, Charlie			
HAVE YOU HEARD THE GOSSIP (45) .... Rose 102		16.00	32.00
MEAN MEAN MAMA (45) .... Rose		5.00	10.00
BRUSH ARBOR			
BRUSH ARBOR MEETING (45) .... Capitol 3538		1.00	2.00
BUFFETT, Jim			
COME MONDAY (45) .... Dunhill 4385		1.00	2.00
BULLOCK, Norm			
LIES, LIES, LIES (45) .... M&J 1		13.00	26.00
BURNETTE, Dorsey			
BERTHA LOU (45) .... Surf 5019		7.50	15.00
BERTHA LOU (45) .... Cee Jan 16		4.00	8.00
BURNETTE, Smiley			
DOWN BY THE CANE BRAKE (78)			
UNCLE FRALEY'S FORMULA (78) .... Decca 5633		1.00	3.00
BURNETTE, Johnny Trio			
DRINKIN WINE SPO-DEE-O-DEE, DRINKIN WINE (45) ...... Coral 61869		11.00	22.00
LONESOME TRAIN (45) .... Coral 61758		9.00	18.00
TRAIN KEPT A ROLLIN (45) .... Coral 61719		8.00	16.00
BUTLER, Carl & Pearl			
MY TEARS DON'T SHOW (45) .... Columbia 42893		1.00	2.00
CAMPBELL, Cecile			
ROCK & ROLL FEVER (45) .... MGM 12482		25.00	50.00
CAMPI, Ray			
BALLAD OF DONNA AND PEGGY SUE (45) .... D 1047		4.00	8.00
PLAY IT COOL (45) .... TNT 145		15.00	30.00
CAPEHEART, Jerry			
ROLLIN (With Cochran Bros.) (45) .... Cash 102		12.50	25.00
CARAWAY, Bobby & Terry			
BALL IN KEEN (45) .... Crest 1065		13.00	26.00
CARGILL, Henson			
SKIP A ROPE (45) .... Monument 1041		1.00	2.00
CARLISLE, Bill			
DOLLAR AIN'T A DOLLAR ANYMORE, A (78) .... Federal 10006		1.00	3.00
I DONE IT WRONG (78) .... Bluebird 6568		2.00	6.00
RATTLIN' DADDY (78) .... Bluebird 6478		5.00	15.00
CARLISLE, Cliff			
GET HER BY THE TAIL ON A DOWN HILL DRAG (78) .... Bluebird 6292		5.00	15.00
IT AIN'T NO FAULT OF MINE (78) .... Bluebird 6631		3.00	9.00
MEAN MAMA DON'T WORRY ME, A (78) .... RCA Victor 20-2100		1.00	3.00
NO WEDDING BELLS (78) .... Bluebird 8936		1.50	4.50
ON MY WAY TO LONESOME VALLEY (78) .. Champion (Gennett) 16094		5.00	15.00
TROUBLE ON MY MIND (78) .... Decca 5593		1.50	4.50

Albums by most of these C/W artists appear in the second edition of *Record Albums 1948 1978*.

Johnny Cash

Dorsey Burnette

TITLE	LABEL & No.	GOOD	NEAR MINT
CARLISLES			
NO HELP WANTED (45)	Mercury 70028	1.50	3.00
SHAKE A LEG (45)	Mercury 70351	4.00	8.00
CARROL, Johnny			
HOT ROCK (45)	Decca 30013	18.00	36.00
SWING, THE (45)	Warner Bros. 5042	6.00	12.00
CARTER FAMILY			
KEEP ON THE SUNNY SIDE (78)	Bluebird 5006	7.50	22.50
MY DIXIE DARLING (78)	Decca 5240	7.50	22.50
CARTER, June			
ROOT HOG OR DIE (45)	RCA Victor 0355	1.00	2.00
CARTER SISTERS			
WILDWOOD FLOWER (45)	Columbia 21138	1.50	3.00
CARTER, Wilf (The Yodeling Cowboy)			
MY LITTLE SWISS AND ME (78)	Bluebird 4600	5.00	15.00
WAITING FOR A TRAIN (78)	Bluebird 55-3201	4.00	12.00
CARTER, Wilf as Montana Slim			
JUST A WOMAN SMILE (45)	RCA Victor 0419	3.00	6.00
SWEET LITTLE LOVE (45)	RCA Victor 5045	2.00	4.00
CARVER, Johnny			
YOUR LILY WHITE HANDS (45)	Imperial 66268	1.00	2.00
CASEY, Al			
TEENAGE BLUES (45)	Highland 1002	2.50	5.00
WILLA MAE (45)	Liberty 55117	5.00	10.00
CASH, Eddie			
DOING ALL RIGHT (45)	Peak 1002	12.50	25.00
CASH, Johnny			
HEY PORTER (45)	Sun 221	3.50	7.00
I WALK THE LINE (45)	Sun 241	1.00	2.00

The left hand price column represents the true value of the average, used record.

TITLE	LABEL & No.	GOOD	NEAR MINT
CLAY, Joe			
DUCKTAIL (45)	Vik 0211	13.00	26.00
CLINE, Patsy			
HIDIN OUT (45)	Four Star 11	2.00	4.00
I FALL TO PIECES (45)	Decca 31205	1.00	2.00
COCHRAN BROTHERS (Eddie & Hank)			
ROLLIN' (WITH JERRY CAPEHART) (45)	Cash 1021	12.50	25.00
TIRED AND SLEEPY (45)	Ekko 3001	37.50	75.00
COCHRAN, Hank			
SALLY WAS A GOOD OLD GIRL (45)	Liberty 54461	1.00	2.00
COCHRAN, Jack or Jackie Lee			
HIP SHAKIN MAMA (45)	Sims 107	13.00	26.00
RUBY PEARL (45)	Decca 30206	10.00	20.00
COLLINS KIDS			
BEETLE BUG BOP (45)	Columbia 21470	6.00	12.00
SUGAR PLUM (45)	Columbia 41329	3.00	6.00
COLTER, Jessie			
I'M NOT LISA (45)	Capitol 4009	1.00	2.00
COPAS, Cowboy			
ALABAM (45)	Starday 501	1.00	2.00
GUN TOTIN' MAMA (78)	King 516	1.00	3.00
CRADDOCK, Billy "Crash"			
BIRDDOGGIN (45)	Colonial 721	3.00	6.00
RUB IT IN (45)	ABC 11437	1.00	2.00
CRAFFORD, Cliff			
THERE AIN'T NOTHING HAPPNING TO ME (45)	Tally 1001	10.00	20.00
CRAMER, Floyd			
JOLLY CHOLLY (45)	Abbott 159	1.00	2.00
CRUM, Simon			
BOB CAT HOP (45)	Capitol 3460	1.50	3.00
COUNTRY MUSIC IS HERE TO STAY (45)	Capitol 4073	1.00	2.00
CUPP, Pat			
DO ME NO WRONG (45)	RPM 461	10.00	20.00
CURTIS, Mac			
DANCE HER BY ME (45)	Dot 16315	1.50	3.00
GRANDADDY'S ROCKIN' (45)	King 4949	15.00	30.00
LITTLE MISS LINDA (45)	King 5121	4.00	8.00
DALHART, Vernon			
DON'T MARRY A WIDOW (78)	Columbia 969D	1.50	4.50
LINDBERG (THE EAGLE OF THE U.S.A.) (78)	Columbia 1000D	3.50	10.50
PRISONER'S SONG (78)	Victor 19427	2.50	7.50
Recorded in 1924, this was the first country record to sell a million copies.			
THREE DROWNED SISTERS, THE (78)	Brunswick 100	1.50	4.50
WRECK OF THE ROYAL PALM (78)	Brunswick 101	2.50	7.50
YUKON STEVE AND ALASKA ANN (78)	Clarion 5027	2.00	6.00
DARBY, Tom & Jimmie Tarlton			
BIRMINGHAM TOWN (78)	Columbia 15197 D	5.00	15.00
DARRELL, Johnny			
WITH PEN IN HAND (45)	United Artists 50292	1.00	2.00
DAVIS, Bo			
LET'S COAST AWHILE (45)	Crest 1027	10.00	20.00

TITLE	LABEL & No.	GOOD	NEAR MINT
DAVIS, Dale & His Tomcats			
GONNA ROCK (45)	Stardale 333	10.00	20.00
DAVIS, Jimmie			
BEAR CAT MAMA FROM HORNERS CORNERS (78)	Bluebird 5005	10.00	30.00
RIPPIN' OUT (45)	Abbott 175	1.00	2.00
WHEN A BOY FROM THE MOUNTAINS (78)	Decca 6100	2.00	6.00
YO YO MAMA (78)	Bluebird 6437	5.00	15.00
DAVIS, Mac			
I'M A POOR LOSER (45)	Jamie 1227	1.00	2.00
DAVIS SISTERS			
GOTTA GET AGAIN (45)	RCA Victor 5607	1.50	3.00
ROCK-A-BYE BOOGIE (45)	RCA Victor 5345	2.50	5.00
DAVIS, Skeeter			
(I CAN'T HELP YOU) I'M FALLING TOO (45)	RCA Victor 7767	1.00	2.00
DAWSON, Ronnie			
ROCKIN BONES (45)	Rockin Records 1	15.00	30.00
DAY, Bing			
MARY'S PLACE (45)	Mercury 71494	3.50	7.00
PONY-TAIL PARTNER (45)	Federal 1282	15.00	30.00
DEAN, Bobby			
IT'S A FAD MA (45)	Profile 4006	10.00	20.00
DEAN, Jimmy			
BUMMING AROUND (45)	Four Star 1613	1.00	2.00
FREIGHT TRAIN BLUES (45)	Mercury 70786	4.00	8.00
DEATON, Frank & The Mad Lads			
JUST A LITTLE BIT MORE (45)	Bally 1042	15.00	30.00
DELMORE, Alton			
GOOD TIMES IN MEMPHIS (45)	Linco 1315	10.00	20.00
DELMORE BROTHERS			
GAMBLER'S YODEL (78)	Bluebird 8230	4.00	12.00
GOT THE KANSAS CITY BLUES (78)	Columbia 15724	10.00	30.00
LONESOME YODEL BLUES (78)	Bluebird 5299	7.50	22.50
PRISONER'S FAREWELL (78)	King 503	2.50	7.50
THERE'S TROUBLE ON MY MIND TODAY (78)	Decca 5878	3.00	9.00
WALKING WITH THE BLUES (78)	King 884	1.50	4.50
DEMAR, Jerry			
LOVERMAN (45)	Ford 501	13.00	26.00
DICKENS, "Little" Jimmy			
I GOT A HOLE IN MY POCKET (45)	Columbia 41137	4.00	8.00
MAY THE BIRD OF PARADISE FLY UP YOUR NOSE (45)	Columbia 43388	1.00	2.00
DOLAN, Ramblin Jimmy			
HOT ROD RACE (45)	Capitol 1322	3.00	6.00
DOVE, Ronnie			
LILACS IN WINTER (45)	Decca 33038	1.00	2.00
DOWD, Larry			
BLUE SWINGIN MAMA (45)	Spinning 6009	14.00	28.00
DRAPER, Rusty			
GAMBLER'S GUITAR (45)	Mercury 70167	1.50	3.00

Samples chosen for each artist represent the range of high and low values that artist's records usually bring.

"Little" Jimmy Dickens

Big Jimmy Dean with The Louvin Bros.

TITLE	LABEL & No.	GOOD	NEAR MINT
DRIFTWOOD, Jimmy			
GRAPEVINE NEWS (45)	CD 5000	2.00	4.00
JOHN PAUL JONES (45)	RCA Victor 7603	1.00	2.00
DRUSKY, Roy			
SUCH A FOOL (45)	Starday 185	1.50	3.00
DUDLEY, Dave			
MAYBE I DO (45)	Vee 7003	1.50	3.00
POOL SHARK (45)	Mercury 73029	1.00	2.00
DUNCAN, Herbie			
HOT LIPS BABY (45)	Marvel 1400	25.00	50.00
EATON, Connie			
ANGEL OF THE MORNING (45)	Chart 5048	1.00	2.00
ELDRIDGE, Billy			
LET'S GO BABY (45)	United Artists 2011	13.00	26.00
FAIRBURN, Werly			
EVERYBODY'S ROCKIN' (45)	Columbia 21528	8.00	16.00
IT'S A COLD WEARY WORLD (45)	Capitol 3101	1.50	3.00
TELEPHONE BABY (45)	Savoy 1521	4.00	8.00
FAIRCHILD, Barbara			
LOVE IS A GENTLE THING (45)	Columbia 44797	1.00	2.00
FARGO, Donna			
HAPPIEST GIRL IN THE WHOLE U.S.A., THE (45)	Dot 17409	1.00	2.00

TITLE	LABEL & No.	GOOD	NEAR MINT
FEATHERS, Charlie			
I'VE BEEN DECEIVED (45) .... Sun 503		87.50	175.00
I'VE BEEN DECEIVED (45) .... Flip 503		75.00	150.00
STUTTERIN CINDY (45) .... Philwood 223		1.50	3.00
FELTS, Narvel			
DARLING SUE (45) .... Pink 706		1.00	2.00
KISS A ME BABY (45) .... Mercury 71140		2.50	5.00
FENDER, Freddie			
WASTED DAYS AND WASTED NIGHTS (45) .... Duncan 1001		3.50	7.00
FERRIER, Al & His Bopping Billies			
HEY BABY (45) .... Excello 2105		13.00	26.00
MONEY BABY (45) .... Goldband 1212		5.00	10.00
FISHER, Sonny			
ROCKIN DADDY (45) .... Starday 179		7.50	15.00
ROCKIN' & ROLLIN' (45) .... Starday 207		20.00	40.00
FLATT, Lester & Earl Scruggs			
BALLAD OF JED CLAMPETT, THE (45) .... Columbia 42606		1.00	2.00
COME BACK DARLING (45) .... Columbia 20777		4.00	8.00
FLOYD, Frank			
ROCK A LITTLE BABY (50's release) (45) .... F&L 100		42.50	85.00
ROCK A LITTLE BABY (70's reissue) (45) .... F&L 100		1.00	2.00
FOLEY, Red			
BIRMINGHAM BOUNCE (45) .... Decca 46234		1.00	2.00
CHATTANOOGIE SHOE SHINE BOY (45) .... Decca 46205		1.00	2.00
I'M GOING TO MAKE HEAVEN MY HOME (78) .... Mercury 6161		2.50	7.50
WILL YOU WAIT FOR ME LITTLE DARLIN' (78) .... Decca 6010		1.50	4.50
FORD, Tennessee Ernie			
SHOTGUN BOOGIE (45) .... Capitol 1295		2.00	4.00
SIXTEEN TONS (45) .... Capitol 3262		1.00	2.00

Narvel Felts

Red Foley

TITLE	LABEL & No.	GOOD	NEAR MINT
FORSE, Beanon			
YOU BETTER GO NOW (45)	Rodney 514	15.00	30.00
FORT WORTH DOUGHBOYS--see Wills, Bob and Milton Brown			
FRAZIER, Dallas			
LOVE LIFE AT 14 (45)	Capitol 2895	1.00	2.00
GALLAGHER, James			
CRAZY CHICKEN (45)	Decca 29984	13.00	26.00
GAYLE, Crystal			
WRONG ROAD AGAIN (45)	United Artists 555	1.00	2.00
GEEZINSLAW BROTHERS			
CHUBBY (PLEASE TAKE YOUR LOVE TO TOWN) (45)	Capitol 2002	1.00	2.00
GENTRY, Bobbie			
OKOLONA RIVER BOTTOM BAND (45)	Capitol 2044	1.00	2.00
GIBSON, Don			
OH LONESOME ME (45)	RCA Victor 7133	1.00	2.00
SWEET DREAMS (45)	MGM 12194	2.00	4.00
GILLEY, Mickey			
OOH WEE (45)	Minor 106	25.00	50.00
WILD SIDE OF LIFE (45)	Princess 4006	2.50	5.00
GLASER, Tompall & The Glaser Brothers			
RINGS (45)	MGM 14291	1.00	2.00
YOU'RE IN MY HEART AGAIN (45)	Robbins 1001	2.00	4.00
GORDON, Curtis			
CRY CRY (Black label) (45)	Mercury 71121	4.00	8.00
SITTIN ON TOP (Black label) (45)	Mercury 71097	13.00	26.00
GRAY, Claude			
LETTER OVERDUE (45)	D 1059	1.00	2.00
GRAYZELL, Rudy "Tutti"			
DUCK TAIL (45)	Starday 241	13.00	26.00
LOOKING AT THE MOON (45)	Abbott 145	2.00	4.00
GREENE, Jack			
THERE GOES MY EVERYTHING (45)	Decca 32033	1.00	2.00
GREENE, Lorne			
RINGO (45)	RCA Victor 8444	1.00	2.00
GUITAR, Bonnie			
WOMAN IN LOVE, A (45)	Dot 17029	1.00	2.00
GUNTER, Hardrock			
FALLEN ANGEL (45)	Sun 201	40.00	80.00
IS IT TOO LATE (45)	Cullman 6410	1.50	3.00
HAGERS			
GOTTA GET TO OKLAHOMA ('CAUSE CALIFORNIA'S GETTIN' TO ME) (45)	Capitol 2647	1.00	2.00
HAGGARD, Merle			
OKIE FROM MUSKOGEE (45)	Capitol 2626	1.00	2.00
SING A SAD SONG (45)	Tally 155	1.50	3.00
HAGGETT, Jimmy			
NO MORE (45)	Sun 236	125.00	250.00 Tie

50

Albums by most of these C/W artists appear in the second edition of *Record Albums 1948-1978*.

TITLE	LABEL & No.	GOOD	NEAR MINT
HALL, Roy & His Jumpin Cats			
DON'T STOP NOW (45)	Decca 29786	15.00	30.00
THREE ALLEY CATS (45)	Decca 30060	10.00	20.00
THREE ALLEY CATS (45)	Hi-Q 5045	1.00	2.00
HALL, Tom T			
YEAR THAT CLAYTON DELANY DIED, THE (45)	Mercury 73221	1.00	2.00
HAMBLEN, Stuart & His Covered Wagon Jubilee			
POOR UNLUCKY COWBOY (78)	Decca 5001	1.00	3.00
THIS OLE HOUSE (45)	RCA Victor 5739	1.00	2.00
YHINH, THE (45)	RCA Victor 3968	2.50	5.00
HAMILTON, George IV			
ABILENE (45)	RCA Victor 8181	1.00	2.00
EVERYBODY'S BABY (45)	ABC 9838	8.00	16.00
HARRIS, Phil			
LONG WAY, THE (45)	RCA Victor 5333	2.00	4.00
PIECE OF PUDDIN' (45)	RCA Victor 4993	1.50	3.00
HARRIS, Ray			
COME ON LITTLE MAMA (45)	Sun 254	10.00	20.00
GREENBACK DOLLAR, WATCH & CHAIN (45)	Sun 272	3.50	7.00
HART, Freddie			
EASY LOVING (45)	Capitol 3115	1.00	2.00
HAWKINS, Hawkshaw			
LIFE OF HANK WILLIAMS (78)	King 1190	5.00	15.00
LONESOME 7-7203 (45)	King 5712	1.00	2.00
MARK 'ROUND MY FINGER (45)	RCA Victor 5444	2.00	4.00
SINCE YOU WENT AWAY (78)	King 611	1.00	3.00
WAY I LOVE YOU, THE (78)	King 544	2.50	7.50
HEAD, Roy			
GET BACK (45)	Scepter 12124	1.00	2.00
HELMS, Bobby			
TENNESSEE ROCK 'N ROLL (45)	Decca 29947	1.50	3.00
HEROLD, Dennis			
HIP HIP BABY (45)	Imperial 5482	14.00	28.00
HESS, Bennie			
TRUCKER'S BLUES (45)	Musicode 5691	5.00	10.00
WILDHOG HOP (45)	Major	25.00	50.00
WILDHOG HOP (45)	Musicode	12.50	25.00
HOMER & JETHRO			
FIVE MINUTES MORE (78)	King 571	1.00	3.00
HEART BROKE MOTEL (45)	RCA Victor 6542	2.50	5.00
THAT HOUND DOG IN THE WINDOW (45)	RCA Victor 5280	1.50	3.00
WHEN IT'S LONG-HANDLE TIME IN TENNESSEE (78)	Federal 10004	1.50	4.50
HORTON, Johnny			
BATTLE OF NEW ORLEANS, THE (45)	Columbia 41339	1.00	2.00
I'M COMING HOME (45)	Columbia 40813	5.00	10.00
HOUSTON, David			
BABY BABY (I KNOW YOU'RE A LADY) (45)	Epic 10539	1.00	2.00
SUGAR SWEET (45)	RCA Victor 6611	8.00	16.00
HUSKEY, Ferlin			
WINGS OF A DOVE (45)	Capitol 4406	1.00	2.00

All artists shown in photos appear with listings in the guide these samples were taken from.

"Grandpa" Jones

Homer & Jethro

Sleepy La Beef

TITLE	LABEL & No.	GOOD	NEAR MINT
INMAN, Autry			
BALLAD OF TWO BROTHERS (45)	Epic 10389	1.00	2.00
BE BOP BABY (45)	Decca 29936	11.00	22.00
JACKSON, Stonewall			
WATERLOO (45)	Columbia 41393	1.00	2.00
JACKSON, Wanda			
RIGHT OR WRONG (45)	Capitol 4553	1.00	2.00
RIOT IN CELL BLOCK NUMBER NINE (45)	Capitol 4520	5.00	10.00
JAMES, Sonny			
AIN'T GONNA TAKE NO CHANCE (45)	Capitol 3112	1.50	3.00
HERE COMES HONEY AGAIN (45)	Capitol 3174	1.00	2.00
JENNINGS, Waylon			
JOLE BLON (45)	Brunswick 55130	10.00	20.00
RAVE ON (45)	A&M 722	2.00	4.00
JIMMY & JOHNNY			
IF YOU DON'T SOMEBODY ELSE WILL (45)	Chess 4859	1.50	3.00
LOVE ME (45)	Chess 4863	15.00	30.00
SWEET LOVE ON MY MIND (45)	Decca 30061	15.00	30.00
JOHNNY & JACK			
HEART TROUBLE (45)	RCA Victor 4765	1.00	2.00
THAT'S WHY I'M LEAVING (45)	RCA Victor 6932	2.50	5.00
JOHNSON, Joe. D.			
RATTLESNAKE DADDY (Black & silver label) (45)	Acme 47	15.00	30.00
RATTLESNAKE DADDY (Black & orange label) (45)	Acme 47	1.50	3.00
JONES, Corky--see Owens, Buck			
JONES, Louis M. as George Jones			
WHY BABY WHY (45)	Starday 202	2.00	4.00
TENDER YEARS (45)	Mercury 71804	1.00	2.00
JONES, Louis M. as "Grandpa" Jones			
I'M ON MY WAY SOMEWHERE (78)	King 717	1.50	4.50
IT'S RAINING HERE THIS MORNING (78)	King 502	2.00	6.00
MOUNTAIN LAUREL (78)	RCA Victor 20-4505	1.00	3.00
MY HEART IS LIKE A TRAIN (45)	RCA Victor 5475	1.00	2.00
T.V. BLUES (45)	RCA Victor 4660	2.00	4.00
JONES, Louis M. as Thumper Jones			
ROCK IT (45)	Starday	17.50	35.00
JOY, Benny			
ITTY BITTY EVERYTHING (45)	Ram 10001	5.00	10.00
SPIN THE BOTTLE (45)	Dixie 2001	12.50	25.00
KING, Claude			
SHE KNOWS WHY (45)	Specialty 705	1.50	3.00
WOLVERTON MOUNTAIN (45)	Columbia 42352	1.00	2.00
KING, Pee Wee			
SILVER AND GOLD (45)	RCA Victor 4458	1.00	2.00
STEEL GUITAR RAG (78)	Bluebird 58-0025	1.00	3.00
TENNESSEE TEARS (45)	RCA Victor 0037	1.50	3.00
KRISTOFFERSON, Kris			
LOVING ARMS (45)	A&M 8572	1.00	2.00
LA BEEF, Sleepy			
ALL ALONE (45)	Starday 292	10.00	20.00
ALL THE TIME (45)	Mercury 71179	15.00	30.00
LA BEEF, Tommy			
TORE UP (45)	Wayside 1654	12.50	25.00

TITLE	LABEL & No.	GOOD	NEAR MINT
LAMIE, Tony			
WORE TO A FRAZZLE (45) .... Sunset 706		12.50	25.00
LANDERS, Dizie			
UNCLE JOHN'S BONGOS (45)........................ Do Ra Me 1412		15.00	30.00
LARUE, Roc			
BABY TAKE ME BACK (45).............................. Rama 226		15.00	30.00
LAWRENCE, Vicki			
NIGHT THE LIGHTS WENT OUT IN GEORGIA, THE (45).....Bell 45,303		1.00	2.00
LEE, Dickie			
FOOL, FOOL, FOOL (45)..................................Sun 297		1.00	2.00
STAY TRUE BABY (45) .... Tampa 10016		4.00	8.00
LEE, Wilma			
I DREAMED ABOUT MOM (45) ...:................Columbia 20654		1.00	2.00
LEWIS, Jerry Lee			
BABY BABY BYE BYE (45) ....Sun 337		1.00	2.00
GREAT BALLS OF FIRE (45) ....Sun 281		2.00	4.00
WHOLE LOTTA SHAKIN GOIN ON (45) ....Sun 267		1.50	3.00
LOCKLIN, Hank			
PLEASE HELP ME, I'M FALLING (45)................. RCA Victor 7692		1.00	2.00
SAME SWEET GIRL (45) .... Four Star 1747		2.00	4.00
LONESOME DRIFTER			
EAGER BOY (45) .... K 303		25.00	50.00
LONG, Huey			
ELVIS STOLE MY BABY (45) .... Fidelity 4055		23.00	46.00
LONG, Jimmy			
THAT'S WHY I LEFT			
THE MOUNTAINS (78)................... Champion (Gennett) 16117		3.00	9.00
LONS, Curtis			
HOOTCHY COOTCHY (45)................................ Linco 1314		15.00	30.00
LORD, Bobby			
FIRE OF LOVE (45) .... Columbia 40666		1.00	2.00
HIGH VOLTAGE (45) ....Columbia 40927		3.50	7.00
NO MORE, NO MORE, NO MORE (45) .... Columbia 21339		8.00	15.00
LOUDERMILK, John D.			
OH HOW SAD (45) .... RCA Victor 8054		1.00	2.00
SUSIE'S HOUSE (45) ....Columbia 41165		5.00	10.00
LOUVIN BROTHERS			
I DON'T BELIEVE YOU'VE MET MY BABY (45)............ Capitol 3300		1.00	2.00
MY LOVE SONG (45)...................................MGM 11221		1.50	3.00
LUKE THE DRIFTER--see Hank Williams			
LUMAN, Bob			
LET'S THINK ABOUT LIVING (45) .... Warner Bros. 5172		1.00	2.00
RED HOT (45)...Imperial 8313		10.00	20.00
LYNN, Loretta			
DARKEST DAY, THE (45)................................Zero 112		2.00	4.00
HONKY TONK GIRL (45) .... Zero 1011		1.50	3.00
MACON, Uncle Dave			
CROSS-EYED BUTCHER AND			
THE CACKLING HEN (78)...........................Supertone 2041		15.00	45.00
DEATH OF JOHN HENRY (78) .... Brunswick 112		15.00	45.00
DELIVERANCE WILL COME (78) ....Vocalion 5001		17.50	52.50
HE'S UP WITH THE ANGELS NOW (78) .... Decca 6369		15.00	45.00

TITLE	LABEL & No.	GOOD	NEAR MINT
ONE MORE RIVER TO CROSS (78)	Bluebird 5842	12.50	37.50
STOP THAT KNOCKING AT MY DOOR (78)	Vocalion 5006	15.00	45.00
WHEN THE HARVEST DAYS ARE OVER (78)	Montgomery Ward 4819	12.50	37.50
WHEN THE TRAIN COMES ALONG (78)	Champion 16805	15.00	45.00
WRECK OF THE TENNESSEE GRAVY TRAIN (78)	Okeh 45507	15.00	45.00

MADDOX BROTHERS
I'LL NEVER DO IT AGAIN (45)	Four Star 1664	1.50	3.00
UNCLOUDED DAY (45)	Decca 28784	2.50	5.00

MADDOX, Rose
GAMBLER'S LOVE (45)	Capitol 4177	1.00	2.00
HEY LITTLE DREAMBOAT (45)	Columbia 21990	3.00	6.00

MAINER'S MOUNTAINEERS, J.E.
MAPLE ON THE HILL (78)	Bluebird 6065	5.00	15.00
NOBODY'S DARLING BUT MINE (78)	Bluebird 6385	3.00	9.00
WHAT'LL I DO WITH THE BABY-O (78)	King 538	2.50	7.50

MANDRELL, Barbara
MIDNIGHT OIL, THE (45)	Columbia 45904	1.00	2.00

MANN, Carl
GONNA ROCK & ROLL TONIGHT (45)	Jackson	17.50	35.00
I AIN'T GOT NO HOME (45)	Phillips Int'l 3569	1.00	2.00

McAULIFFE, Leon
JELLY BEAN RAG (45)	Columbia 20755	2.50	5.00
THIS SIDE OF TOWN (45)	Columbia 20952	1.50	3.00

McDONALD, Skeets
DON'T LET THE STARS GET IN YOUR EYES (45)	Capitol 2216	1.50	3.00
YOU OUGHTA SEE GRANDMA ROCK (45)	Capitol 3461	13.00	26.00

McKOWEN, Gene & Tune Twisters
ROCK-A-BILLY RHYTHM (45)	Aggie 101	15.00	30.00

McMICHEN, Clayton & McMichen's Melody Men
CORN LICKER STILL IN GEORGIA, PT. 1 (78)	Columbia 15201 D	10.00	30.00
LET ME CALL YOU SWEETHEART (78)	Columbia 15111 D	7.50	22.50

MILLER, Jody
HE'S SO FINE (45)	Epic 10734	1.00	2.00

MILLER, Roger
WHEN TWO WALLS COLLIDE (45)	RCA Victor 7878	1.50	3.00

MILLER SISTERS
FLIP SKIP, THE (45)	Acme 111	4.00	8.00
SOMEDAY YOU WILL PAY (45)	Sun 504	35.00	70.00
SOMEDAY YOU WILL PAY (45)	Flip 504	15.00	30.00

MILSAP, Ronnie
ONE ROOM COUNTRY SHACK (45)	Scepter 12127	1.50	3.00

MITCHELL, Guy
WIMMIN' (45)	Columbia 39639	1.50	3.00

MONROE, Bill as Bill Monroe's Blue Grass Boys
CHANGING PARTNERS (78)	Decca 20921	1.50	4.50
COUNTRY WALTZ (45)	Decca 28749	2.50	5.00
I'M ON MY WAY TO THE OLD HOME (78)	Decca 28045	2.50	7.50
MOTHER'S ONLY SLEEPING (78)	Columbia 20107	5.00	15.00
MY ROSE OF OLD KENTUCKY (78)	Columbia 20423	4.00	12.00

MONROE BROTHERS
THIS WORLD IS NOT MY HOME (78)	Bluebird 6309	5.00	15.00
WHERE IS MY SAILOR BOY? (78)	Bluebird 6762	10.00	30.00

MONTANA SLIM--see Carter, Wilf

Halfway between good and mint is the true value and the best condition usually available in old records. Mint is rare.

TITLE	LABEL & No.	GOOD	NEAR MINT
MORGAN, George			
ALMOST (45)	Columbia 20906	1.00	2.00
CANDY KISSES (45)	Columbia 20547	1.50	3.00
MULLICAN, Moon			
CHEROKEE BOOGIE (Red label) (45)	King 965	5.00	10.00
I'LL SAIL MY SHIP ALONE (45)	King 830	2.00	4.00
LONESOME HEARTED BLUES, THE (78)	King 565	1.50	4.50
MONA LISA (45)	Starday 562	1.00	2.00
MURPHY, Jimmy			
SIXTEEN TONS OF ROCK AND ROLL (45)	Columbia 21534	20.00	40.00
NELSON, Willie			
NIGHT LIFE (Red vinyl record) (45)	Bellaire 107	7.50	15.00
TOUCH ME (45)	Liberty 55439	1.00	2.00
NEWMAN, Jimmy			
CARRY ONE (45)	Dot	8.00	16.00
FALLEN STAR, A (45)	Dot 1289	1.00	2.00
NORMA JEAN			
GO CAT GO (45)	RCA Victor 8433	1.00	2.00
NORMAN, Gene			
NIGHT TRAIN (45)	Snag 101	13.00	26.00
NOWLIN, Ernie			
TALLY HO (45)	Missouri 640	15.00	3.00
ORBISON, Roy			
ALMOST EIGHTEEN (45)	RCA Victor 7447	2.00	4.00
CHICKEN HEARTED (45)	Sun 284	2.50	5.00
ORBISON, Roy & The Teen Kings			
OOBIE DOOBIE (45)	Jewel	60.00	120.00
OVERSTREET, Tommy			
I DON'T KNOW YOU (ANYMORE) (45)	Dot 17387	1.00	2.00
OWENS, Bonnie			
DON'T TAKE ADVANTAGE OF ME (45)	Tally 156	1.00	2.00
OWENS, Buck			
DOWN ON THE CORNER OF LOVE (45)	Pep 105	5.00	10.00
UNDER YOUR SPELL AGAIN (45)	Capitol 4245	1.00	2.00
OWENS, Buck as Corky Jones			
HOT DOG (45)	Pep 107	12.50	25.00
RHYTHM & BOOZE (45)	Dixie 505	7.50	15.00
RHYTHM & BOOZE (45)	Pep 107	12.50	25.00
PARSONS, Bill--see Bare, Bobby			
PARTON, Dolly			
JOSHUA (45)	RCA Victor 9928	1.00	2.00
PATTON, Jimmy			
OAKIE IN THE POKIE (45)	Sims 117	25.00	50.00
YAH, I'M MOVIN (45)	Sage 261	25.00	50.00
PEARL, Minnie			
GIDDYUP-GO ANSWER (45)	Starday 754	1.00	2.00
ON TOP OF OLD SMOKY (78)	King 590	1.50	4.50
PENNY, Hank			
HADACILLIN BOOGIE (45)	RCA Victor	2.50	5.00
I WANT MY RIB (45)	RCA Victor 4363	1.50	3.00

This section represents approximately 5% of the artists and songs listed in *55 Years of Recorded Country/Western Music.*

TITLE	LABEL & No.	GOOD	NEAR MINT
PERKINS, Carl			
BLUE SUEDE SHOES (45)	Sun 234	2.50	5.00
GONE GONE GONE (45)	Sun 224	15.00	30.00
MOVIE MAGG (45)	Flip 501	50.00	100.00
PETERSON, Earl			
BOOGIE BLUES (45)	Sun 197	17.50	35.00
PHANTOM, The			
LOVE ME (With picture cover) (45)	Dot 16056	25.00	50.00

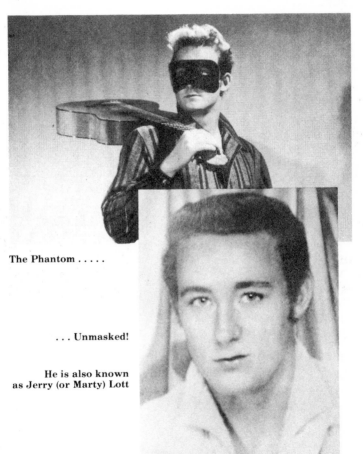

The Phantom . . . . .

. . . Unmasked!

He is also known
as Jerry (or Marty) Lott

TITLE	LABEL & No.	GOOD	NEAR MINT
PIERCE, Webb			
LOVE, LOVE, LOVE (45)	Decca 29662	1.00	2.00
SO USED TO LOVING YOU (78)	Decca 28091	1.00	3.00
TEENAGE BOOGIE (45)	Decca 30045	3.00	6.00
PILLOW, Ray			
THANK YOU, MA'AM (45)	Capitol 5518	1.00	2.00
POE, Bobby			
ROCK & ROLL BOOGIE (45)	Whiterock 1112	11.00	22.00

TITLE	LABEL & No.	GOOD	NEAR MINT

POOLE, Charlie & The North Carolina Ramblers
CAN I SLEEP IN YOUR BARN TONIGHT, MISTER BLUES (78) ....Columbia 15038 D		10.00	30.00
SWEET SUNNY SOUTH (78) ....Columbia 15425 D		5.00	15.00

POOVEY, Joe "Groovy"
MOVE AROUND (45)..Dixie 733		20.00	40.00

PRESLEY, Elvis
48 GOOD ROCKIN' TONIGHT (45) ....Sun 210		135.00	270.00
37 I'M LEFT, YOURE RIGHT, SHE'S GONE (45) ....Sun 217		115.00	230.00
MILKCOW BLUES BOOGIE (45) ....Sun 215		155.00	310.00

The second side "You're A Heartbreaker" was the hit.

38 MYSTERY TRAIN (45)..Sun 223		90.00	180.00
THAT'S ALLRIGHT (MAMA) (45)..............................Sun 209		150.00	300.00 Tie

Elvis

PRICE, Ray
CRAZY ARMS (45) ....Columbia 21510		1.00	2.00
HEART ACHING BLUES (45) ....Columbia 20863		2.00	4.00

PRIDE, Charley
ALL I HAVE TO OFFER YOU (IS ME) (45) ....RCA Victor 0167		1.00	2.00
KISS AN ANGEL GOODMORNIN' (45) ....RCA Victor 0550		1.00	2.00

PUCKETT, Riley
BUCKIN' MULE (78) ....Columbia 110 D		7.50	22.50
CURLY HEADED BABY (78) .... Bluebird 6134		5.00	15.00
ROCK ALL YOUR BABIES TO SLEEP (78) ....Columbia 107 D		5.00	15.00
Recorded in 1923.			
SHORT LIFE OF TROUBLE (78) ....Decca 5442		2.50	7.50
WAITIN' FOR THE EVENIN' MAIL (78) ....Bluebird 5432		4.00	12.00

RAINWATER, Marvin
GONNA FIND ME A BLUEBIRD (45) ....MGM 12412		1.50	3.00
HOT & COLD (45) ....MGM 12240		4.00	8.00

RATCLIFFE, Bozo
LET ME IN (45) .... Space 100		17.50	35.00

RAY, David
JITTER BUGGIN BABY (45)............................... Kliff 105		25.00	50.00
LONESOME BABY BLUES (45) .... Kliff 101		12.50	25.00

Elvis Presley records are listed in all three of our guides on pop singles, albums and country/western.

TITLE	LABEL & No.	GOOD	NEAR MINT
RAY, Wade			
CALL ME UP (45)	RCA Victor 5199	2.00	4.00
TWO RED RED LIPS (45)	Dot 15600	1.00	2.00
REED, Jerry			
WHEN I FOUND YOU (45)	Capitol 3429	5.00	10.00
WHEN YOU'RE HOT, YOU'RE HOT (45)	RCA Victor 9976	1.00	2.00
REEVES, Glenn & Rockabillies			
ROCKIN COUNTRY STYLE (45)	Atco 6080	13.00	26.00
REEVES, Jim			
BILLY BAYOU (45)	RCA Victor 7380	1.00	2.00
MEXICAN JOE (45)	Abbott 115	1.50	3.00
WHERE DOES A BROKEN HEART GO (45)	Abbott 174	2.00	4.00
RENO, Don & Red Smiley			
HEAR JERUSALEM MOURN (78)			
I'M USING MY BIBLE FOR A ROAD MAP (78)	King 1045	1.00	3.00
RHODES, Slim			
DO WHAT I DO (45)	Sun 256	3.50	7.00
HOUSE OF SIN (45)	Sun 225	17.50	35.00
RICH, Charlie			
BEHIND CLOSED DOORS (45)	Epic 10950	1.00	2.00
PHILADELPHIA BABY (45)	Phillips 3532	2.00	4.00
RILEY, Billy Lee			
GOT THE WATER BOILING (45)	Sun 322	10.00	20.00
WOULDN'T YOU KNOW (45)	Sun 289	3.50	7.00
RILEY, Jeannie C.			
HARPER VALLEY P.T.A. (45)	Plantation 3	1.00	2.00
RITTER, Tex			
BE NOBODY'S DARLIN' BUT MINE (78)	Champion 45153	2.50	7.50
RIDING OLD PAINT, A (78)	Conqueror 8073	2.50	7.50
I DREAMED OF HILL-BILLY HEAVEN (45)	Capitol 4567	1.00	2.00
MY BUCKET'S BEEN FIXED (45)	Capitol 1388	1.50	3.00
RITTER, Tex & His Texans			
SAM HALL (78)	Decca 5076	1.00	3.00
ROBBINS, Marty			
EL PASO (45)	Columbia 41511	1.00	2.00
PRETTY MAMA (45)	Columbia 21461	6.00	12.00
SINGING THE BLUES (45)	Columbia 21545	1.50	3.00
ROBERTSON, Texas Slim			
BEWARE (45)	MGM 11591	1.50	3.00
GONE FISHIN (45)	RCA Victor 3824	2.50	5.00
ROBISON, Carson			
NOLA (78)	Columbia 840D	1.00	3.00
RED RIVER VALLEY (78)	Clarion 5109	1.50	4.50
RODGERS, Jimmie			
BLUE YODEL #1 (78)	Victor 21142	7.50	22.50
BLUE YODEL #5 (78)	Victor 22072	10.00	30.00
COWHAND'S LAST RIDE (78)	Victor 18-6000	250.00	750.00
This is a very rare picture record released June 24, 1933.			
IN THE HILLS OF TENNESSEE (78)	Victor 23736	20.00	60.00
JIMMIE RODGERS LAST BLUE YODEL (78)	Bluebird 5281	10.00	30.00
SLEEP BABY SLEEP (78)	Victor 20864	12.50	37.50
SOMEWHERE BELOW THE DIXON LINE (78)	Victor 23840	25.00	75.00
WHY THERE'S A TEAR IN MY EYE (78)	Bluebird 6698	12.50	37.50

⑨

The left hand price column represents the true value of the average, used record.

Halfway between good and mint is the true value and the best condition usually available in old records. Mint is rare.

Rare Picture Record

TITLE	LABEL & No.	GOOD	NEAR MINT
RODRIGUEZ, Johnny			
RIDIN' MY THUMB TO MEXICO (45)	Mercury 73416	1.00	2.00
ROGERS, Kenny			
LADY, PLAY YOUR SYMPHONY (45)	Jolly Roger 1001	1.00	2.00
ROGERS, Rock			
THAT AIN'T IT (45)	Starday 245	13.00	26.00
ROGERS, Roy			
ALONG THE NAVAJO TRAIL (78)	RCA Victor 20-1730	1.00	3.00
HAPPY TRAILS (45)	RCA Victor 4709	2.00	4.00
NOBODY'S FAULT BUT MY OWN (78)	Decca 5876	1.00	3.00
SAMPLES, Junior			
WORLD'S BIGGEST WHOPPER, THE (45)	Chart 1460	1.00	2.00
SCOTT, Jack			
BABY SHE'S GONE (45)	ABC Paramount 9818	12.50	25.00
I KNEW YOU FIRST (45)	Groove 0031	1.50	3.00
SCRUGGS, Earl			
EARL'S BREAKDOWN (45)	Columbia 20886	3.00	6.00
PIKE COUNTY BREAKDOWN (45)	Mercury 6396	2.50	5.00
SEELY, Jeannie			
DON'T TOUCH ME (45)	Monument 933	1.00	2.00
SELF, Ronnie			
AIN'T I'M A DOG (45)	Columbia 40989	3.00	6.00
PRETTY BAD BLUES (45)	ABC 9714	13.00	26.00
SHEPARD, Jean			
SATISFIED MIND (45)	Capitol 3118	1.00	2.00
SIMMONS, Gene			
DRINKIN WINE (45)	Sun 299	12.50	25.00

All records are listed by rpm speed, (45) or (78).

TITLE	LABEL & No.	GOOD	NEAR MINT
SISCO, Bobby			
GO, GO, GO (45)	Chess 1650	17.50	35.00
SKINNER, Jimmy			
PENNY POST CARD (45)	Capitol 1889	2.00	4.00
SMITH, Carl			
HEY, JOE (45)	Columbia 21129	1.00	2.00
LOOSE TALK (45)	Columbia 21317	1.00	2.00
SMITH, Connie			
ONCE A DAY (45)	RCA Victor 8416	1.00	2.00
SMITH, Sammi			
HELP ME MAKE IT THROUGH THE NIGHT (45)	Mega 615-0015	1.00	2.00
SMITH, Warren			
I DON'T BELIEVE I'LL FALL IN LOVE TODAY (45)	Liberty 55248	1.00	2.00
MISS FROGGIE (45)	Sun 268	2.50	5.00
ROCK & ROLL RUBY (45)	Sun 239	7.50	15.00
SNOW, Hank			
BLUE VELVET BAND, THE (78)	Bluebird 4635	5.00	15.00
CAN'T HAVE YOU BLUES (45)	RCA Victor 0059	2.50	5.00
I DON'T HURT ANYMORE (45)	RCA Victor 5698	1.50	3.00
WHEN IT'S OVER I'LL BE COMING BACK TO YOU (78)	Bluebird 55-3203	4.00	12.00
SONS OF THE PIONEERS			
COOL WATER (45)	Decca 46027	3.00	6.00
COOL WATER (78)	RCA Victor 20-1724	1.00	3.00
RIVER OF NO RETURN (45)	Coral 61186	1.50	3.00
TUMBLIN TUMBLEWEEDS (45)	RCA Victor 4081	2.50	5.00
'WAY OUT THERE (78)	Decca 5013	1.00	3.00
SOVINE, Red			
GIDDYUP GO (45)	Starday 737	1.00	2.00
JUKE JOINT JOHNNY (45)	Decca 30239	3.00	6.00
SPEARS, Billie Jo			
MR. WALKER IT'S ALL OVER (45)	Capitol 2436	1.00	2.00
SPELLMAN, Jimmy			
IT'S YOU, YOU, YOU (45)	VIV 1002	2.50	5.00
WHAT A WAY TO DIE (45)	Rev 3521	1.00	2.00
STAFFORD, Jim			
WILDWOOD WEED (45)	MGM 14737	1.00	2.00
STAFFORD, Terry			
HOPING (45)	Crusader 110	1.00	2.00
STANLEY BROTHERS			
TRAIN 45 (78)	King 5155	1.50	4.50
STARR, Andy			
ROCKIN ROLLIN STONE (45)	MGM 12263	20.00	40.00
SHE'S A GOING JESSIE (45)	MGM 12315	15.00	30.00
STARR, Frankie			
DIG THEM SQUEEKY SHOES (45)	Lin 1009	12.50	25.00
LITTLE BITTY FEELING (45)	Holiday Inn 108	1.50	3.00
STATLER BROTHERS			
FLOWERS ON THE WALL (45)	Columbia 43314	1.00	2.00
STEVENS, Ray			
HIGH SCHOOL YEARBOOK (45)	NRC 031	1.50	3.00
ROCKIN' TEENAGE MUMMIES (45)	Mercury 72382	1.00	2.00

TITLE	LABEL & No.	GOOD	NEAR MINT
STRUNK, Jud			
DAISY A DAY (45) ....MGM 14463		1.00	2.00
STUCKEY, Nat			
WHISKEY WHISKEY (45) ....RCA Victor 9884		1.00	2.00
SURF-RIDERS			
I'M OUT (45)...Masco 6008		13.00	26.00
SWAN, Billy			
I CAN HELP (45) ....Monument 8621		1.00	2.00
SWATELY, Hank			
OAKIE BOOGIE (45) ....Aaron 101		18.00	36.00
TANNER, Gid & His Skillet Lickers			
BE KIND TO A MAN WHEN HE'S DOWN (78)........Columbia 15010D		7.50	22.50
MISSISSIPPI SAWYER (78) ....Bluebird 5433		5.00	15.00
TAYLOR, Bill			
NELDA JANE (45) ....Trophy 500		3.50	7.00
SPLIT PERSONALITY (45) ....Flip 502		62.50	125.00
TAYLOR, Ray			
CONNIE LOU (45) ....Clix 2207		18.00	36.00
THOMPSON, Ernest			
WRECK OF THE SOUTHERN OLD 97 (78) ....Columbia 130D		5.00	15.00
THOMPSON, Hank			
LOST JOHN (45) ....Capitol 4649		2.50	5.00
WILD SIDE OF LIFE, THE (45) ....Capitol 1942		1.50	3.00
THOMPSON, Junior			
RAW DEAL (45) ....Meteor 5029		18.00	36.00
THOMPSON, Sue			
CANDY AND ROSES (45)...............................Hickory 1652		1.00	2.00
TILLIS, Mel			
HEART OVER MIND (45) ....Kapp 2086		1.00	2.00
TEENAGE WEDDING (45) ....Columbia 41115		5.00	10.00
TILLMAN, Floyd			
DON'T BE BLUE (78)			
I DIDN'T KNOW (78)....................................Decca 5741		1.00	3.00
TODD, Johnny			
PINK CADILLAC (45) ....Modern		13.00	26.00
TOROK, Mitchell			
REDLIGHT, GREEN LIGHT (45) ....Decca 29863		3.50	7.00
TRAIL, Buck			
HONKY TONK ON SECOND STREET (45).....................Trail 100		33.00	66.00
TRAMMELL, Bobby Lee			
ARKANSAS TWIST (45) ....Alley 1001		2.50	5.00
SHIRLEY LEE (45) ....Fabor 4038		10.00	20.00
TRASK, Diana			
SAY WHEN (45) ....Dot 17448		1.00	2.00
TRAVIS, Merle			
LOUISIANA BOOGIE (45) ....Capitol 2902		5.00	10.00
RE-ENLISTMENT BLUES (45) ....Capitol 2563		1.50	3.00

This section represents approximately 5% of the artists and songs listed in *55 Years of Recorded Country/Western Music.*

TITLE	LABEL & No.	GOOD	NEAR MINT
TUBB, Ernest			
BLUE CHRISTMAS (45)	Decca 46186	1.50	3.00
BLUE EYED ELAINE (78)	Decca 5825	3.00	9.00
MEAN OLD BED BUG BLUES (78)	Bluebird 8899	25.00	75.00
MISSING IN ACTION (45)	Decca 46389	1.00	2.00
PASSING OF JIMMIE RODGERS, THE (78)	Bluebird 6693	40.00	120.00
SINCE THAT BLACK CAT CROSSED MY PATH (78)	Bluebird 7000	30.00	90.00
SO ROUND, SO FIRM, SO FULLY PACKED (78)	Decca 46040	1.50	4.50
TUBB, Justin			
PEPPER HOT BABY (45)	Decca 29895	1.00	2.00
TUCKER, Tanya			
WHAT'S YOUR MAMA'S NAME (45)	Columbia 45799	1.00	2.00
TWITTY, Conway			
DOUBLE TALK BABY (Blue label) (45)	Mercury 71384	3.00	6.00
HELLO DARLIN' (45)	Decca 32661	1.00	2.00
SUCH A NIGHT (45)	ABC Paramount 10550	2.00	4.00
TYLER, T. Texas			
DECK OF CARDS (78)	King 5249	1.00	3.00
HE DONE HER WRONG (45)	Decca 28554	2.00	4.00
KISS ME LIKE CRAZY (45)	RCA Victor 1649	1.50	3.00
VAN DYKE, Leroy			
WALK ON BY (45)	Mercury 71834	1.00	2.00
VAUGHN, Dale			
HIGH STEPPIN' (45)	Von 480	15.00	30.00
WAGONER, Porter			
DIG THAT CRAZY MOON (45)	RCA Victor 5527	1.50	3.00
SATISFIED MIND (45)	RCA Victor 6105	1.00	2.00
WAKELY, Jimmy & His Rough Riders			
BEAUTIFUL BROWN EYES (45)	Capitol 1393	1.50	3.00
CIMMARON (ROLL ON) (78)	Decca 5877	1.00	3.00
WALKER, Billy			
ALCOHOL LOVE (45)	Capitol 1097	1.00	2.00
I'VE GOT LEAVING ON MY MIND (45)	Columbia 21531	2.00	4.00
WATSON, Doc & Merle			
BOTTLE OF WINE (45)	United Artists 276	1.00	2.00
WAYNE, Alvis			
DON'T MEAN MAYBE BABY (45)	Westport 138	8.00	16.00
SWING BOP BOOGIE (45)	Westport 132	11.00	22.00
WEAVER, Dennis			
GENESIS THROUGH EXODUS (45)	Warner Bros. 5352	1.50	3.00
HUBBARDVILLE STORE (45)	Ovation 1056	1.00	2.00
WELLS, Kitty			
IT WASN'T GOD WHO MADE HONKY TONK ANGELS (45)	Decca 28232	1.00	2.00
MY MOTHER (45)	RCA Victor 0384	2.00	4.00
WEST, Dottie			
WOULD YOU HOLD IT AGAINST ME (45)	RCA Victor 8770	1.00	2.00
WHEELER, Onie			
GOING BACK TO THE CITY (45)	Columbia 40911	5.00	10.00
RUN EM OFF (45)	OK 18022	1.00	2.00
WHITMAN, Slim			
INDIAN LOVE CALL (45)	Imperial 8156	1.00	2.00

Samples chosen for each artist represent the range of high and low values that artist's records usually bring.

TITLE	LABEL & No.	GOOD	NEAR MINT

WILBURN BROTHERS
DEEP ELM BLUES (45) .... Decca 29887 — 2.50 — 5.00
MY HEART OR MY MIND (45) .... Decca 29459 — 1.00 — 2.00

WILLIAMS, Hank
CALLING YOU (78) .... Sterling 201 — 50.00 — 150.00
HONKY TONKIN' (78) .... Sterling 210 — 25.00 — 75.00
LOVE SICK BLUES (78) .... MGM 10352 — 2.50 — 5.00
MOVE IT ON OVER (78) .... MGM 10033 — 1.50 — 4.50
MY BUCKET'S GOT A HOLE IN IT (45) ... MGM 12635 — 4.00 — 8.00
TAKE THESE CHAINS FROM MY HEART (45) ... MGM 11479 — 2.00 — 4.00

WILLIAMS, Hank as Luke the Drifter
JUST WAITIN' (45) .... MGM 10932 — 3.50 — 7.00

WILLIAMS, Billy
MARY MARRY ME (78) .... RCA Victor 20-2343 — 1.00 — 3.00

WILLIAMS, Tex
BLUEBIRD ON YOUR WINDOWSILL (45) ... Capitol 40225 — 1.50 — 3.00

WILLIAMS, Wayne
RED HOT MAMA (45) .... Sure 1001 — 13.00 — 26.00

WILLIS BROTHERS
GIVE ME 40 ACRES (TO TURN THIS RIG AROUND) (45) ... Starday 681 — 1.00 — 2.00

WILLIS, Don
BOPPIN HIGH SCHOOL BABY (45) .... Satellite 101 — 37.50 — 75.00

WILLIS, Hal
BOPPA-DEE BOPPA-DOO (45) .... Atlantic 1114 — 14.00 — 28.00

WILLS, Bob
STEAMBOAT STOMP (45) .... MGM 11377 — 1.00 — 2.00

WILLS, Bob & His Texas Playboys
ALEXANDER'S RAGTIME BAND (78) ... Vocalion 04275 — 17.50 — 52.50
DUSTY SKIES (78) .... Columbia 20147 — 2.00 — 6.00
OLD FASHIONED LOVE (78) .... Vocalion 03295 — 10.00 — 30.00
SAN ANTONIO ROSE (78) .... Decca 9-29604 — 1.50 — 4.50

WILLS, Bob and Milton Brown as The Fort Worth Doughboys
SUNBONNET SUE (78) .... Bluebird 5257 — 40.00 — 120.00
Rare first record by Bob Wills and Milton Brown. Recorded under the name of Fort Worth Doughboys in 1933.
TAKE ME BACK TO TULSA (78) .... Columbia 37019 — 1.50 — 4.50
WHOSE HEART ARE YOU BREAKING NOW? (78) ... Okeh 6703 — 2.00 — 6.00

WISEMAN, Mac
JIMMY BROWN, THE NEWSBOY (45) ..... Dot 15946 — 1.00 — 2.00
STEP IT UP AND GO (45) .... Dot 15544 — 3.50 — 7.00

WOODY, Don
BIRD DOG (45) .... Decca 30277 — 12.50 — 25.00

WOOLEY, Sheb
HUM DINGER (45) .... MGM 12114 — 3.00 — 6.00
THAT'S MY PA (45) .... MGM 13046 — 1.00 — 2.00

WYATT, Gene
LOVE FEVER (45) .... Ebb 123 — 13.00 — 26.00

WYNETTE, Tammy
D-I-V-O-R-C-E (45) .... Epic 10315 — 1.00 — 2.00

All artists shown in photos appear with listings in the guide these samples were taken from.

TITLE	LABEL & No.	GOOD	NEAR MINT

YELVINGTON, Malcolm
DRINKIN WINE SPO DEE O DEE (45)	Sun 211	13.00	26.00
ROCKIN' WITH MY BABY (45)	Sun 246	5.00	10.00

YOUNG, Faron
COUNTRY GIRL (45)	Capitol 4233	1.00	2.00
FOOLISH PRIDE (45)	Capitol 2133	2.50	5.00

Jimmie Rodgers   **Will Rogers**

Glossary of Terms

BOOTLEG—Any unauthorized issuance of previously released or unre-
leased material.

BOXED SET—A box-style holder for two or more records.

COLORED PLASTIC—A record made of some other color of vinyl than
black, usually red, green, blue or gold.

DOUBLE POCKET—A special jacket made to hold two LP's. Some triple
pockets have been issued.

EP—See Extended Play.

EXTENDED PLAY—A seven-inch 45 rpm disc containing three or more
songs. Some EP's have been made at 33 1/3, and some in stereo. Very few
were being made by 1965.

JACKET—A heavy cardboard sleeve for an LP or EP.

LONG PLAY ALBUM—A 12" record that plays at 33 1/3 rpm, containing
12 to 30 minutes per side. These are not to be confused with the old time
"albums" that packaged several 45's or 78's into one binder.

LP—See Long Play Album.

ORIGINAL CAST—The music from a stage production—usually
"Broadway"—starring the opening night cast.

PICTURE SLEEVE—A paper "sleeve" to hold and protect a 45 record,
usually with a photo of the artist.

PROMO COPY—A promotional release of a record to be sent to radio sta-
tions, usually marked "Not for Sale."

REISSUE—The re-release of an item utilizing more timely merchandising,
such as a new jacket, photos, etc.

RPM—The "revolutions per minute" a particular record makes when
played on a phonograph or turntable.

SINGLE—Either a 45 or 78 rpm, usually with one song on each side.

SOUNDTRACK—Music taken directly from the audio track of a motion
picture or television program.